CATHOLIC RECORD SOCIETY
PUBLICATIONS

MONOGRAPH SERIES
VOLUME 8

The Gages of Hengrave and Suffolk Catholicism 1640–1767

FRANCIS YOUNG

PUBLISHED FOR

THE CATHOLIC RECORD SOCIETY

BY

THE BOYDELL PRESS

2015

First published 2015

ISBN 978–0–902832–29–9

A Catholic Record Society publication
published by The Boydell Press
an imprint of Boydell & Brewer Ltd
PO Box 9, Woodbridge, Suffolk IP12 3DF, UK
and of Boydell & Brewer Inc.
668 Mt Hope Avenue, Rochester, NY 14620–2731, USA
website: www.boydellandbrewer.com

A CIP catalogue record for this book is available
from the British Library

The publisher has no responsibility for the continued existence or
accuracy of URLs for external or third-party internet websites referred to
in this book, and does not guarantee that any content
on such websites is, or will remain, accurate or appropriate

This publication is printed on acid-free paper

Printed and bound in Great Britain by
TJ International Ltd, Padstow, Cornwall

CONTENTS

ILLUSTRATIONS

PREFACE

Between 1662, when Sir Edward Gage received his baronetcy from Charles II, and 1872 when the ninth and last baronet died without an heir, the Gage family were the socially and financially pre-eminent Catholics of the county of Suffolk. They lived at Hengrave Hall, two-and-a-half miles north of Bury St Edmunds, between 1640 and 1767, and again from 1843–72. This book traces the history of the Gages from their arrival at Hengrave to the inheritance of the baronetcy by a more junior branch of the family, the Rookwood Gages, in 1767. It is also a history of the Catholic community in the western half of Suffolk during that period, which was able to thrive largely because of the influence, patronage and protection of the Gages of Hengrave.

This book has been a long time in the making. I began writing it in the summer of 2010, but the idea of a history of the Gage family after 1640 was a much older ambition. Many years ago, shortly after I first encountered John Gage's *The History and Antiquities of Hengrave* (1822), the starting point for anyone interested in the history of Hengrave Hall, I conceived the idea of 'completing' Gage's work by taking his history up to 1767, when the senior line of the family died out. However, the scope of this book has expanded somewhat beyond that original ambition, and its title, *The Gages of Hengrave and Suffolk Catholicism, 1640–1767*, reflects the fact that it is also about other Catholics who interacted with the Gages, principally in Bury St Edmunds and its immediate environs. A 'companion volume' on Suffolk's other great Catholic dynasty, the Rookwood family, is to be published by the Suffolk Records Society.

Together, the present volume and my forthcoming *Rookwood Family Papers, 1606–1761* represent the culmination of over a decade's historical work on the history of Catholicism in Suffolk. My interest in Suffolk's Catholics began when I was studying for my A levels and working as a volunteer at Hengrave Hall, which was then an ecumenical retreat and conference centre. I owe my first debt of gratitude to my then History teacher, Alan Dures, who inspired my interest in Reformation history, as well as to the late Sr Mary Aquinas and the Rev. Eleanor Whalley, who was then education co-ordinator at Hengrave. Eleanor encouraged me to pursue my interest in Hengrave's history, and it was she who first introduced me to the Hengrave Manuscripts in Cambridge University Library in 1998.

I owe a second and equal debt of gratitude to Joy Rowe, who has pioneered the study of Suffolk Catholicism since the 1950s, and who graciously shared her knowledge, wisdom and personal collection of papers in order to allow me to complete this book. Joy's work forms the foundation for this monograph, and without her I would certainly not have been able to accomplish it. I am also very grateful for her comments on an earlier draft of the book.

Many others have contributed, in large or small ways, to the success of this project. The members of the Catholic Record Society, especially Prof. Alan McLelland and Dr Leo Gooch, helped to nurture my initial studies in Catholic history, and I am indebted to Michael Hodgetts for his comments on specific details of the text. I thank Dr Peter Doyle and his successor as CRS Volumes Editor, the Rev. Dr John Broadley, for their work in guiding this book towards publication. I am grateful to the staff of the Manuscripts and Rare Books rooms at Cambridge University Library and the British Library, the staff of the Suffolk Record Office in Bury St Edmunds, Fr John Sharp of Birmingham Archdiocesan Archives, Fr Nicholas Schofield of the Archives of the Archbishop of Westminster and Abbot Geoffrey Scott of Douai Abbey.

I am especially grateful to the Abbot and community of Downside Abbey and Dr Simon Johnson for giving me access to the archives of the South Province of the English Benedictine Congregation, as well as for the monks' hospitality on my visits there. I am grateful to Dr Gabriel Glickman and Edward Davis for reading and commenting on the draft manuscript. I am likewise grateful to Dr Kendra Packham for her encouragement of my early research, whether at Catholic Record Society conferences or in the tearoom of Cambridge University Library. I thank Prof. Maurice Whitehead for his helpful comments and insight on Jesuit missions in the reign of James II, and Dr Pat Murrell and Dr John Sutton for directing me to important sources regarding the late seventeenth century in Bury St Edmunds. Lastly, I thank my wife Rachel Hilditch for her unfailing support for all my academic endeavours and her tolerance of my sometimes recondite historical preoccupations. Naturally, I take full responsibility for any errors or omissions in the text.

This book is dedicated to all members of the Community of Reconciliation at Hengrave Hall, 1974–2005, whether still living or now deceased.

Qui amat Deum ambulat super mare.

Ely, Cambridgeshire
November 2014

ABBREVIATIONS

Bellenger	D. A. Bellenger (ed.), *English and Welsh Priests 1558–1800* (Bath: Downside Abbey, 1984)
BL	British Library
Bury Register	Jesuit mission register for Bury St Edmunds kept by John Gage SJ, 1756–89 (now in private ownership)
Catalogue	*A Catalogue of the Whole of the Very Interesting and Historical Contents of Hengrave Hall, Bury St Edmunds* (London: Hampton and Sons, 1897)
CPCC	M. A. Green (ed.), *Calendar of Proceedings of the Committee of Compounding, 1643–1660* (London: HMSO, 1889–92), 5 vols
CRS	Catholic Record Society
CSPD	Calendar of State Papers, Domestic Series
CUL	Cambridge University Library
Diary	Diary of Dom Alexius Jones, 1732–43 (CUL Hengrave MS 69)
EANQ	*East Anglian Notes and Queries*
Foley	H. Foley (ed.), *Records of the English Province of the Society of Jesus* (London: Burns and Oates, 1877–83), 8 vols
Gage, *Hengrave*	J. Gage, *The History and Antiquities of Hengrave in Suffolk* (Bury St Edmunds, 1822)
Gage, *Thingoe*	J. Gage, *The History and Antiquities of Suffolk: Thingoe Hundred* (London, 1838)
Hengrave Register	Benedictine mission register for Hengrave and Bury St Edmunds kept by Dom Francis Howard, 1734–51 (Downside Abbey MSS)
Lords MSS	Various eds., *The Manuscripts of the House of Lords* (London, 1887–1977)
ODNB	*The Oxford Dictionary of National Biography* (Oxford: Oxford University Press, 2004)
OFM	Order of Friars Minor (Franciscan)
OSA	Order of St Augustine (Augustinian Canoness)
OSB	Order of St Benedict (Benedictine)
PSIA(H)	*Proceedings of the Suffolk Institute of Archaeology (and History)*

St James Baptisms	S. H. A. Hervey (ed.), *Bury St. Edmunds, St. James Parish Registers, Baptisms 1558–1800* (Bury St Edmunds: Paul and Mathew, 1915)
St James Burials	S. H. A. Hervey (ed.), *Bury St. Edmunds St. James Parish Registers: Burials 1562–1800* (Bury St Edmunds: Paul and Mathew, 1916)
St James Marriages	S. H. A. Hervey (ed.), *Bury St. Edmunds, St. James Parish Registers, Marriages 1562–1800* (Woodbridge: G. Booth, 1916)
SJ	Society of Jesus (Jesuit)
SRO(B)	Suffolk Record Office, Bury St Edmunds
SRS	Suffolk Records Society
Suffolk in 1674	S. H. A. Hervey (ed.), *Suffolk in 1674, being the Hearth Tax Returns* (Woodbridge: G. Booth, 1905)

A Note on Names and Dates

I have chosen to refer to married women throughout the text by their maiden surnames in order to avoid the confusion that can be caused by multiple marriages and consequent changes of surname. Thus Penelope, the mother of Sir Edward Gage, 1st Baronet, who was married three times, is referred to as Penelope Darcy throughout the text. Names in direct quotations from documents remain unaltered. Religious names of clergy are given after the Christian name, thus John Jones (Alexius Jones in religion) is referred to in the first instance as John Alexius Jones, and thereafter as Alexius Jones.

All dates before 1752 are given according to the Julian Calendar (OS). However, for the sake of clarity I have taken the year as beginning on 1 January rather than 25 March, thus 1 January 1737 or 1737/8 becomes 1 January 1738.

West Suffolk

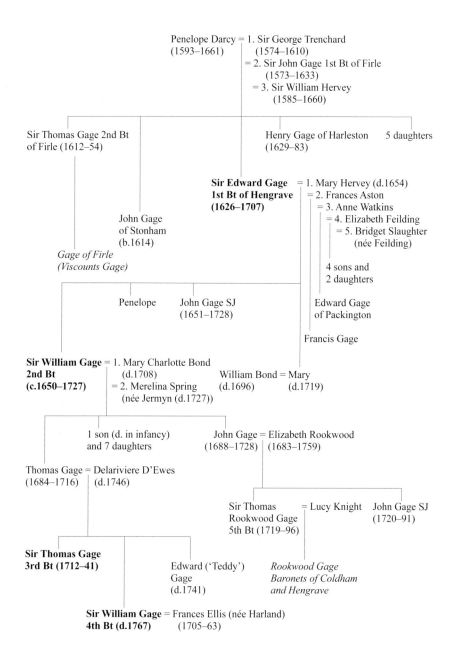

Penelope Darcy = 1. Sir George Trenchard
(1593–1661)   (1574–1610)
              = 2. Sir John Gage 1st Bt of Firle
                   (1573–1633)
              = 3. Sir William Hervey
                   (1585–1660)

Sir Thomas Gage 2nd Bt   Henry Gage of Harleston   5 daughters
of Firle (1612–54)   (1629–83)

Sir Edward Gage   = 1. Mary Hervey (d.1654)
1st Bt of Hengrave   = 2. Frances Aston
(1626–1707)   = 3. Anne Watkins
                         = 4. Elizabeth Feilding
                            = 5. Bridget Slaughter
                                 (née Feilding)

John Gage
of Stonham
(b.1614)

*Gage of Firle
(Viscounts Gage)*

                                              4 sons and
                                              2 daughters

Penelope   John Gage SJ   Edward Gage
              (1651–1728)   of Packington

                                   Francis Gage

Sir William Gage = 1. Mary Charlotte Bond
2nd Bt   (d.1708)
(c.1650–1727)   = 2. Merelina Spring   William Bond = Mary
                          (née Jermyn (d.1727)) (d.1696)   (d.1719)

         1 son (d. in infancy)   John Gage = Elizabeth Rookwood
         and 7 daughters   (1688–1728) (1683–1759)

Thomas Gage = Delariviere D'Ewes
(1684–1716)   (d.1746)

                          Sir Thomas   = Lucy Knight   John Gage SJ
                          Rookwood Gage   (1720–91)
                          5th Bt (1719–96)

Sir Thomas Gage
3rd Bt (1712–41)   Edward ('Teddy')   *Rookwood Gage*
                        Gage   *Baronets of Coldham*
                        (d.1741)   *and Hengrave*

Sir William Gage = Frances Ellis (née Harland)
4th Bt (d.1767)   (1705–63)

INTRODUCTION

It is a peculiar feature of the history of English Catholicism that it is often teased out of domestic documents such as family pedigrees, deeds and conveyances rather than the kind of 'official' ecclesiastical records that exist for the Established Church. English Catholic history is, unavoidably, family history. This book is an attempt to reconstruct the story of one Catholic family, and its relationship to other Catholics, during a crucial period from the start of the Civil War to the threshold of the first Catholic Relief Act in 1778. It is an avowedly local study, but the Gages, like most Catholic families, differed from their Protestant neighbours in having a strikingly cosmopolitan outlook and lifestyle. The Gages were as much at home in Paris or Brussels as they were in rural Suffolk. This book is a case study of the Gages of Hengrave as a fairly successful recusant family of the middle-ranking gentry, as well as an attempt to reconstruct the Catholic community of an English market town in the mid-eighteenth century.

Bury St Edmunds was unusual in England as whole, by being a market town with an established, cohesive and enduring Catholic community. In the seventeenth century, Bury was one of only three such towns with a medium-sized community of between forty and fifty Catholics; the others were Baldock in Hertfordshire and Walsall in Staffordshire.[1] Neither of these places had much in common with Bury other than their market status. It is impossible to apply generalisations, social or geographical, to a community as marginalised as English Catholics. Evidence such as the Compton Census of 1676 makes it plain that there was a small but vibrant 'plebeian' Catholic community in Bury St Edmunds in the seventeenth century, but adequate records of ordinary Catholics in Bury do not become available until the 1730s; up to that point, our evidence mainly concerns the Catholic gentry, and it is from their family documents that the story of the entire community must be told.

Marie Rowlands noted that seeing English Catholicism exclusively in terms of the gentry leads to an impression of a highly fragmented community, with isolated landowners clinging on to the faith amid a sea of conformity.[2] The addition of the lower orders to the picture reveals that there were other Catholics 'filling in the gaps', although this was not always so, and genuine examples of gentry isolation can be found

---

[1] M. B. Rowlands (ed.), *English Catholics of Parish and Town 1558–1778* (London: CRS, 1999), pp. 105–6.

[2] Ibid. p. 3.

in south Suffolk. However, in West Suffolk,[3] the gentry and 'plebeian' Catholic communities cannot be pulled apart, and it is better, when possible, to study high and low together in the hope that light may be shed on the development of both. Certainly, this is preferable to ignoring either gentry or ordinary Catholics on account of ideological presuppositions concerning the significance or insignificance of either group.

The Gage family's relationship with the Catholic community was often far from the 'seigneurial' model of gentry Catholicism proposed by John Bossy in the 1970s.[4] Combining the historic occasional conformity of the Kytson and Darcy families of Suffolk and Essex with the passionate recusancy of the Sussex Gages, the Hengrave Gages drew strength from both approaches to penal legislation and shrewdly avoided political confrontation. The family interacted with, and in many ways depended on, the small yet growing Catholic community of Bury St Edmunds, and in the early 1760s it was the Jesuit John Gage, a cousin of the then baronet, who built a chapel for that community and re-established a Jesuit mission free from the patronage of his own family.

Peter Marshall and Geoffrey Scott recently noted that studies are needed of 'how ... the elites of the Catholic community stand in relation to the social topography around them'.[5] In order to define the nature and extent of English Catholicism during the seventeenth and eighteenth centuries, Rowlands argued in *English Catholics of Parish and Town*, 'we have to reconstruct histories of families, parishes and congregations'.[6] This book fulfils those aims for one region and brings interpretative methodology to bear on Suffolk's Catholics, with a focus on the west of the county. The evidence itself demands that the gentry and their social inferiors be treated as a single community. The gentry were prepared to act as godparents to the children of ordinary families, while the humblest labourer acted as witness to the historically important union of the Gage and Rookwood families in 1718. The Catholic faith united social classes rather than dividing them, and Suffolk makes an eminently suitable case study of a socially interdependent Catholic

---

3   In this book 'West Suffolk' refers to the eight and half hundreds covered by the ancient Liberty of St Edmund, which remained a judicial division of the county of Suffolk and was almost exactly coextensive with the county of West Suffolk created in 1889 (abolished and merged with East Suffolk in 1974). See E. Martin, 'Hundreds and Liberties' in D. Dymond and E. Martin (eds), *An Historical Atlas of Suffolk* (Ipswich: Suffolk County Council, 1988), pp. 18–19.

4   See J. Bossy, *The English Catholic Community 1570–1850* (London: Darton, Longman and Todd, 1975), pp. 149–81.

5   P. Marshall and G. Scott, 'Introduction: The Catholic Gentry in English Society' in idem (eds), *Catholic Gentry in English Society: The Throckmortons of Coughton from Reformation to Emancipation* (Farnham: Ashgate, 2009), p. 4.

6   Rowlands, *English Catholics of Parish and Town*, pp. 5–6.

community. Whereas plebeian Catholicism had the strength to exist in isolation from gentry involvement in a county like Lancashire, neither the gentry nor the common people could survive without the other in Suffolk, where the Catholic population was always small.[7]

The recusant family in Catholic history

To date very few studies of individual Catholic families have been produced, although it is now recognised that the contribution of the gentry and their kinship networks to the survival (and indeed growth) of English Catholic society was at least as important as the organisation of clergy and missions.[8] Some families have attracted the attention of historians for reasons other than their Catholicism. An early example relating to Suffolk was G. H. Ryan and L. J. Redstone's 1931 study of the Timperleys of Hintlesham,[9] while a more recent one can be found in Nesta Evans's 1980 article on the Tasburghs of Flixton.[10] The value of these two studies for understanding Catholicism in Suffolk is limited, however. Ryan and Redstone were admiring yet uncomprehending of the Timperleys' recusancy, while Evans saw the recusancy of the Tasburghs as an oddity that could only lead a family into a spiral of decline. The idea that remaining or becoming Catholic could have been a positive choice, rather than a recondite preoccupation, was alien to these historians.

By contrast with local historians at a loss to comprehend Catholic families, the focus of historians of the Catholic community such as Bossy and J. C. H. Aveling was on 'the society of Catholics' as a whole.[11] Individual family studies, often relegated to the pages of *Recusant History*,[12] gave way to broader analysis of recusancy rolls and an 'inter-

---

7   Bossy, *The English Catholic Community 1570–1850*, estimated that between 6% and 10% of households in Suffolk were Catholic in 1641–42, falling to between 1% and 5% in 1767 (p. 408).

8   Marshall and Scott, *Catholic Gentry in English Society*, p. 1.

9   G. H. Ryan and L. J. Redstone, *Timperley of Hintlesham: A Study of a Suffolk Family* (London: Methuen, 1931).

10 N. Evans, 'The Tasburghs of South Elmham: The Rise and Fall of a Suffolk Gentry Family', *Proceedings of the Suffolk Institute of Archaeology and History* 34 (1980), pp. 269–80.

11 J. Bossy, *The English Catholic Community 1570–1850* (London: Darton, Longman and Todd, 1975); J. C. H. Aveling, *The Handle and the Axe* (London: Blond and Briggs, 1976).

12 Examples include M. B. Joyce, 'The Haggerstons: The Education of a Northumberland Family', *Recusant History* 19 (1978), pp. 175–92; M. Hodgetts, 'The Yates of Harvington, 1631–1696', *Recusant History* 22 (1994), pp. 152–81; M. Murphy, 'A

nalist' national history of the Catholic community. Recent years have seen some detailed family studies whose emphasis is less on the internal dynamics of English Catholicism than on the relationship between Catholic families and the world around them. Michael Questier's *Catholicism and Community in Early Modern England* (2006) has approached issues of national Catholic history through the Brownes of Cowdray and Battle between 1550 and 1640,[13] while Lyn Boothman and Richard Hyde Parker's volume on the Savages of Long Melford (relatives of the Gages) traces the family to the Civil War period, although the Catholicism of the Savages is not a strong focus of the book.[14] My own articles on the Tasburghs of Flixton and Bodney have illuminated the influence of that family on the survival of Catholicism in north-east Suffolk and the Duke of Norfolk's political dominance of south Norfolk.[15]

One of the rare studies to take the history of a Catholic family beyond the Civil War, through the Restoration and the 1688 Revolution and on into the eighteenth century and beyond is Peter Marshall and Geoffrey Scott's 2009 collection of essays on the Throckmortons of Coughton, which makes a persuasive case for the value of tracing the fortunes of individual families.[16] Some scholars have focussed on the gentry in one particular locality rather than on an individual family and its immediate connections,[17] although works addressing the relationship between gentry and urban Catholicism, and between Catholic and Protestant gentry, are scarce.[18]

House Divided: The Fall of the Herberts of Powys 1688–1715', *Recusant History* 26 (2002–3), pp. 88–101.

[13] M. Questier, *Catholicism and Community in Early Modern England: Politics, Aristocratic Patronage and Religion, c.1550–1640* (Cambridge: Cambridge University Press, 2006).

[14] L. Boothman and R. Hyde Parker (eds), *Savage Fortune: An Aristocratic Family in the Early Seventeenth Century* (Woodbridge: SRS, 2006), pp. xiii–lxxxvi.

[15] F. Young, 'The Tasburghs of Flixton and Catholicism in North-east Suffolk, 1642–1767', *Proceedings of the Suffolk Institute of Archaeology and History* 42 (2012), pp. 455–70; F. Young, 'The Tasburghs of Bodney: Catholicism and Politics in South Norfolk', *Norfolk Archaeology* 46 (2011), pp. 190–98.

[16] Marshall and Scott, *Catholic Gentry in English Society*; another example of a family study of this period is J. Callow, 'The Last of the Shireburnes: The Art of Life and Death in Recusant Lancashire 1690–1754', *Recusant History* 26 (2002–3), pp. 589–615.

[17] See J. C. H. Aveling, *Northern Catholics: The Catholic Recusants of the North Riding of Yorkshire 1558–1790* (London: Chapman, 1966); S. Bastow, *The Catholic Gentry of Yorkshire, 1536–1642: Resistance and Accommodation* (Lampeter: Edwin Mellen Press, 2007); L. Gooch, '"The Religion for a Gentleman": The Northern Catholic Gentry in the Eighteenth Century', *Recusant History* 23 (1997), pp. 543–68.

[18] Two examples are S. Bastow, 'The Catholic Gentry and the Catholic Community in the City of York, 1536–1642: The Focus of a Catholic Country?', *York Historian* 18 (2001), pp. 12–22 and B. G. Blackwood, 'Lancashire Catholics, Protestants and Jacobites in the 1715 Rebellion', *Recusant History* 22 (1994), pp. 41–59.

Bossy and Aveling established an orthodoxy that presented the post-Revolution period as a time of decay and decline for English Catholicism, and this may explain why historians have been reluctant to investigate individual families and localities in the period after 1688. However, Gabriel Glickman has recently defended the vitality of post-Revolution Catholicism; he draws attention to the cultural and spiritual contribution of Jacobitism and continental links to the English Catholic community as well as the dynamism of lay Catholicism.[19] In the context of renewed interest in the role of the Catholic gentry and greater recognition of the eighteenth century as an age of positive development rather than inevitable decline, studies of Catholic families that trace their role in local communities from the early modern into the modern period are essential.

There is no such thing as a 'typical' English Catholic family of the early modern period, largely because the embattled post-Reformation community lived under a different set of conditions in each region and county and different families adopted different strategies for survival. These included church papistry or occasional conformity, stubborn recusancy, marriage alliances with other Catholics, marriage alliances with Protestants, cultivating good relations with Protestant neighbours, surrounding themselves with Catholic servants and retainers, foreign exile and even participation in armed rebellion. The ability or willingness of any Catholic family to adopt one or all of these strategies depended on such factors as status, wealth, location and confidence. Marshall and Scott have argued that marriage strategy, kinship networks, the management and expansion of estates, patronage, consumption, expenditure and concepts of honour and ideological commitment all contributed to the gentry's role and identity – the same concerns that affected their Protestant neighbours.[20]

In spite of the diversity of Catholic gentry families, some broad categorisation by means of comparison must be attempted. In contrast to the 'new money' of the Kytsons, who built Hengrave Hall, the Gages were untitled but ancient landed gentry from Sussex who, like the Bedingfields, Cornwallises, Drurys, Jerninghams and Sulyards in East Anglia, had served the regime of Mary Tudor. They became baronets in the reign of Charles II but, unlike the senior line of Sussex Gages, they never rose to the peerage through conformity. Largely owing to the caprice of Mary Kytson, who favoured her daughter Elizabeth over her daughter Penelope, the Savages came to own lands in Cheshire and Devon as well as Suffolk and Essex. The Gages differed from Catholic families such

[19] G. Glickman, *The English Catholic Community 1688–1745: Politics, Culture and Ideology* (Woodbridge: Boydell Press, 2009), pp. 53–86, 121–57.

[20] Marshall and Scott, *Catholic Gentry in English Society*, p. 3.

as the Rookwoods and Tasburghs who owned lands beyond the county boundaries. On the other hand, the wealth of the Gages did allow them to own a London townhouse, and there is evidence to suggest that Sir Edward Gage kept fellow Catholics informed of events in the capital.[21]

It is probably fair to say that the Suffolk Gages were middle-ranking Catholic gentry who occupied a position of local rather than national leadership. Yet the relative insignificance of the Gages on a national scale does not make them less interesting. English Catholicism never had a uniform texture across all localities, and in order to understand the national picture, local studies are essential. So far they are particularly scarce for the south of England. The north, where 'popular Catholicism' was a more significant phenomenon, has understandably attracted the attention of historians keen to overturn the perception of a gentry-dominated and inward-looking community. However, the south was not without its modest Catholic enclaves, and it is a mistake to assume that gentry Catholics there survived in isolation without a wider Catholic community. In Suffolk, the number of Catholics was small but sustained; the community was not focussed on Ipswich and the Stour Valley but on Bury St Edmunds in the west of the county, where the Gages enjoyed influence.

Catholicism in Suffolk

The portrayal of Catholicism in Suffolk as a gentry phenomenon, in which Catholics of lower social status could survive only as appendages of high-status households, is inaccurate with respect to the Gages' relationship with the Catholic community in Bury St Edmunds and the surrounding area.[22] Whilst the conclusions of John Walter's studies of the Stour Valley (south Suffolk and north Essex) are valid for that small geographical area, they have coloured the way in which East Anglian Catholicism as a whole has been perceived.[23] Joy Rowe has observed that most Catholics lived in Bury St Edmunds 'or scattered about the countryside around the houses of known Catholic gentry, especially

---

[21] Sir Edward Gage to Sir Francis Mannock, 13 March 1678, Cambridge University Library (hereafter CUL) Hengrave MS 88/2/182.

[22] J. J. Scarisbrick, *The Reformation and the English People* (London: Blackwell, 1984), p. 149; J. Walter, 'Anti-Popery and the Stour Valley Riots of 1642', in D. Chadd (ed.), *Religious Dissent in East Anglia III* (Norwich: University of East Anglia, 1996), p. 124; G. Blackwood, *Tudor and Stuart Suffolk* (Lancaster: Carnegie, 2001), p. 122.

[23] Walter, 'Anti-Popery and the Stour Valley Riots of 1642'; Walter, *Understanding Popular Violence in the English Revolution: The Colchester Plunderers* (Cambridge: Cambridge University Press, 1999).

in the villages of High Suffolk and along the Norfolk border'.[24] These demographic facts are important when estimating the genuine impact of localised anti-Catholicism on Catholics in Suffolk as a whole.

Major manifestations of anti-Catholic feeling such as the Stour Valley Riots of 1642 were exceptional, however, and the militant godliness of south Suffolk and north Essex did not characterise the entire county. Catholics remained a tiny minority in the region, but there were pockets of popular Catholicism in East Anglia, most notably at Norwich and, as previously noted, Bury St Edmunds, which Gordon Blackwood has described as the 'spiritual capital' of Suffolk Catholicism in the late seventeenth century.[25] During the reign of James II, Bury became the setting for a Jesuit College in the ruins of the Abbey of St Edmund, entirely independent of gentry control. Where it had been a hotbed of Protestant enthusiasm in the 1580s, by the time of the outbreak of the Civil War, Bury was on the whole a politically and religiously conservative town in comparison with others in the Eastern Association, and it was the scene of a brief Royalist uprising in May 1648.

Joy Rowe, whose contribution to the history of Catholicism in Suffolk is of inestimable value, was the first to draw attention to clusters of Catholics in the county independent of the gentry, ministered to by 'riding priests' rather than sedentary domestic chaplains.[26] The geographical concentration of Catholics in High Suffolk and the Liberty of St Edmund is significant; Patrick Collinson remarked upon 'the insubordination characteristic of the mixed economy of High Suffolk, with its weak manorial organisation and lack of gentry control'.[27] (The mixed economy consisted of woodland on the sandy Breckland and pasture on the chalk uplands, and freeholdings abounded.) As Rowe has suggested, 'stiff-necked independence and conservatism' were characteristics that Catholics and the godly had in common, and they may have been linked to economic factors partly dependent on geography.[28] If post-Reformation

---

[24] J. Rowe, 'Roman Catholic Recusancy' in D. Dymond and E. Martin (eds), *An Historical Atlas of Suffolk* (Ipswich: Suffolk County Council, 1988), p. 88.

[25] Blackwood, *Tudor and Stuart Suffolk*, p. 230.

[26] Rowe, 'Roman Catholic Recusancy', p. 88; J. Rowe, 'The 1767 Census of Papists in the Diocese of Norwich: The Social Composition of the Roman Catholic Community' in Chadd, *Religious Dissent in East Anglia III*, p. 189; J. Rowe, '"The Lopped Tree": The Re-formation of the Suffolk Catholic Community' in N. Tyacke (ed.), *England's Long Reformation 1500–1800* (Abingdon: UCL Press, 1998), pp. 174–75.

[27] P. Collinson, 'Godly Preachers and Zealous Magistrates in Elizabethan East Anglia: The Roots of Dissent' in idem (ed.), *From Cranmer to Sancroft* (London: Continuum, 2006), p. 30.

[28] Rowe, '"The Lopped Tree": The Re-formation of the Suffolk Catholic Community', pp. 167–94.

Catholicism was 'a haven for the nonconformist conscience',[29] then Suffolk was a tiny but significant stronghold.

Suffolk's post-Reformation Catholic population was always small, yet it proved 'perdurable', particularly in Bury St Edmunds, where it was sustained by the Short family, a sprawling medical dynasty that was at the heart of the town's Catholic community from the late sixteenth to the late eighteenth century.[30] The Gages depended on the self-made Shorts, as well as on incomers such as the Bonds, Burtons, Staffords and Tyldesleys, to maintain the strength of the Catholic community in which they enjoyed social rather than religious pre-eminence. The Gages even married into these newer Catholic families and they cannot be considered apart from the wider Catholic community. To the south, the Rookwoods of Stanningfield enjoyed periods of prosperity and they were one of the few families who certainly maintained a chaplain and chapel consistently throughout the eighteenth century. However, the Rookwoods' trenchant Jacobitism and prolonged periods of exile ensured that their influence on the local community was small. Blackwood's suggestion that 'Catholics in urban Bury were as much under gentry domination as Catholics in rural Suffolk' runs contrary to the evidence, and is based on surface assumptions about the influence of the Gages, derived from the extent of their wealth and property holdings.[31]

Some historical discussions of Catholicism's dependence on the gentry have tended to assume a broad definition of gentility; they have failed to distinguish between gentry proper (those who lived on income from inherited land) and the 'middling sort' who might well have been called gentry (and self-defined as such), but enjoyed a slightly less exalted social status. Physicians such as the Shorts were defined as gentry by their profession rather than by inherited wealth, and they should not be lumped together with titled and untitled landed families. Gentility was to some extent a relative concept, and the leading man in any rural community might be labelled a gentleman by his social inferiors. Catholics' social status, especially as they entered the more socially mobile eighteenth century, was sometimes fluid and the historian cannot apply rigid categories.[32] In some cases the gentry depended on Catholic tradesmen who would not, by convention, have been described as gentlemen but

---

[29] J. C. H. Aveling, *The Handle and the Axe* (London: Blond and Briggs, 1976), p. 21.

[30] Rowe, 'Roman Catholic Recusancy', p. 88; F. Young, 'The Shorts of Bury St Edmunds: Medicine, Catholicism and Politics in the Seventeenth Century' in *The Journal of Medical Biography* 16 (2008), pp. 188–94. The Shorts were originally from Timworth and had been conformists in the reign of Elizabeth; see Rowe, '"The Lopped Tree": The Re-formation of the Suffolk Catholic Community', pp. 172–73.

[31] Blackwood, *Tudor and Stuart Suffolk*, p. 231.

[32] Rowlands, *English Catholics of Parish and Town*, p. 6.

could wield considerable influence in a community (a 'Lady Russell' occupied one of the four tenements into which the Bury tailor George Birch had divided his house in 1715).[33] In the seventeenth and eighteenth centuries virtually anyone with wealth, however acquired, aspired to live from an income derived from land and thereby be considered a gentleman; families such as the Prettymans and Staffords straddled social boundaries since they were at once landowners, tradesmen and participants in civic politics. Whether they ought to be labelled 'gentry' is debateable.

The seigneurial character of Suffolk Catholicism cannot be inferred from the fact that the vast majority of Suffolk-born Catholic clergy were of gentle birth. Only the wealthy could afford to send their sons and daughters to be educated abroad, a necessary precursor to profession and ordination in most continental religious houses; in addition, many convents required dowries for nuns.[34] The clergy were not in any way representative of the social make-up of the Catholic community in Suffolk, and as so often in early modern history, the mass of poor, uneducated Catholics remained largely hidden from sight until the concerted efforts of the government to count them in 1745. Like a continental education, recusancy was a luxury available only to those who could afford the fines involved throughout most of the early modern period. The church papistry and occasional conformity of the gentry were probably dwarfed by the prevalence of the practice among other less visible social groups, and Michael Questier has argued persuasively that Catholic belief and practice was not coextensive with the legal definition of recusancy.[35] In the case of the Gages, their recusancy or conformity may have had more to do with the political and financial feasibility of refusing to attend church at any particular time than with zealous conviction.

The Gages never adhered to the pattern of endogamous marriage that historians have recognised within some Catholic families who reso-

---

[33] E. E. Estcourt and J. O. Payne (eds), *The English Catholic Non-Jurors of 1715* (London: Burns and Oates, 1885), p. 257. This may have been the same Lady Russell whom Elizabeth Feilding, the fourth wife of Sir Edward Gage, suggested as a suitable wife for her brother William, Earl of Desmond (CUL Hengrave 1/4, fol. 316).

[34] There were exceptions, such as the Bury-born Emmanuel Christmas (d.1748) who entered Douai on a burse, was ordained in 1710 and became chaplain to the 'Blue Nuns' in Paris; see Rowe, '"The Lopped Tree": The Re-formation of the Suffolk Catholic Community', p. 186. In 1745 his Bury relatives were simple labourers (Suffolk Record Office, Bury St Edmunds (hereafter SRO(B)), D8/1/3, bundle 2).

[35] M. Questier, 'Conformity, Catholicism and the Law' in P. Lake and M. Questier (eds), *Conformity and Orthodoxy in the English Church, c.1560–1660* (Woodbridge: Boydell Press 2000), pp. 237–61.

lutely refused to marry Protestants,[36] and they deliberately and repeatedly allied themselves with the Jermyns of Rushbrooke as well as other local Protestants such as the Herveys of Ickworth and the Springs of Pakenham. The Jermyns, a family whose members included all shades of religious opinion, were closely associated with the court of the Dowager Queen Henrietta Maria. Thomas Jermyn, 1st Baron St Edmundsbury was known for his ambivalent attitude to the Protestant religion even before his son Henry Jermyn, 1st Baron Dover converted to Catholicism in the 1670s. However, it was the Jermyns' considerable local influence (as the deciding factor in elections, for instance), as well as their consistent Royalism, that made them an attractive alliance. For the Gages, the normal ties of gentry sociability undoubtedly cut across the confessional divide, and this became clearly evident when the Gages were protected by their Protestant friends and relatives before and during the Civil War. Interconfessional relations are thus illuminated by the relationship of the Gages with their Protestant relatives and neighbours.[37]

In the later seventeenth century, Bury was the centre of the activities of the Jesuit College of the Holy Apostles, founded by Sir Francis Petre in 1633. Petre was the son-in-law of Penelope Darcy, the dynastic foundress of the Hengrave Gages. From the 1670s the Jesuits ministered in West Suffolk relatively unmolested, and it was quite natural for them to acquire permanent and imposing premises in the form of the old Abbot's Palace when de facto toleration of Catholicism arrived in 1685. The 1688 Revolution disrupted but did not end Jesuit activity in the area, although over time the financial impact of the loss of their assets in Bury may have induced the Jesuits to relocate to the Stour Valley, where they enjoyed the patronage of the Daniels of Acton and the Mannocks of Gifford's Hall.

In the 1730s the Gages and Bonds presided over a revival of Catholic fortunes in the Bury area. They supported two Benedictine monks between them who worked closely with (and eventually replaced) a secular priest attached to a 'town mission' that may have been patronised by the Short family. The register kept by the Benedictines during this period was one of the earliest Benedictine mission registers in the country. On the death of the last of the monks the Jesuit mission in Bury was revived under Fr John Gage, the nephew of the 2nd Baronet and brother of the 5th Baronet. However, John Gage was never a gentry chaplain and he was as much the spiritual successor of the Jesuits of

36   Walter, 'Anti-Popery and the Stour Valley Riots of 1642', p. 123; G. Scott, 'The Throckmortons at Home and Abroad, 1680–1800' in P. Marshall and G. Scott (eds), *Catholic Gentry in English Society: The Throckmortons of Coughton from Reformation to Emancipation* (Farnham: Ashgate, 2009), p. 179.

37   Marshall and Scott, *Catholic Gentry in English Society*, p. 6.

the old Abbot's Palace as he was of the Benedictines. Gage funded the mission with his own income, derived from lands bequeathed to him by his mother Elizabeth Rookwood. In 1762 he completed the building of a house and chapel (which he owned himself) with financial help from Sir William Gage, 4th Baronet, his brother Thomas Rookwood Gage, and the Provincial of the English Jesuits, James Dennett. The role of gentry chaplains and rural centres such as Hengrave in sustaining Bury Catholicism was over, and the present Catholic parish of St Edmund King & Martyr in Bury is the unbroken successor to John Gage's mission.

A close examination of the Gages and their interaction with other Catholics and the clergy reveals that John Spurr's characterisation of the Catholic community as 'introspective, gentry dominated and politically loyal' holds true in only one respect for the Gages.[38] More than one of the women who married into the family from strongly Protestant backgrounds converted to Catholicism on doing so, which hardly suggests a religion in stagnation; Delariviere D'Ewes, the granddaughter of a Parliamentarian and a Presbyterian, became the driving force behind the Benedictine mission. The Gages were certainly politically loyal and supported the Hanoverian regime, a fact that must have made the penal laws particularly obnoxious when the Mannocks of Gifford's Hall and members of the Rookwood family were deeply implicated in the Jacobite cause.

The Gages aided rather than hindered the Catholic community's establishment of an identity in the eighteenth century, and the dynastic decline of the senior line of the family from the 1740s onwards hastened the process of change. In 1767 the baronetcy, and with it lay leadership of the local Catholic community, passed to the Rookwood Gages of Coldham Hall, Stanningfield. The reality, however, was that Thomas Rookwood Gage had, through his Jesuit brother, long been more important than his cousin in sustaining Catholicism in the area.

Hengrave Hall

The Hengrave estate lies on the south side of the river Lark, which marks the boundary between the sandy soils of Breckland and the chalkland on which Bury St Edmunds is built; Hengrave is just on the chalkland side. At some point in the reign of St Edward the Confessor the land was inherited by a monk of Westminster, but the Provost of the Abbey of St Edmund confiscated it from him; thereafter it was the property of the Abbey until Abbot Anselm (ruled 1119–48) granted it to a certain Leo,

---

[38] J. Spurr, *The Restoration Church of England 1646–1689* (New Haven, CT: Yale University Press, 1991), p. 65; Blackwood, *Tudor and Stuart Suffolk*, p. 236.

whose heirs, known as De Hemegrethe or De Hemegrave, held the land in the male line until their extinction in 1411.[39] The manor then passed to the Hethe family of Little Saxham and was sold to Humphrey Stafford, later created Duke of Buckingham. A year before Buckingham was attainted in 1522 Thomas Kytson (c.1490–1540), a London mercer originally from Wharton in Lancashire, bought the manor of Hengrave from the Duke. It was duly confiscated from him by the Crown, since Henry VIII saw fit to postdate Buckingham's attainder, but Kytson appealed and managed to persuade the Privy Council to restore his property.[40]

Sir Thomas Kytson the Elder built the present Hengrave Hall between 1525 and 1538. As Sheriff of London, Kytson assisted with the dissolution of the London Charterhouse in 1535 and he built his house using stone from the dissolved priories of Ixworth, Burwell and Thetford,[41] hardly an auspicious start for a house destined to be a centre of the Catholic faith for centuries. The hall he built was a showpiece for new wealth, 'a country house for a London merchant who had made his mark and who announced his status to his neighbours by the size and materials he was able to afford and the cleverness of the decorative conceits that his craftsmen provided for him'.[42] However, Sir Thomas Kytson the Elder died soon after the dissolution of the Abbey of St Edmund, leaving his wife Margaret Donnington pregnant with his posthumous son and heir, Thomas Kytson the Younger (1540/1–1602).

When Hengrave Hall was first built it was a sprawling complex consisting of three main sections, well described by John Gage the antiquary:

> The approach was by a straight causeway, fenced on each side by a deep ditch, lined with a triple row of trees, and terminating at a large semicircular foss, over which a stone bridge led, at some little distance, to the outer court. This court was formed by a central or outer lodge, the residence of the keepers and falconers, and by a range of low surrounding buildings used for offices, including a stable for the horses of pleasure. Beyond was a moat, inclosing the mansion, which is a quadrangular structure, of freestone and white brick, embattled, having an octagonal turret at each angle, with turrets larger and more ornamented that flank the gate-house or entrance to the inner court. By the removal, in the seventeenth century, of the outer court, and, in 1775, of a mass of building which projected at the east and north sides of the

---

[39] By the marriage of Beatrix de Hemegrave to Robert de Thorpe in the fourteenth century the Pastons (and later the Bedingfields) were descended from the de Hemegraves in the female line. See J. Gage, *The History and Antiquities of Hengrave in Suffolk* (Bury St Edmunds, 1822), pp. 80–94.

[40] Gage, *Hengrave*, pp. 95–106.

[41] Ibid. p. 54.

[42] M. Airs, 'The Designing of Five East Anglian Country Houses, 1505–1637', *Architectural History* 21 (1978), p. 66.

mansion, together with a high tower, the house has been reduced one-third, at least, from its original size. The moat has been filled up; there was a bridge over it at the inner gate, figured with devices in polished flint-work, and also a drawbridge communicating with the church.[43]

The main part of the house was built around a central courtyard with a great hall and, innovatively, a cloister running around the courtyard both on the ground floor and the first floor. The moat enclosed this central building and the bowling green behind it to the north. Sir Thomas Kytson the Elder included a domestic chapel on the west side of the south front of the Hall, complete with twenty-one lights of custom-made Flemish stained glass, which were shipped to Ipswich in sections and assembled in situ.

Following the death of Thomas Kytson the Elder, Margaret Donnington remarried John Bourchier, Earl of Bath, who was a strong supporter of Mary I's claim to the throne. On 6 July 1553 Mary may have stayed at Hengrave for one night while on her way to Kenninghall, where she rallied the gentry of East Anglia, including Sir Thomas Cornwallis, Sir Henry Jerningham and Sir John Sulyard, who then rode to Framlingham Castle, where Mary raised her standard.[44] Each of these three surnames would be found in the rolls of East Anglian recusancy for centuries thereafter. Diarmaid MacCulloch has argued that the West Suffolk gentry's loyalty to Mary was due to historic connections with the Abbey and with Mary's Lord Chancellor, the Bury-born Stephen Gardiner, Bishop of Winchester, as well as 'sunny memories of that epicurean prelate', Abbot Reeve, who left generous legacies of wine to the mothers of Sir William Drury and Sir John Tyrrell of Gipping.[45]

It was in Mary's reign that the seeds of Sir Thomas Kytson the Younger's religious conservatism were sown. Kytson married first Jane Paget, and second Elizabeth Cornwallis of Brome, the daughter of Sir Thomas Cornwallis, who rode with Queen Mary from Kenninghall to Framlingham. Cornwallis was a local magnate whose sprawling and ancient family owned vast tracts of land in East Anglia, particularly along the Suffolk–Norfolk border, and it was a step up the social ladder for a Kytson to ally himself to the Cornwallises. The Kytsons hosted Queen Elizabeth I at Hengrave during her progress through East Anglia in 1578, when Sir Thomas presented the Queen with 'a rich jewel' during

---

[43] J. Gage, *The History and Antiquities of Suffolk: Thingoe Hundred* (London, 1838), p. 215.

[44] Gage, *Hengrave*, p. 131; A. Whitelock and D. MacCulloch, 'Princess Mary's Household and the Succession Crisis, July 1553', *Historical Journal* 50 (2007), pp. 265–87.

[45] D. MacCulloch, *Suffolk and the Tudors: Politics and Religion in an English County 1500–1600* (Oxford: Clarendon Press, 1986), p. 210.

a masque.[46] This gesture seems to have purchased him some temporary favour, but Kytson and his wife experienced a good deal of persecution for their occasional relapses into recusancy during the 1580s and 1590s. During the 'Bury Stirs' of the 1580s, when Puritans and anti-Puritans strove for control of Bury's two parish churches, Sir Thomas Kytson and Henry Drury of Lawshall, both Catholics, allied with Bishop Freke of Norwich to oppose a Puritan nominee as minister of St James's Church. It is no surprise that Kytson and Drury's candidate was Giles Wood, the Rector of Brome and a creature of Kytson's brother-in-law Sir Thomas Cornwallis.[47] Cornwallis was notorious for his patronage of non-preaching and 'popish' incumbents, but Kytson and Cornwallis's direct opposition to the Puritans and alliance with Freke is evidence that recusants took an active part in Elizabethan church politics rather than just idly standing by.

Elizabeth Cornwallis and Sir Thomas Kytson the Younger had two surviving children, both daughters: Margaret and Mary. Since Margaret died without issue, it was Mary Kytson (1567–1644) and her children who inherited Hengrave Hall.[48] In 1583 Mary Kytson married Thomas Darcy of Chiche (otherwise known as St Osyth) in Essex (1565–1639).[49] The Darcys, like the Kytsons, had a history of occasional conformity and church papistry. While Mary and Thomas's eldest surviving daughter, Elizabeth, married Thomas Savage, their younger daughter Penelope (1593–1661) married three times.[50] Penelope had children only by her second husband, Sir John Gage, 1st Baronet of Firle, whom she married in 1611. The Gages were an ancient Sussex family, and Sir John Gage's grandfather had been Lord Chamberlain of the Household and Constable of the Tower under Mary.[51] Thus the Gages shared the Kytsons' and Cornwallises' association with the Marian regime and their hereditary religious conservatism. Sir John Gage and Penelope Darcy's eldest son, Thomas, inherited the Firle baronetcy and became the ancestor of the present Viscounts Gage. However, Hengrave was inherited by Penelo-

---

[46] Z. Dovey, *An Elizabethan Progress: The Queen's Journey into East Anglia, 1578* (Stroud: Sutton, 1996), pp. 104–9.

[47] MacCulloch, *Suffolk and the Tudors*, p. 210. On the Bury Stirs see pp. 200–11.

[48] A portrait of Mary Kytson as a young woman is reproduced as Plate II in Boothman and Hyde Parker, *Savage Fortune*.

[49] Ibid. p. xviii.

[50] According to a fanciful story that seems to occur first in E. Kimber and R. Nicholson, *The Baronetage of England* (London, 1771), vol. 2, p. 249 and repeated in Gage, *Hengrave*, p. 224, Penelope was courted by Sir George Trenchard, Sir John Gage and Sir William Hervey at St Osyth before 1610, and in order to discourage them from fighting over her Penelope promised to marry each of them in turn, which was how it turned out.

[51] Gage, *Hengrave*, p. 229.

pe's third son, Edward (1626–1707), on whom she settled it in 1648 when he married Mary Hervey, a daughter of Penelope's third husband, Sir William Hervey of Ickworth, by his first marriage.

The outer court at Hengrave was demolished some time after 1661, when an inventory of the Hall's contents makes clear that Hengrave still retained its original dimensions. Also in the seventeenth century, Hengrave's spacious rooms were subdivided and the Tudor interior was largely obliterated. The original chapel, which had ostensibly served for Church of England worship during the era of the occasional conformist Kytsons, was divided into two rooms, one above the other; the great hall was similarly split. It seems likely that these changes were occasioned by the large number of relatives and friends of the Gages who took refuge at Hengrave during the 1640s and 1650s.

The Gages of Hengrave

Edward Gage of Hengrave was created a baronet by Charles II at his coronation on 15 July 1662. Sir Edward had twelve surviving children by five wives, and Hengrave was inherited by his eldest son by Mary Hervey, Sir William Gage, 2nd Baronet (c.1650–1727). William married Mary Charlotte Bond in 1675 and, subsequently, Merelina Jermyn, the widow of Sir Thomas Spring. On his death in 1727 Hengrave was inherited by his grandson, Sir Thomas Gage, 3rd Baronet (1712–41), the son of Sir William's eldest son Thomas (1684–1716) and Delariviere D'Ewes (d.1746). When the 3rd Baronet died unmarried he was succeeded by his brother William (d.1767) as 4th Baronet. Sir William Gage, 4th Baronet married the widow Frances Ellis (née Harland) in 1741 but had no issue, so on his death in 1767 Hengrave passed to his first cousin, Sir Thomas Rookwood Gage, 5th Baronet. This branch of the family had styled itself Rookwood Gage in 1728 following the death of Thomas Rookwood, the father-in-law of John Gage who married Elizabeth Rookwood in 1718, and the Rookwood Gages had inherited the Rookwoods' Coldham Hall.[52] Thus Hengrave gave way to Coldham as the principal seat of the family, the hub of an estate and a centre of local recusancy.

The Gage family had numerous branches by the end of the seventeenth century, most of them Catholic recusants, and this has sometimes caused confusion among historians. For instance, an error perpetrated by the seventeenth- or eighteenth-century author of a life of the Jesuit William Wright passed into Henry Foley's *Records* and is even to be found in T. M. McCoog's article on Wright in the *Oxford Dictionary*

---

[52] For a more detailed account of the Gage pedigree see Gage, *Hengrave*, pp. 238–47.

of National Biography.[53] This story has 'Edward Gage of Hengrave' receive Fr Wright in his house for eight months in 1606; this was twenty years before 'Edward Gage of Hengrave' was even born. The confusion of the original author may owe something to the fact that Peter Wright, S.J. was chaplain to Sir Henry Gage, Governor of Oxford during the Civil War.[54]

Although less politically significant than the Firle Gages, who eventually conformed to the Church of England, the Gages of Hengrave were a family of great local significance to East Anglia's web of Catholic gentry families, as well as the maintenance and protection of the small 'urban' Catholic community of Bury St Edmunds. Penelope Darcy's marriage to Sir John Gage, described by Michael Questier as an 'unambiguously separatist' recusant,[55] cemented the ties of the occasional conformist and church papist Darcys and Kytsons with confirmed recusants.

The recusancy of Sir Thomas Kytson the Younger has been noticed by historians largely on account of his involvement in Queen Elizabeth's 'progress' of 1578. However, the Gages were no less important than the Kytsons had been in the Catholic life of Suffolk. They were forced to cope with the challenges of the Civil War, the Popish Plot, the 1688 Revolution and the suspicion that fell on Catholics in 1715 and 1745. The tolerance that the Catholic community enjoyed at so early a date is testament to the good relations that Catholic families, and the Gages in particular, had cultivated over many years with the local Protestant establishment.

John Gage the antiquary and the Hengrave manuscripts

Sir Thomas Rookwood Gage, 7th Baronet first recognised the importance of the papers of the Kytson, Gage and Rookwood families and began to compile and index them in the first decade of the nineteenth century. Sir Thomas was a keen naturalist, antiquary, draughtsman and calligrapher. By 1818 he had handwritten four volumes entitled 'Some Account of

---

53   T. M. McCoog, 'Wright, William' in *The Oxford Dictionary of National Biography* (Oxford: Oxford University Press, 2004) (hereafter *ODNB*), vol. 60, p. 503.

54   The original account of William Wright is found in the Jesuits' 1607 report to Robert Persons, *News from England*, which tells us only that '3 members of the leading family of Gage, who are likewise constant guests to the Clink' testified that Wright was making converts; the later author seems to have elaborated this. See H. Foley (ed.), *Records of the English Province of the Society of Jesus* (London: Burns and Oates, 1877–83), 8 vols (hereafter Foley), vol. 7:2, p. 1004.

55   M. Questier, 'Conformity, Catholicism and the Law' in Lake and Questier, *Conformity and Orthodoxy in the English Church*, p. 242. Sir John Gage's house in Clerkenwell was under surveillance by government informants in 1630; see Calendar of State Papers, Domestic Series (hereafter *CSPD*), 1629–1631, p. 429.

the Manor and Parish of Hengrave in the County of Suffolk'.[56] These contained transcriptions of documents (and, in some cases, the original documents pasted in) pertaining to the history of Hengrave and its occupants, as well as pedigrees, family trees and, occasionally, family anecdotes. On Sir Thomas Gage's death in 1820, his work was taken up by his brother John Gage Rokewode (1786–1842), a barrister of Lincoln's Inn, President of the Society of Antiquaries and the fourth son of Sir Thomas Gage, 6th Baronet.[57] John's nephew became 8th Baronet and inherited Coldham Hall, while his brother Robert inherited Hengrave.[58]

In 1822 John Gage published *The History and Antiquities of Hengrave, in Suffolk* (hereafter referred to as *Hengrave*), which followed the conventional pattern of antiquarian works of the time by tracing the history of the site, followed by the history and pedigrees of the families who had lived there. However, John Gage also included accurate transcriptions of original documents such as the great domestic inventory of 1603 and letters written by Margaret Donnington, Elizabeth Cornwallis and Mary Kytson, as well as Henry VIII, Queens Mary and Elizabeth and Sir Philip Sidney. In 1838 John Gage published the first part of a projected monumental county history of Suffolk, *The History and Antiquities of Suffolk: Thingoe Hundred* (hereafter referred to as *Thingoe*). This covered only the parishes of Thingoe Hundred on the west and north sides of Bury. The material on Hengrave that was included in *Thingoe* largely reproduced what Gage had written in *Hengrave*, although there was some additional matter.[59]

Gage's *Hengrave* depended heavily on Sir Thomas Gage's four-volume manuscript history. However, none of the documents published in *Hengrave* dated from after 1643, and John Gage focussed, understandably, on the splendour of Tudor Hengrave and the Kytsons' and Bourchiers' royal connections and role in English history. John Gage attempted to trace the pedigree of the Gage family and provided a wealth of genealogical information, whilst giving only a bare outline of the family's history after 1643, unsupported by documents.

John Gage himself claimed that he was inspired to write *Hengrave* by the antiquarian efforts of another gentleman local to the Bury St Edmunds area, Sir John Cullum, who published *A History of Hawstead* in 1784.[60] However, Gage's abiding ambition was to write a county history of Suffolk, and he asked that *Hengrave* 'be taken as a portion

56 CUL Hengrave MS 1.
57 T. Cooper (rev. J. M. Blatchly), 'Rokewode, John Gage' in *ODNB*, vol. 47, pp. 605–6.
58 See 'Obituary: John Gage Rokewode, Esq.', *The Gentleman's Magazine* (December 1842), pp. 660–61.
59 Gage, *Thingoe*, pp. 164–201.
60 Gage, *Hengrave*, p. vii.

of a general history, much wanted, of the county of Suffolk'. It was to be another sixteen years before Gage would partially fulfil his ambition in the form of *Thingoe*, but the antiquary did not live to complete his work. The first county history of Suffolk was Alfred Suckling's more modest two-volume *History and Antiquities of the County of Suffolk* of 1846, which was heavily dependent on Gage for information on Thingoe Hundred.

John Gage was fortunate that he had access to an archive of original papers as rich as the Hengrave manuscripts. Sir Thomas Kytson the Elder's widow, Margaret Donnington, who subsequently married John Bourchier, 1st Earl of Bath, began the tradition of carefully preserving the letters she received. The practice was continued faithfully by Elizabeth Cornwallis, wife of Sir Thomas Kytson the Younger, and then by Mary Kytson until her death in 1644. The keeping of letters thereafter was more sporadic; they reappear in the late 1660s and early 1670s, when there is a large gap in personal correspondence until 1729. Thereafter, Delariviere D'Ewes and Sir William Gage, 4th Baronet retained most of the letters they received, and the Rookwood Gages continued this practice after 1767 (most of the surviving letters from the period 1640–1767 are reproduced as Appendix 1 of this volume). The Kytsons and Gages were scrupulous in their storage of documents relating to the family and the estate, and Hengrave had its own muniment room, known as the Evidence Room, at least as early as 1727, when a list was made of the documents stored there shortly after the death of Sir William Gage, 2nd Baronet.[61] The list is somewhat vague, but it indicates that the room contained a rental book of the manor of Hengrave,[62] a rental book of other lands held in the parish of Hengrave, deeds, leases and maps relating to the manors of Hengrave, Chevington, Flempton, Lackford and Risby, and the letters patent of Charles II creating Sir Edward a baronet.[63] The compiler of the list made no effort to ascertain the nature of other smaller papers mentioned, and they could well have been the Kytson letters later collected by John Gage.

The Evidence Room was labelled on the plan of 1775,[64] and John Gage the antiquary used the abbreviation *Hengrave Evid.* ('Hengrave Evidence Room') for many of his maunscript sources, implying that the Evidence Room still existed in the 1820s. It was located at the east end

---

[61] Sir William died on 8 February (Gage, *Hengrave*, p. 245) and the audit of documents was made on 15 April (SRO(B) HA 528/40) at the request of a certain John Coggeshall, gentleman. There is no mention of the Evidence Room in the 1661 inventory, CUL Hengrave MS 86.

[62] Now SRO(B) HA 528/40.

[63] Now CUL Hengrave MS 67.

[64] Gage, *Hengrave*, facing p. 18; Gage, *Thingoe*, facing p. 212.

of the south front of the Hall, between the Winter Parlour and the Still House. This same room had a safe and, as late as 2005, was still in use for storing documents. In the first half of the nineteenth century, John Gage augmented the papers in the Evidence Room with documents relating to the Gage family acquired from other sources, such as the diary of Dom Alexius Jones given to him by Margaret, Lady Bedingfield. John Gage created his own library of manuscripts, and his meticulous efforts are responsible for the completeness of the Hengrave manuscripts today.

The widow of Sir Edward Gage, 9th Baronet died in 1887 and thereafter the Hall was let to tenants. Sir John Wood saved the manuscripts by buying them, together with the Hall, in 1897. After Sir John Wood's death, in 1952 the Hengrave manuscripts passed into the possession of his insurers who lent the personal letters and household documents to Cambridge University Library, while the Suffolk Records Office in Bury St Edmunds acquired by purchase the manuscripts relating to land ownership such as wills, maps and deeds. The Hengrave manuscripts deposited there were bought by the University Library in 2005 and this remarkable archive was saved from being broken up.[65] The survival of the Hengrave manuscripts is surprising, given Hengrave's period of abandonment in the eighteenth century, the extinction of the Gage Rokewodes in 1872, Hengrave's subsequent period as a rented house and the two sales of the entire contents in 1897 and 1952. They constitute one of the most complete sets of personal papers belonging to an English Catholic family.

Sources for the Catholic community

In addition to the Gages' personal documents, there are seven key sources for the wider Catholic community in Bury St Edmunds in the eighteenth century:

1. Returns of the annual value of estates of Catholic nonjurors in 1715. These were published in 1745 as *The Names of the Roman Catholics, Nonjurors, and others, who refus'd to take the Oath of Allegiance to his late Majesty King George*. A more complete edition, *The English Catholic Nonjurors of 1715*, was produced by E. E. Estcourt and J. O. Payne in 1885.
2. The Benedictine mission register (referred to hereafter as *Hengrave Register*) kept by Dom Francis Howard, the chaplain at Hengrave and subsequently missionary priest in Bury, from 1734–51. This manuscript probably survived accidentally, as the book in which it

---

[65] 'Hengrave Hall manuscripts saved', *Cambridge University Library Readers' Newsletter* 34 (October 2006).

was written was reused as the English Benedictine Congregation's North Province Cash Book from 1806–9. It is now in the Abbot's Archives at Downside Abbey.

3. The diary of Dom Alexius Jones (referred to hereafter as *Diary*) kept from 1731–43. Jones was chaplain to the Bond family in Bury and worked alongside Francis Howard. This diary was given to John Gage the antiquary by Lady Bedingfield in the early nineteenth century and therefore forms part of the Hengrave manuscripts in Cambridge University Library.

4. Constables' lists of Catholic nonjurors to the quarter sessions of 1745. These lists are in the Suffolk Record Office, Bury St Edmunds Branch.

5. The Jesuit mission register (known hereafter as *Bury Register*) kept by John Gage the Younger, S.J. from 1756 until his death in 1790, and thereafter by his successors. This register is in private hands.

6. The 'Galloway Letters', a collection of letters written to the Norwich Jesuit Edward Galloway by John Gage and others between 1763 and 1780.[66] The letters pertaining to the Bury mission were published by Geoffrey Holt in *Recusant History* in 1983, and the original letters are in the Jesuit Archives in Mount Street, London.

7. Returns of papists compiled by incumbents and sent to the Bishop of Norwich in 1767. These are retained by the Norfolk Record Office but have also been published as an appendix to Joy Rowe's 1996 article on Suffolk Catholics.[67]

Documents that are not specific to the Catholic community, such as the 1674 hearth tax returns and the 1695 tax assessment for the Parish of St James are also crucial sources. Compared with many locales, Bury's Catholic history is well-documented from 1734 onwards, and the distribution of these documents across the century allows us to trace the extent to which the community was sustained by the same families or by new blood. Chapter 5 provides an analysis of the extent of change and continuity in the town.

In addition to these sources I have drawn on printed sources relating to other families, Catholic and non-Catholic, in the Bury area. These

---

[66] G. Holt, 'Some Letters from Suffolk, 1763–80: Selection and Commentary', *Recusant History* 16 (1983), pp. 304–15.

[67] J. Rowe (ed.), 'Norwich Diocesan Return of Papists 11 November 1767 (NRO: DN/ DIS 9/16)', in D. Chadd (ed), *Religious Dissent in East Anglia III* (Norwich: University of East Anglia, 1996), pp. 202–34.

include the letters of John Hervey, 1st Earl of Bristol,[68] the autobiographies of the nuns Catharine Burton and Mary Charlotte Bond,[69] as well as obituaries and necrologies of religious orders, contemporary newspapers, parish registers and the 1674 hearth tax returns. Other detail is provided in official records such as the reports on the manuscripts of the House of Lords, the *Calendar of State Papers Domestic* and the *Calendar of the Committee of Compounding*.

Relatively little has been written on the Catholic community in Suffolk, with the notable exception of a series of studies produced between 1959 and 2004 by Joy Rowe. These began with a pamphlet on the history of Catholic Bury St Edmunds (revised and reprinted in 1981),[70] and followed by contributions to *A Historical Atlas of Suffolk* and the third volume of essays edited by David Chadd, *Religious Dissent in East Anglia*, in 1996.[71] Rowe's 1996 article compared the evidence for Bury's Catholic community at the time of the Compton Census in 1676 with the Returns of Papists of 1767. Her 1998 article in Nicholas Tyacke's *England's Long Reformation* took a similar approach, comparing snapshots of Suffolk's Elizabethan Catholic community with its state at the end of the eighteenth century.[72] Rowe also contributed several articles on Suffolk Catholics and Catholic families to the new *Oxford Dictionary of National Biography*, published in 2004.[73] Geoffrey Holt's 1983 article on the 'Galloway Letters' has already been mentioned. My 2006 article on Catholicism in Bury in the late seventeenth century brought together an analysis of the political efforts of supporters of James II with the missionary efforts of the Jesuits,[74] while in 2008 I examined the influence of the Short family on the survival of Catholicism in Bury.[75]

---

[68] S. H. A. Hervey (ed.), *Letter-Books of John Hervey, First Earl of Bristol* (Wells: E. Jackson, 1894).

[69] T. Hunter, *An English Carmelite. The Life of Catharine Burton, Mary Xaveria of the Angels, of the English Teresian Convent at Antwerp* (London, 1876); N. Hallett, *Lives of Spirit: English Carmelite Self-Writing of the Early Modern Period* (Aldershot: Ashgate, 2007).

[70] J. Rowe, *The Story of Catholic Bury St. Edmunds, Coldham and Surrounding District* (Bury St Edmunds, 1981).

[71] Rowe, 'Roman Catholic Recusancy', pp. 88–89; J. Rowe, 'The 1767 Census of Papists in the Diocese of Norwich, pp. 187–234.

[72] Rowe, '"The Lopped Tree": The Re-formation of the Suffolk Catholic Community', pp. 167–94.

[73] J. Rowe, 'Drury family' in *ODNB*, vol. 16, pp. 997–1000; J. Rowe, 'Everard, Thomas' in *ODNB*, vol. 18, p. 788; J. Rowe, 'Kitson family' in *ODNB*, vol. 31, pp. 845–46.

[74] F. Young, '"An Horrid Popish Plot": The Failure of Catholic Aspirations in Bury St. Edmunds, 1685–88', *Proceedings of the Suffolk Institute of Archaeology (and History)* (hereafter *PSIAH*), 41 (2006), pp. 209–55.

[75] Young, 'The Shorts of Bury St Edmunds', pp. 188–94.

Although the Catholic community in Suffolk is not entirely unexplored terrain, therefore, the relationship between gentry and urban Catholicism has not been treated in detail, and the story of the Gage family has not been integrated into the history of the Catholic community as a whole. Whilst they did a great deal to ensure the survival of the Catholic faith in Suffolk (by providing clergy from the family, patronising chaplains and providing Mass centres), the resilience of the small community in Bury was such that it could and did survive independently of the patronage of the Gages at times (such as the first three decades of the eighteenth century) when the family withdrew its overt support. It is the aim of this book, through a case study of the Gages and the Catholic community in West Suffolk, to contribute to an ongoing debate about the relative significance of the gentry in the survival of local Catholic communities. Whilst it may challenge the 'hagiographical' view of a zealous lay leadership sustaining the faith against all odds, my argument does not diminish the influence and symbolism of the Gage family as *primus inter pares* among the Catholic families of the locality. Their wealth and marriage connections brought respect and, ultimately, de facto tolerance to their fellow Catholics long before it became enshrined in the law of the land.

1

'SOE GREAT A RESORT OF PAPISTS': THE HOUSEHOLD AT HENGRAVE, 1640–60

From 1639 to 1644 Hengrave Hall was the property of Mary Kytson, Countess Rivers; during that period it became the home of her daughter Penelope Darcy with her children by Sir John Gage, 1st Baronet of Firle. In 1643 Penelope married Sir William Hervey of Ickworth, who made Hengrave his seat. Penelope eventually inherited Hengrave in her own right in 1644, following the failure of a Parliamentary attempt to sequestrate the estate, and thereafter it became a place of refuge for Penelope's married children and their families, as well as Sir William Hervey's children by his first wife and other Royalists seeking a quiet retreat. On the marriage of Edward Gage to his stepsister Mary Hervey in 1648, Hengrave was settled on Edward, who inherited the estate on Penelope's death in 1661.

The period before and during the outbreak of the Civil War was a time of great insecurity for Catholics, when the certainties of income from land and inheritance were threatened by sequestration, summary searches and the malice of neighbours. As the daughter of Earl Rivers, a favourite of Charles I, it is hardly surprising that Penelope Darcy, along with almost the entire Gage family, was an instinctive (albeit non-belligerent) Royalist. In this, the Gages differed from some other Suffolk Catholic families who, perhaps on account of the massive compositions for recusancy extracted during the 1630s, remained neutral.[1] Alan Everitt counted seventy-five 'Royalist delinquents and neutrals' in Suffolk.[2] The number was small compared with other counties, although as Everitt has pointed out, Royalist families such as the Cornwallises, Herveys, Mannocks and Timperleys could often make

1 Rowe, 'Roman Catholic Recusancy', p. 88; Blackwood, *Tudor and Stuart Suffolk*, p. 115.
2 A. Everitt, *Suffolk and the Great Rebellion 1640–1660* (Ipswich: SRS, 1960), p. 11.

more of an impact on their local area through ingrained deference and custom than could the grand religious and political ideals of the godly.[3]

The Parliamentarian policy of sequestration was carried out, in Suffolk, by the County Committee. In theory, properties belonging to 'popish recusants' and Royalist 'malignants' (landowners in arms in the service of King Charles, or known to have given their financial support to the King) were subject to automatic sequestration. In reality, however, the situation was more complicated. In some cases, properties owned by Catholics were rented or occupied by non-Catholic relatives. The sequestration of these properties was unpopular and threatened support for Parliament among tenants who might otherwise have been loyal.[4] In other cases the recusancy of a landowner was unproven, and consequently sequestration could not go ahead.[5] Some Catholic families were able to avoid sequestration by means of pre-existing legal arrangements, such as the Rookwoods of Stanningfield whose estate had been in trust since before 1606.[6] However, there were certainly Catholic families who suffered greatly from sequestrations. The Rookwoods of Euston were bled dry by Parliament,[7] albeit the eventual sale of Euston Hall to the Earl of Desmond later proved fortuitous for the marriage prospects of Sir Edward Gage. The Tasburghs of Flixton, although they managed to regain their property, were forced to run up enormous debts during the 1640s and 1650s,[8] while the Savages of Long Melford suffered the ultimate indignity of eviction by a mob.

Penelope Darcy was a Catholic occupying a property owned by her mother, an outward conformist from 1642, yet both her recusancy and the Royalist connections of her father's family rendered her vulnerable. Sir Thomas Gage, 7th Baronet, well described her grim situation:

> Lady Penelope as a Papist Recusant Convict was exposed to the payment of double Taxes and to the severe Penalties for not attending divine service in her Parish Church and also lay at the mercy of the sequestrators named by

3   Ibid. p. 13.
4   See, for example, the protest of Sir Thomas Barker to the Committee of Compounding; Barker rented the Essex estate of Elsenham from the Catholic Cressy Tasburgh of Flixton, in M. A. Green (ed.), *Calendar of Proceedings of the Committee of Compounding, 1643–1660* (London: HMSO, 1889–92), 5 vols (hereafter *CPCC*), vol. 3, p. 2235.
5   Cressy Tasburgh was eventually allowed to keep Elsenham because his recusancy could not be proved.
6   See Sir Robert Rookwood's 1636 appeal against recusancy fines (SRO(B) 326/48). There is no reference to the Rookwoods' Suffolk estates in the *CPCC*.
7   *CPCC*, vol. 2, p. 1425.
8   Evans, 'The Tasburghs of South Elmham', p. 279; *CPCC*, vol. 4, pp. 2708–9.

the Parliament appointed to take two fifths of the yearly value of Catholic Estates.[9]

However, unlike her sister Elizabeth, Penelope escaped the most frightening manifestations of anti-Catholicism, and she was eventually able to transmit her property to her son intact. Penelope's good fortune owed a great deal to the character of West Suffolk compared with the Stour Valley; John Walter has drawn attention to the inevitable friction between 'godly townsmen' and the Catholic households at the fringes of East Anglian towns such as Sudbury and Colchester.[10] One reason why this tension was not so pronounced around Bury St Edmunds was the Royalist affiliation of many of the Protestant gentry, forming a buffer between the extremes of godly townsfolk and Catholic gentry that proved to be such an explosive mix on the Essex–Suffolk border. The Gages were, to a certain extent, protected by the support of local gentry and the occasional expedient of religious conformity.

Penelope Darcy at Hengrave

Penelope Darcy did not come to live at Hengrave willingly, but rather because her mother, Mary Kytson, gave her no choice: 'I submitted to live in Hengrave with my owne poor fortunes,' she wrote to Lady Rivers in 1640, 'rather then to molest your ladyship because you were unwilling to alter your wrightings.'[11] The house that Penelope moved into with her three youngest, unmarried children (Edward, Ann and Dorothy) had been empty since 1628, the year of the death of Penelope's maternal grandmother, Elizabeth Cornwallis, the widow of Sir Thomas Kytson the Younger. Thereafter Hengrave passed to Penelope's father, Thomas Darcy, 1st Earl Rivers, by virtue of his marriage to Mary Kytson. Elizabeth Cornwallis had maintained a splendid household at Hengrave after her husband's death in 1602; she even continued to employ the madrigalist John Wilbye as her musician and composer.[12] However, Earl

---

[9] CUL Hengrave MS 1/3, fol. 297.

[10] Walter, 'Anti-Popery and the Stour Valley Riots of 1642', p. 126.

[11] Penelope Darcy to Mary Kytson, 28 November 1640, CUL Hengrave MS 88/2/147.

[12] Wilbye left Hengrave in 1628 after Lady Kytson's death and lived for the remainder of his life with Mary Kytson in Colchester. On Wilbye see E. H. Fellowes, 'John Wilbye', *Proceedings of the Musical Association* 41 (1915), pp. 55–86; D. Brown, 'John Wilbye, 1574–1638', *The Musical Times* 115 (1974), pp. 214–16.

Fig. 1. Penelope Darcy (1593–1661) as a young woman, engraving from John Gage, *History and Antiquities of Hengrave* (1822) after an original portrait now at Firle Place, Sussex

Rivers broke up the household and there are no unambiguous references to occupation at Hengrave during the intervening period.[13]

In 1640 Penelope, a widow since the death of her second husband, Sir John Gage, 1st Baronet of Firle, on 3 October 1633, was largely financially dependent on the provisions of his will. Sir John left her a jointure of £500 a year, £100 in coin, the furniture of her chamber, a carriage and his house in the parish of St John's, Clerkenwell.[14] This house may in fact have been brought to the marriage by Penelope anyway, since she married her short-lived first husband, Sir George Trenchard,[15] in the same parish and she could have inherited from him any house he had in the area. Penelope lived at Clerkenwell with her children by Sir John Gage from 1633. During that time she was repeatedly prosecuted for recusancy at the Middlesex quarter sessions at the Old Bailey or the Shire Hall in St John's Street, Clerkenwell. A document of 1 December 1646, remitting the payment of arrears in her recusancy fines, records no less than nine convictions between 1625 and 1642.[16]

Penelope's father, Earl Rivers, died on 21 February 1639. The Earl's death was good news for his wife, Mary Kytson, who had been formally separated from her husband just a few months after Penelope's birth in 1594. Mary could now dispose of her maternal inheritance from the Kytsons as she pleased. It was less welcome news for Penelope, whose mother now controlled what would otherwise have been her inheritance, had the Earl not predeceased her mother.[17] Penelope wrote to her mother

---

[13] On the dissolution of the household, see John Wilbye to Mrs Camocke, September 1628, CUL Hengrave MS 88/2/131, 'I think Mr Crofts w[i]t[h] some others wilbe att Hengrave to prise the stuffe'. The only reference to Hengrave between 1628 and 1640 in the Hengrave MSS is in an undated letter of Katherine Colwell to Mary Kytson, according to which Sir John Gage was meant to meet Viscount Savage at Hengrave, CUL Hengrave MS 88/2/136.

[14] Gage, *Hengrave*, n. p. 239. On Penelope Darcy see also J. Rowe, 'Kitson family' in *ODNB*, vol. 31, pp. 845–46.

[15] Penelope Darcy married Sir George Trenchard of Wolverton, Dorset at the church of St James, Clerkenwell on 11 June 1610; Sir George died in December 1610 and Penelope married Sir John Gage at Firle on 28 June 1611. See R. Hovenden, *A True Register of all the Christenings, Marriages and Burials in the Parishe of St. James, Clarkenwell* (London: Mitchell and Hughes, 1884–93), p. 36 and W. Berry, *County Genealogies: Pedigrees of the Families in the County of Sussex* (London, 1830), p. 294.

[16] British Library (hereafter BL) Add. MS 30267. Penelope was convicted on 1 December 1625, 17 April 1630, 5 December 1638, 14 January 1639, 1 and 9 August 1639, 29 August 1639, 1 September 1640, 20 August 1641 and 1 and 5 August 1642.

[17] Penelope Darcy to Mary Kytson, 28 November 1640, CUL Hengrave MS 88/2/147: 'If my L[ord] my father had survived halfe your fortunes had been my byrthright.'

from London about alterations to Lady Rivers's mourning gown. This was probably just after the Earl's death, as Penelope confessed to a growing sense of insecurity about the future: 'my selfe growes now [h]ourlie aff[e]ard of that which must needs bee[.] god give me pacience to suffer his will'.[18] Penelope seems to have endured an unhappy childhood with her father at St Osyth's Priory in Essex, while her mother had her own household in the parish of Holy Trinity, Colchester.[19] In later life she would reflect bitterly on 'my fathers want of affection'.[20]

Following the death of Earl Rivers, Mary Kytson seems to have turned against Penelope, favouring instead the family of Penelope's elder sister, Elizabeth Darcy (1581–1651), who had married Sir Thomas Savage (c.1586–1635), created Viscount Savage in 1626 and subsequently inheriting his father-in-law's title of Earl Rivers. Through Viscount Savage's mother, Mary Allington, the Savages inherited Melford Hall between Bury St Edmunds and Sudbury.[21] The family enjoyed considerable royal favour, and Elizabeth was created *suo jure* Countess Rivers on 21 April 1641, while her mother Mary Kytson, also Countess Rivers, was still living.[22] The duplication of titles has understandably caused confusion amongst historians, since both women were associated with St Osyth's Priory in Essex.

Around 1640 Mary Kytson decided to give the manor of Fornham St Martin (adjacent to Hengrave) to her son-in-law Thomas Savage, 2nd Earl Rivers,[23] and in November 1640 Penelope received word that her mother intended to settle her lands in Devon on the Savages as well.[24] Penelope seems to have believed that her mother was considering giving to them the inheritance that Mary Kytson had earlier promised

---

[18] Penelope Darcy to Mary Kytson, undated, CUL Hengrave MS 88/2/138.

[19] Gage, *Hengrave*, p. 215.

[20] Penelope Darcy to Mary Kytson, 28 November 1640, CUL Hengrave MS 88/2/147.

[21] On the Savage family see Boothman and Hyde Parker, *Savage Fortune*, pp. xiii–lxxxvi. Melford Hall should not be confused with Melford Place, the seat of the Catholic Martin family.

[22] J. Walter, 'Savage [née Darcy], Elizabeth, suo jure Countess Rivers' in *ODNB*, vol. 49, pp. 67–68.

[23] George Gilbert (?) to Mary Kytson, undated, referring to a gift of land to Savage in Fornham St Martin, CUL Hengrave MS 88/2/167. The letter is signed 'G. G.'; George Gilbert is mentioned in conjunction with Savage in the letter of 28 November 1640.

[24] As part of the Kytson inheritance Mary Kytson held the Devon manors of Ipplepen and Torbryan. By a deed of settlement of 27 November 1640 Mary settled them on Thomas Savage with the condition that he should pay £2,000 to Edward Gage, £1,000 to Ann Gage and £100 to Henry Gage. On the Savages' Devon manors see Boothman and Hyde Parker, *Savage Fortune*, p. lxxii.

to Penelope's son Edward, which included Hengrave. In an indenture of 1640, subsequently revoked, Mary had 'conveyed her Suffolk estates to Trustees ... charged with an annual sum of £1000 to Francis Petre and Elizabeth his wife to the use of Lady Penelope Gage in fee'.[25] Penelope wrote to her mother an earnest letter:

> Remember how many yeares you withstood it [i.e. the sale of the manors] & now at last were pleased out of your love to settle it on my beloved sonne Edward. I beseech you let not him bee the first on whom you repent your guift bestowed, who is the last and all that God hath left me of my nurselings.[26]

Penelope pleaded 'let not my poor children suffer for my faulte', which seems to refer to some resentment Mary Kytson held against her; we can only guess what this might have been, but an inscription from Psalm 27 on a miniature portrait of Mary Kytson from this period suggests that she was prone to imagine slights against her: 'Unjust witnesses have risen up against me, and iniquity has lied to itself':[27] a motto for the paranoid if ever there was one.

Although Hengrave remained her mother's property, Penelope lived there by virtue of the fact that Mary Kytson, for the time being at least, had settled it on Penelope's son Edward. However, as the political storm clouds gathered over East Anglia and the Civil War erupted, Penelope's vulnerability as a Catholic widow became increasingly apparent. At the beginning of 1643 her known recusancy, or at least the reputation of her dead husband Sir John Gage, attracted the attention of informants who told Parliament that at Hengrave 'were an 100 armes & soe great a resort of papists as the countrie about it were much troubled at it'.[28] Any report of a Catholic threat was likely to produce a strong reaction from a fearful Parliament, but there is no evidence to suggest that there was anyone at Hengrave at this time, apart from Penelope and her children. Nevertheless, on 14 January 1643 Parliament issued an order for the High Sheriff of Suffolk to search Hengrave 'and seize all such arms as they shall find there, and put them in safe custody'.[29] In practice it was the de facto local government, the Committee of Suffolk, which carried out this order.

The local Royalist gentry came to Penelope's aid in the form of Sir William Hervey of Ickworth, soon to be her third husband, who

25 CUL Hengrave MS 1/3, fol. 257.
26 Penelope Darcy to Mary Kytson, 28 November 1640, CUL Hengrave MS 88/2/147.
27 'Insurrexerunt in me testes iniqui, et mentita est iniquitas sibi', Gage, *Hengrave*, p. 218.
28 Walter, 'Anti-Popery and the Stour Valley Riots of 1642', p. 136.
29 CUL Hengrave MS 88/2/148 (copy of warrant).

rode up to Hengrave on the evening of 25 January 1643 to give her advance warning that a party was on its way to confiscate the armour. Penelope was unwell and had been confined to her bed for the last six days. Fifteen minutes after Sir William's arrival, three members of the Committee of Suffolk, the High Sheriff Sir William Castleton, Sir William Spring,[30] Maurice Barrow and thirty men arrived at Hengrave. Penelope told them that the house was her mother's and that she was only there to recover from illness; she suggested that the officers should present their authorisation from Parliament to her mother. The officers declined to put off the search and confiscation and Penelope 'told them, if theyr authoritie would reach so farr, I could not gainesay anything the Parliam[en]t commanded'.[31] Peed, the armourer, was called from his sickbed at home and told to find the key to the armoury and an inventory, but he was unable to locate either.[32] The Parliamentary officers broke down the door and 'tooke up carts in the highe way' for the arms. Penelope tried to persuade them to leave the drum, since it was used to train horses not to bolt at sudden noises, but 'they by no means would leave it, but tooke it into the coach with them'.

The Sheriff thought that they should leave a guard on the armoury and empty the rest of it the next day, but Barrow offered to stay until midnight and finish the job. Penelope observed that: 'They made great apologies to me at theyr coming inne, saying they hoped I would pardon theyr unwilling employment, and that they wer forced to what they did.' Penelope replied that, 'the armes had been 100 yeares in catholike's hands, and never hurt a finger of any body, and I wished they never might'. The officers agreed to write a letter to Mary Kytson that apologised for the confiscation and assured her that the arms were treated 'with so joint a care both in the loadings, carriage, and laying up, as may well express our due respect to your honour, and our tenderness not to neglect the Parliament'.[33] Penelope included her own letter to her mother, written in haste in a large hand.

---

[30]   Sir William was Penelope's second cousin; he was the son of Sir William Spring of Lavenham and Anne Kytson, third daughter of Sir Thomas Kytson the Elder and Margaret Donnington.

[31]   Penelope Darcy to Mary Kytson, 29 January 1643, CUL Hengrave MS 88/2/150.

[32]   An inventory of the armoury from 1603 survives, including such items as 40 lances, 24 powder flasks, 4 'dagges' (apparently handguns), 2 'snaphaunces' (firelocks), 3 'pethernells' (a horseman's gun), 7 'partisans' (a type of halberd), 9 halberds, 33 pikes, 19 swords, 14 daggers and 4 'long pistols'; Gage, *Hengrave*, p. 31.

[33]   Sir William Castleton et al. to Mary Kytson, 25 January 1643, CUL Hengrave MS 88/2/149. Penelope Darcy to Mary Kytson, 29 January 1643, CUL Hengrave MS 88/2/150; also printed in Gage, *Hengrave*, pp. 219–20.

A number of factors may have contributed to the conspicuous politeness with which the Committee of Suffolk conducted its raid on Hengrave in January 1643. Henry Becket's letter confirms that Mary Kytson was a 'Protestant' at this time, having continued the Kytson and Darcy families' practice of occasional conformity,[34] and this threw the legitimacy of any raid on her property into doubt, as she was technically neither a malignant nor a recusant. Furthermore, Sir William Spring was her cousin and she had powerful connections in the House of Commons and on the Committee of Suffolk. Respect for Mary Kytson and her aristocratic status was just as important to the Committee members as securing popish arms.[35] Penelope hinted that not all were as deferential as the three officers, when she wrote at the end of her letter to her mother: 'We are daily threat[e]ned by the common sort of people, and for our defence have nothing left us.'

January 1643 was a time of heightened awareness of the supposed popish threat, and the home of the Daniels at Acton was searched for 'popish arms' at around the same time as Hengrave.[36] At Stoke-by-Nayland, 'Sir Francis Mannocke's house was pillaged of all goods, and as is said not his writings spared … nor his dogs'.[37] In John Walter's view there was some justification for the alarm; arms were intercepted at Sudbury, apparently on their way to Acton, and Mr Tempest of Whaddon in Cambridgeshire was supposedly overheard commenting on the importance of Catholics arming themselves.[38] However, the disarming of Catholics need not be seen as an activity done for any practical purpose; Brian Quintrell suggested that in the period before the Civil War, Catholics deliberately kept old arms in case they were confiscated. On this reading, disarming was a ritualised, 'neighbour-shaming' activity.[39] The Committee of Suffolk seems to have had no desire to

---

[34] See J. Walter, *Understanding Popular Violence in the English Revolution: The Colchester Plunderers* (Cambridge: Cambridge University Press, 1999), p. 215.

[35] Mary Kytson was not presented as a recusant until the Colchester summer quarter sessions of 1642, even though the order to indict all recusants had gone out from Parliament in December 1640, see Walter, 'Anti-Popery and the Stour Valley Riots of 1642', p. 132.

[36] J. Walter, *Understanding Popular Violence in the English Revolution: The Colchester Plunderers* (Cambridge: Cambridge University Press, 1999), p. 226.

[37] Everitt, *Suffolk and the Great Rebellion 1640–1660*, p. 11.

[38] Walter, *Understanding Popular Violence in the English Revolution*, n. 77, p. 226.

[39] B. Quintrell, 'The Practice and Problems of Recusant Disarming', *Recusant History* 17 (1983), p. 219; P. Croft, 'The Catholic Gentry, the Earl of Salisbury and the Baronets of 1611' in Lake and Questier, *Conformity and Orthodoxy in the English Church*, p. 281.

shame Mary Kytson, but in the build-up to the Civil War national interests had begun to supervene on neighbourly resentments. However, Penelope herself said that the arms at Hengrave were a century old, and they may well have been examples of useless weapons deliberately preserved for show or confiscation.

The political context: the 'Stour Valley Riots' of August 1642

The events of January 1643 were at least partly a reaction to the collective violence that erupted in Suffolk, particularly in the Stour Valley, in August 1642. Crowds originating in 'godly' urban communities, particularly Colchester, roamed the countryside in large armed groups destroying the property and threatening the lives of both Catholic and Protestant Royalists. Penelope's sister Elizabeth Darcy, Countess Rivers became one of the crowd's most famous targets. The Royalist clergyman and pamphleteer Bruno Ryves, in his newssheet *Mercurius Rusticus*, gave a vivid account of the actions of a mobile crowd that picked up followers as it moved across the countryside:

> Being met, their next plundering expedition is to the Countesse of Rivers house at S. Osyth, a rich prize: there they enter the house, and being entred, they pull downe, cut in pieces, and carry away her costly Hangings, Beds, Couches, Chaires, and the whole furniture of her house, rob her of her Plate and Monies: They teare downe her Wainscote, Leads, and Windowes, they leave not a door, not so much as a barre of a window behind them. The Countesse with her family, forewarned of their intensions to come thither, made an escape, and retired to her house at Melford in Suffolke: thither within a day or two they pursue her, Essex is too narrow to bound the madnesse of the Essex Schismaticks; in Suffolke they meet with some that are as mad as themselves: Few Counties (the more is the pity) but can yeeld companion in such outrages. From thence she hardly escapes with her life: she abandons her house, and leaves it to the mercy of these new ministers of justice, who not onely rifle the house, but make strict search for her person. And that you may guess what spirituall men they were, and likewise in what danger this honourable Person was in, they express themselves in this rude unchristian language, That if they found her they would try what flesh she had. From thence she fled to S. Edmunds Bury, where the Gates were shut against her an hour at least: at length she was suffered to lodge there that night, and next day with a strong guard was conveyed out of Town, and so keeping her selfe as private as she could, made an escape to London. Her losses at both her houses were valued at an hundred thousand pounds at least, though some that knew the rich furniture that adorned both, affirm it to be no lesse then an hundred and fifty thousand pounds, besides her Parks in both places were utterly spoiled.[40]

---

[40] B. Ryves, *Mercurius Rusticus: Or, The Countries Complaint of the barbarous*

Ryves and his audience were outraged not so much by the religious persuasion of the mob as by its disrespect for the sanctity of property, a matter of concern for Royalist and Parliamentarian gentry alike. The events of 1642 fulfilled the prophecy of the Suffolk MP Sir Simonds D'Ewes that overturning the constitution would lead to an 'inundation of the vulgar'.[41] It may be significant that Elizabeth Darcy sought refuge in Bury; there were no riots there in 1642, as there were further south, although the Parliamentarian newsbook *Speciall Passages* reported that the town had 'been in great feares a long time' because the county magazine for western Suffolk was in an inconvenient place and its keys in the possession of those suspected of loyalty to the King.[42] On 18 August Parliament ordered the Committee of Suffolk to secure the magazine at Bury.[43]

However, Bury was a town more conspicuously divided in its loyalties than many in the region, and the fact that Elizabeth Darcy was given an armed escort is indicative of the respect that the Committee members had for her status. At the summer quarter sessions on 30 July 1642, both Royalist and Parliamentarian petitions had been presented by the townsfolk, although Walter observed that neither petition featured the names of prominent gentry of the area.[44] This may be an indication of the grass-roots nature of Bury Royalism and Parliamentarianism; alternatively, it indicates that the most important players in local politics were not prepared to declare their views openly but instead spoke and acted through others. This may have been the case at Christmas 1647, when the radical Protestant Thomas Lansetter opened his shop on Christmas Day, provoking a disturbance in which apprentice boys smashed the windows of any shops who dared to open for trade according to Parliament's order.

The meeting of JPs at Bury on 6 September 1642 to discuss the prevention of any repeat of the attacks of August demonstrates the seriousness with which the Parliamentarian authorities treated the socially transgressive violence against persons and property. Walter has compared the 'mobile crowds' of 1642 to the ad hoc armies of sixteenth-century rebels rather than the symbolic protests of the pre-Civil War

Out-rages Committed by the Sectaries of this late flourishing Kingdome (London, 1646), pp. 13–14.

[41] C. Holmes, *The Eastern Association in the English Civil War* (Cambridge: Cambridge University Press, 1974), p. 43.

[42] Walter, *Understanding Popular Violence in the English Revolution*, pp. 38–39.

[43] Ibid. p. 140.

[44] Ibid. pp. 131–32.

era.[45] Penelope Darcy was right to fear 'the common sort of people' far more than the Committee of Suffolk; the danger was not the government itself, but rather the government's failure to keep law and order.

Following the raid on the armoury Henry Becket, a servant, wrote to Mary Kytson from Hengrave on the same day as Penelope, pointing out that the Countess was setting a worrying precedent if she allowed arms that belonged to a Protestant to be confiscated, since no law permitted this. He suggested that she appeal to Sir Harbottle Grimston '& other your friends in the howse' in order to get the arms back; she could then store them at Sir Thomas Jermyn's house at Rushbrooke, 'he being a Parlament man'.[46] Becket's confidence in Rushbrooke's security may have been misplaced; Sir Thomas Jermyn's house had been searched in October 1642 as his loyalty to Parliament was considered suspect. His son Thomas Jermyn was one of two Suffolk MPs to join the Royalist cause, while Sir Thomas himself stayed away from the Long Parliament along with three others, out of a total of fourteen representatives for the county.[47]

By January 1643 Mary Kytson had learned to deal deftly with the authorities and with anti-Catholicism through the practice of occasional conformity. Although she was presented for recusancy at the Colchester quarter sessions in July 1642,[48] Becket certainly thought she was a Protestant in January 1643. The Countess apparently went to some lengths to convince others of the genuineness of her Protestantism; on 25 July 1640 she provided for an annuity of £8 from the manor of Fornham St Martin to be paid to the Bury Corporation so that a sermon should be preached four times a year on 'the distinctive doctrines of the Church of Rome'.[49] The first such sermon was preached by Thomas Newcomen of her own parish of Holy Trinity, Colchester. However, as Samuel Tymms observed in the nineteenth century, the purpose of these sermons was far from clear;[50] and Edmund Gillingwater was inaccurate when he

[45] Ibid. pp. 64–65.
[46] Henry Becket to Mary Kytson, 29 January 1643, CUL Hengrave MS 88/2/151. Penelope's fourth son, Henry Gage of Harleston, was married to Henrietta Jermyn, Sir Thomas Jermyn's daughter; Gage, *Hengrave*, p. 240.
[47] Holmes, *The Eastern Association in the English Civil War*, p. 49.
[48] Walter, 'Anti-Popery and the Stour Valley Riots of 1642', p. 132 observes that this was rather late, given that the order to indict all recusants had gone out from Parliament in December 1640.
[49] S. Tymms, *An Architectural and Historical Account of the Church of St. Mary, Bury St. Edmunds* (Bury St Edmunds: Jackson and Frost:, 1854), pp. 134–35.
[50] Ibid.

described them as being sermons 'against popery'.[51] The ambiguous wording of the endowment was probably deliberate; Mary Kytson seems to have been one of those church papists to whom Michael Questier has drawn attention, manipulating concepts of conformity and the recusancy laws to her own ends with the help of advisers such as Henry Becket, whilst at the same time vulnerable to malicious prosecution for recusancy as a known papist from a papist family.[52]

It was probably the raid on Hengrave in January 1643 that finally convinced Mary Kytson of the need to put Hengrave and her other estates in trust, which she did by an indenture of 21 July 1643. This vested her Suffolk lands in Sir Nicholas Bacon and Richard Green and stipulated that, after her death, they were to be held in trust for the benefit of her daughter Penelope.[53] In the unstable conditions of the early 1640s it is hardly surprising that Penelope sought the security of marriage to Sir William Hervey shortly after the raid. Following their marriage, the couple seem to have gone to live in London at Penelope's house in St John's, Clerkenwell. Penelope was reluctant to live at Hengrave and Sir William tried to get hold of a house for her in Bury, 'but cannot light on anie fitt for a familie'. Penelope confessed, 'I would fayne have been in a Towne these dayngerous times, and I can find n[o] waye but to retire to the Towne at Hengrave', implying that she considered Hengrave close enough to Bury to be in danger from the townsfolk. However, Penelope was forced to leave London on account of the pressure of 'taxes and payments'.[54] Penelope was borrowing money from her mother at this time and was unable to repay it,[55] so Sir William Hervey's resources were evidently either insufficient or unreliable.

For Penelope, the threat to her life and property from anti-Catholic rioters was not her only worry. Her eldest son, Sir Thomas Gage, 2nd Baronet of Firle had succeeded his father as head of the great Sussex recusant family when he was twenty-one years old. He was sent to be educated in Paris with a priest as his governor, but in January 1636 an informant claimed that Sir Thomas Gage and Mr Yate, a gentleman in his company, had designs against the life of the King of France. The Earl of Leicester interceded on Gage's behalf, insisting that he was 'a

51 E. Gillingwater, *An Historical and Descriptive Account of St. Edmund's Bury, in the County of Suffolk* (Bury St Edmunds, 1804), p. 251. Gillingwater misidentified Mary Kytson as 'Penelope, Countess of Rivers'.

52 M. Questier, 'Conformity, Catholicism and the Law', pp. 237–61.

53 CUL Hengrave MS 1/3, fols 261–62.

54 Penelope Darcy to Mary Kytson, 11 July 1643, CUL Hengave MS 88/2/157.

55 Penelope Darcy to Mary Kytson, 7 July 1643, CUL Hengrave MS 88/2/156: 'You shall foinde I will most willingly returne all or what you please soo soone as possible I can'.

very youth and a ward' but the French authorities 'had heard that he frequented much the jesuites'. Gage was arrested and incarcerated in the Bastille with Yate.[56] By 3 February Leicester had effected Gage's release (but not Yate's),[57] and on 24 February Penelope wrote to thank him for his intervention.[58]

On his return from France, Sir Thomas Gage was a young, inexperienced landowner dependent on the advice of his servants and he may have suffered from epilepsy as well; his stay in the Bastille seems to have affected his health. His servant Thomas Harrison wrote to Penelope after 1642: 'S[i]r Thomas Gage hath beene much trouble[d] w[i]th his fitts since his returne into England so we he forced to Bee lett bloud, he hopes the worst is past.'[59] Penelope remained in touch with the household at Firle and it must have been a further source of anxiety to her. However, the servants there, rather like Henry Becket, seem to have devised means of fending off the attentions of hostile parties. Harrison, a servant with thirty-three years' service at Firle, referred to 'my service w[hi]ch I p[er]formed in suppressing many noxious occurrences by my owne policy, or giveing notice to avoyde the dangers, the p[ar]ticulers wheirof I will not commit to paper'.[60] Sir Thomas Gage died on 2 July 1654,[61] fortunately with a son and heir to continue the senior branch of the family.

The threat of sequestration

More money was raised through sequestrations in Suffolk between 1643 and 1649 than in any other county, which is surprising given the relatively small number of 'delinquents' in the county.[62] One reason for this was the efficiency of administration and relative stability of Suffolk; another was that the value of land was simply higher in an agricultural county where farming was well-developed. The third reason for the high

---

[56] Robert, Earl of Leicester to Secretary Coke, 27 January 1636, copied by John Gage the antiquary, CUL Hengrave MS 21/1/197.

[57] Robert, Earl of Leicester to Secretary Coke, 4 February 1636, copied by John Gage the antiquary, CUL Hengrave MS 21/1/197.

[58] Penelope Darcy to Robert, Earl of Leicester, 24 February 1636, copied by John Gage the antiquary, CUL Hengrave MS 21/1/197.

[59] Thomas Harrison to Penelope Darcy, undated (1640s), CUL Hengrave MS 88/2/168.

[60] Thomas Harrison to Penelope Darcy, undated (1640s), CUL Hengrave MS 88/2/168. Walter (1999), p. 64, mistakenly identified Harrison as a servant at Hengrave.

[61] Gage, *Thingoe*, p. 205.

[62] Sequestrations in Suffolk raised £40,917 compared with £21,750 in Norfolk; see Everitt, *Suffolk and the Great Rebellion 1640–1660*, p. 13.

yield from sequestration was the wealth of recusants, who automatically fell under suspicion in spite of their evident neutrality in many cases, whether or not they or their followers had actually taken up arms against Parliament. Penelope Darcy was fortunate to escape the financial fate of the likes of Edward Rookwood of Euston (d.1662). Edward fought for the Royalist cause and on 4 August 1646 he 'was taken prisoner at Woodstock by the forces under the command of the garrison at Northampton, and kept prisoner 18 months'. Edward was obliged to compound 'for delinquency in arms' and in 1647 he also had to pay a heavy fine of £706.[63] In 1652 he compounded his estate once more, this time for recusancy fines. This time, the financial burden proved too much and Edward surrendered the estate, which in 1655 passed to George Feilding, 1st Earl of Desmond.[64]

The purpose of sequestration was not so much to divest recusants of their estates as to raise money, and consequently Parliament rented estates back to their original owners whenever possible. Rookwood was probably unable to pay his rent when he finally surrendered Euston in 1655. On the death of Mary Kytson in 1644 her will and former property naturally became the subject of discussion by Parliament's Committee for Sequestrations. Edmund Harvey of Hinton,[65] a member of the Committee of Suffolk, came to Sir William and Penelope's aid by going to London to act on Penelope's behalf and intercede with MPs. On 13 November Edmund wrote to Penelope from Gray's Inn, telling her that he had spoken to Sir Thomas Trencher who was withholding his rent to Penelope on some property, 'you being a recusant'. Presumably Sir Thomas thought that, as a Catholic, she had no hope of avoiding sequestration and he saw no reason to waste his money paying her rent. Edmund also spoke to Sir Nathaniel Barnardiston, a leading member of the Committee of Suffolk, 'touching St Martin'; probably he was attempting to reverse Mary Kytson's settlement of Fornham St Martin on the Savage family.[66]

When the Committee met on 23 December 1644, Penelope and Edmund's efforts at persuasion rather surprisingly paid off. Those to whom Mary Kytson left legacies were ordered to appear before the Committee but, having failed to do so, they were considered 'delin-

[63] *CPCC*, vol. 2, p. 1425.

[64] Blackwood, *Tudor and Stuart Suffolk*, p. 198.

[65] A. Kingston, *East Anglia and the Great Civil War* (London: E. Stock, 1897), p. 389. It does not seem that Edmund Harvey was any relation of the Herveys of Ickworth.

[66] Edmund Hervey to Penelope Darcy, 13 November 1644, CUL Hengrave MS 88/2/171. Another letter from Edmund to Penelope survives (88/2/169) but it is too damaged to be legible.

quents', and the Committee declared that any trusts, together with 'the resydue of the p[er]sonall estate over and above the debtt' were sequestrated.[67] However, Sir Harbottle Grimston testified that there were no trusts, and that the residue of the estate was worth no more than £400, which did not exceed the debt. Since 'ought appeared to them by way of Sequestration' the Committee of Lords and Commons for Sequestrations gave orders that the Committee of Suffolk should be notified that Mary Kytson's estate should not be sequestrated.[68] Sir Harbottle, it would appear, had exercised his influence to ensure that the Kytson inheritance escaped sequestration on a technicality. However, his intervention may have had something to do with the fact that he, with Sir Thomas Honeywood, was Mary Kytson's executor as well as a beneficiary of the residue of her estate.[69]

Nevertheless, it does not seem to have been straightforward for Penelope to get hold of her mother's personal possessions, and as late as 21 September 1647 she wrote to Sir Harbottle: 'I have now received most of the goods from Colchester.' At the same time she asked him for 'the wrightings for the settlement of my estate upon my children',[70] probably in anticipation of her son Edward's marriage to his stepsister Mary Hervey, Sir William's daughter by his first wife, Susan Jermyn. On 1 July 1648, Penelope settled on Edward the manor of Chevington and put Hengrave in trust for him so that he would inherit it upon her death;[71] the trustees were William Hervey, Henry North, Richard Gipps, John Coel and Fitznun Lambe.[72] Mary Hervey bore Edward Gage a son, Edward, who was baptised in the parish church on 24 April 1649.[73] This could suggest (albeit not necessarily) that Edward was a church papist at the time. Edward's first son must have died soon after, but four children did survive from this marriage, including William, Edward's heir. Mary Hervey was buried on 30 July 1654; in July 1654 a servant at Hengrave recorded that she was owed £8: 'As due to me from my

---

67 It is unclear what this debt was; it may be that Mary Kytson was going to compound for recusancy, or alternatively the debt may have been one of Parliament's forced loans.
68 Report of the Committee of Lords and Commons for Sequestrations, 23 December 1644, CUL Hengrave MS 88/2/159.
69 Gage, *Hengrave*, p. 221.
70 Penelope Darcy to Sir Harbottle Grimston, 21 September 1647, CUL Hengrave MS 88/2/162.
71 Gage, *Hengrave*, n. p. 240.
72 CUL Hengrave MS 1/3, p. 302.
73 Gage, *Hengrave*, p. 77.

Lady [i.e. Penelope Darcy], for 8 yards of black cloth, for mourning for mrs Gage.'[74]

Penelope's known recusancy tainted Sir William Hervey, who appealed to the Committee of Compounding on 20 June 1646 against a decision by the Committee of Suffolk to sequestrate £6,000 he had earned from the sale of the manors of Waxham and Horsey, 'as belonging to Lady Gage, and sequestered for her recusancy'. In this case, the fact that he was married to a recusant was the excuse for extracting money from a Protestant landowner. Penelope deposed six days later that the money was not hers, and eventually Sir William was allowed to keep £2,500 of the original £6,000.[75] Under the circumstances, this was a minor victory. However, on 9 February 1652 Sir William Hervey was forced to claim that his wife had made an act of conformity, so her recusancy evidently remained a financial obstacle.[76]

George Gage of Raunds, the second husband of Penelope's eldest daughter Frances, widow of Sir William Tresham, was less successful when he appealed against the sequestration of Frances's jointure of £365 a year for her recusancy on 26 November 1650. In this case, although George Gage was said to be 'a Protestant, and well affected' (in spite of his having compounded for delinquency in 1649), the request was denied, probably because the money pertained directly to the Catholic wife. Undeterred, George Gage made a further claim against the sequestration of lands in Aldwinckle, Northamptonshire in 1654.[77]

The political context: the Royalist rising of May 1648

Bury St Edmunds was a town at the very heart of the Parliamentarian Eastern Association that, nevertheless, experienced the surge of dissatisfaction with Parliamentarian rule in the late 1640s that marked the beginning of the second Civil War. As a consequence of the rising in Bury in May 1648 the attention of the authorities was drawn to the Jermyns and their activities at Rushbrooke Hall; the Gages' association with the Jermyn family might well have brought them similar attention, and the summer of 1648 was a dangerous one for the Royalist and Catholic gentry. On 12 May there was what a contemporary pamphlet described as 'a great combustion in the town about setting up of a Maypole, which grew to that height that by Satterday six or seven hundred men were gotten into Armes'. Shouts of 'for God and King Charles!'

---

[74] CUL Hengrave MS 92.
[75] *CPCC*, vol. 2, p. 1342.
[76] Gage, *Thingoe*, n. p. 206.
[77] *CPCC*, vol. 4, p. 2624.

were heard around the town, and members of the trained bands, probably soldiers of Sir Thomas Barnardiston's Regiment, were captured by the townsfolk. The leaders of the Royalist uprising took control of the county magazine and barricaded themselves inside Bury's two parish churches, St James's and St Mary's. They were apparently joined by other Royalists from Colchester, where a similar and far more serious rising had taken place. Similar events also happened that summer at Linton and Saffron Walden in Cambridgeshire and in Suffolk at Exning, Newmarket and Lidgate.[78] These eruptions of anti-Parliamentarian feeling were not as spontaneous as they seem in contemporary accounts, and they may have been organised by Colonel Thomas Blague, a veteran cavalier from Suffolk and gentleman of the bedchamber to King Charles I, who was charged with organising Royalist uprisings in East Anglia.[79]

On 13 May the Derby House Committee of Parliament ordered Sir Thomas Barnardiston, MP for Bury, and Sir William Playters, MP for Orford, to secure the town and also informed General Fairfax of the uprising. Meanwhile the Royalists made plans of their own; on 14 May Marmaduke Langdale sent out warrants to a local constable, instructing him to send twenty horse to Bury with arms and men to assist in the town's defence against Parliament.[80] However, the relative distance of any Royalist garrison from Bury, combined with the concentration of Parliamentarian forces in the locality, make it unlikely that Langdale's plan could ever have come to fruition. Fairfax, for his part, ordered Colonel Whalley to march to within a few miles of the edge of the town. Here, Whalley's soldiers came into conflict with Barnardiston's, who did not want the town besieged. Barnardiston and Playters, charged with negotiating with the insurgents, promised them indemnity if they would surrender the magazine and lay down their arms in the market house. The Royalists evidently agreed, and Barnardiston and Cromwell's cousin, Major Desborough, subsequently entered the town. It was later reported to Parliament that 'upon a skirmish in a sally out, there were two of the town killed, and none of ours, only two horses'.[81]

In Alan Everitt's view, the rising at Bury 'woke no effective response' and was essentially a failure in its intention of turning Suffolk against Parliamentary rule.[82] Robert Ashton, by contrast, regarded the events at Bury as approaching the rebellion at Norwich in significance. The

---

[78] Everitt, *Suffolk and the Great Rebellion 1640–1660*, p. 94.

[79] G. Smith, *Royalist Agents, Conspirators and Spies: Their Role in the British Civil Wars, 1640–1660* (Farnham: Ashgate, 2011), p. 152.

[80] R. Ashton, *Counter-Revolution: The Second Civil War and its Origins, 1646–8* (New Haven, CT: Yale University Press, 1994), p. 376.

[81] Kingston, *East Anglia and the Great Civil War*, pp. 255–57.

[82] Everitt, *Suffolk and the Great Rebellion 1640–1660*, p. 15.

Derby Committee's fearful reaction to the rising demonstrated the extent of their fear that local revolts could form the nuclei of larger rebellions, and their fears were justified by attempts to foment Royalist revolts in Thetford and Stowmarket later the same month. However, the principal actors in the Bury rising were not actually from the town; Oliver and John Bridgeman were from Exning and Newmarket and Sir Thomas Peyton had been revolved in Royalist resistance in Kent.[83] Whilst the maypole riot was undoubtedly an indicator of local feeling, this evidence casts doubt on the extent to which the armed uprising that followed was genuinely a 'local' phenomenon. Nevertheless, the Committee of Suffolk suspected that the Bury gentry were more directly involved in seditious activities than was immediately evident: 'We cannot yet discover the bottom of this design', they reported.

Sir Thomas Barnardiston's suspicions alighted specifically on the brothers of Thomas Jermyn (1602–59) at Rushbrooke Hall. Thomas, who joined the King at Oxford in 1643 and later went into exile at the court of Henrietta Maria in Paris,[84] was the son of the 'Parliament man' of Henry Becket's letter of 1643, Sir Thomas Jermyn (1573–1645). Both men had sat as MPs for Bury St Edmunds in the Long Parliament. Ironically, where Rushbrooke had seemed a safe place for Mary Kytson's arms in 1643, in 1648 it was seen as a hotbed of Royalist dissent.

On 3 June 1648 Sir Thomas Barnardiston wrote to Sir Nathaniel Barnardiston, his brother and fellow Committee of Suffolk member, that: 'The disaffected in these parts keep still their meetings at Newmarkett under pretence of horse racing, Rushbrooke hall, near Bury, the place of their general rendezvous, and there feasted by the Jermyn family.'[85] Sir Thomas Barnardiston was reacting to the concerns of the Alderman of Bury, who considered these gentlemen a military threat. Sir William Hervey had been married to a Jermyn, he had raised a Royalist regiment in the first Civil War,[86] and his family frequently visited Rushbrooke; it is consequently almost impossible to imagine that he was not somehow party to the Jermyns' conspiracies (if they were real). However, two years later, in 1650, he was appointed High Sheriff of Suffolk. Sir William's appointment may have been a mark of the inability of the Commonwealth to operate without the involvement of influential Royalist gentry, rather than a sign of the extent to which Sir William had rehabilitated himself in the eyes of the regime. On 31 January 1655

---

[83] Ashton, *Counter-Revolution*, pp. 377–78.

[84] S. H. A. Hervey (ed.), *Rushbrook Parish Registers with Jermyn and Davers Annals* (Woodbridge: G. Booth, 1903), p. 240.

[85] Hervey (ed.), *Rushbrook Parish Registers with Jermyn and Davers Annals*, p. 244; Kingston, *East Anglia and the Great Civil War*, pp. 257–58.

[86] Gage, *Hengrave*, n. p. 240.

he was the recipient of an order from the Lord Protector's Council that was as much concerned with the prevention of vagabondage, maypole dancing, bear-baiting and identifying the reputed fathers of bastard children as it was with Royalist adherents and users of the Prayer Book. Evidently there was little concern about papists at this time, as there is no mention of prosecuting recusants or searching out Catholic chapels; the republican government's religious fears converged on Church of England loyalists.[87] For the time being, the threat of popular violence and state persecution against the community at Hengrave had passed.

Family and community at Hengrave Hall, 1643–60

On Penelope's marriage to Sir William Hervey in 1643, her remaining unmarried children by Sir John Gage (Edward, Ann and Dorothy) were joined by Sir William's children by his first wife, Susan Jermyn (1590–1637/8), the sister of Sir Thomas Jermyn MP. Sir William's eldest son, Thomas Hervey, spent his time courting Isabella May (d.1665), daughter of Sir Humphrey May, Vice-Chamberlain to the Household of Charles I,[88] and left behind letters that shed some light on life at Hengrave in the 1650s. Penelope organised bowls matches between the many relations and friends who were staying at Hengrave; the bowling green was on the north side of the Hall, inside the moat, and would have provided the most readily available means of outdoor entertainment. Some of the bowls matches apparently lasted for days. Thomas Hervey wrote to Isabella on 22 May 1652:

> I have been these two days engaged in a match at bowles. Your brother being concerned made me imagine you might have been in the green … The hope of this made me victor the first day; nor could they gain anything upon us the second till it was so late in the evening as I dispair'd and could not attend to those little successes, having fail'd of my greater expectation. On Tuesday next soon after dinner, if you please so to order it as to be ready, my sister Kez and I have agreed to waite on you to Rushbrooke.

When they were not playing bowls the inhabitants may have resorted to a game of billiards under the tower.[89] If Hengrave had not been 'a resort of papists' when it was searched, from the time of the Herveys'

---

[87] CUL Hengrave MS 88/3/98.
[88] Sir Thomas Hervey served as MP for Bury St Edmunds after the Restoration and was the father of the Whig politician John Hervey, 1st Earl of Bristol (1665–1751), see C. Carter, 'Hervey, John, first earl of Bristol' in *ODNB*, vol. 26, pp. 861–62.
[89] CUL MS Hengrave 86 (1661 Inventory). The billiard table seems to have been there in 1603 as well, when we hear of 'one square board w[i]th a frame' and 'one carpet of greene cloth for the same', Gage, *Hengrave*, p. 34.

arrival it did become something of a bolthole for Royalists and Catholics. Sydenham Hervey imagined these refugees 'all stowed away there,
wondering when the clouds would roll away and the king be brought
back'.[90] The claim found in Kimber and Nicholson's *The Baronetage
of England* (1771) (and repeated by John Gage the antiquary) that there
were over a hundred people living under the protection of Penelope and
Sir William Hervey at this time cannot be unsubstantiated,[91] and may
derive from a letter from Dr Francis Gage to Penelope at Hengrave of 25
April 1650, in which the priest referred to 'all the million of acquaintances thereunto belonging'.[92] However, this hardly implies that there
were over a hundred people living at Hengrave, and Dr Francis Gage
mentioned only Penelope, Sir William Hervey, 'my cosen Edward and
his Lady,[93] the Lady Tressam,[94] my cosen Peters'[95] and 'cosen Hbury'.

Hengrave certainly had some appeal as a Royalist refuge; in the
middle of the Eastern Association, it was far away from the probable
marching routes of the armies that did so much damage to properties in
central England. Furthermore, it was owned by the well-respected and
nominally Protestant Mary Kytson; if it was searched again its inhabitants could, like Penelope in 1643, claim ignorance and innocence in a
house that was not their own. One prominent Royalist who stayed at
Hengrave in the 1640s was Sir Thomas Hanmer (1612–78). Hanmer
represented Flintshire in Parliament before the Civil War and had been
appointed one of Prince Rupert's representatives in North Wales, but on
going to France in 1644 he became a Parliamentarian informant, albeit
this remained unknown to his Royalist friends and relatives.[96] On the
death of his first wife, Elizabeth Baker, in Paris in July 1645, Hanmer
secretly returned to England but avoided his Welsh home, Haughton in

[90] Hervey (ed.), *Rushbrook Parish Registers with Jermyn and Davers Annals*,
     p. 246.
[91] E. Kimber and R. Nicholson, *The Baronetage of England* (London, 1771),
     vol. 2, p. 249; Gage, *Hengrave*, n. p. 240.
[92] Dr Francis Gage to Penelope Darcy, 25 April 1650, CUL Hengrave MS
     88/2/163.
[93] Edward Gage and his wife Mary Hervey.
[94] Penelope's eldest daughter Frances Gage married Sir William Tresham,
     1st Baronet of Liveden in Northamptonshire (d.1650). In 1652 she married
     secondly her cousin George Gage of Raunds in Northamptonshire (d.1688);
     Gage, *Hengrave*, p. 240; Gage, *Thingoe*, p. 205.
[95] This is more likely to refer to Penelope's second daughter, Elizabeth Gage,
     and her children by Sir Francis Petre, 1st Baronet of Cranham than to her
     fourth daughter, Ann, and her children by Henry Petre, younger son of
     William, second Lord Petre – on the basis that Ann was the last of Penelope's
     children to marry.
[96] J. Martin, 'Hanmer, Sir Thomas' in *ODNB*, vol. 25, pp. 64–65.

Flintshire, and headed for Hengrave, 'where Sir Thomas [sic] Harvey, a loyal subject, and sufferer for the king, having married my Lady Penelope Gage, whose jointure-house it was, lived with her whole family'.[97] Hanmer courted and eventually married Susan, a daughter of Sir William by his first wife, in Hengrave church on 22 November 1646.[98] Hanmer had left his only daughter, Trevor, with a Huguenot family in France who thought he was dead, having heard nothing from him for a year. To their great surprise he returned, taking Trevor back to England with him.[99] He gave her a choice of living with her grandmother in Wales or living with her new stepmother at Hengrave; Trevor chose her grandmother's house at Haughton, where she first conceived the idea of becoming a nun. When Hanmer heard of this he sent for her to come back to Hengrave.

At Hengrave, Trevor was 'received with all imaginable kindness by my lady her step-mother [i.e. Susan Hervey], which she returned with that dutiful respect and affection she was able'. Trevor begged her father not to give her a servant, since she wanted to perform all menial tasks as a mortification in preparation for entering religious life. On one occasion Hanmer found Trevor on her knees cleaning the floor of her room; Sir Thomas 'took her up in his arms and embraced her, with tears in his eyes, telling her, "God would one day give her a particular blessing, for conforming herself, after so particular a manner, to those circumstances, to which his providence, and her kindness to himself, had reduced her".'[100] Shortly afterwards, Hanmer went with Trevor to Haughton, but Sir William Hervey wanted her to return to Hengrave, so she came back. Here, 'her former desires of a religious life returned'. Trevor began to fast from any food and water one day a week, she woke up to pray at midnight and engaged in hard manual labour; when others asked her why she did it she claimed that it was good for her health.

Eventually Trevor's father sent for her to live with him and Susan Hervey in London, where he agreed to her becoming a Benedictine nun and was prepared to provide her with a suitable dowry. However, Hanmer's wife Susan persuaded him that he would expose himself to too much risk if he sent his daughter overseas, and he reneged on his promise.[101] Trevor married Sir John Warner of Parham in Suffolk in June 1659.[102] However, when she and her husband both later agreed to enter religion she joined the Poor Clares at Gravelines, taking the name

[97]   E. Scarisbrick, *The Holy Life of Lady Warner* (London, 1691), p. 4.
[98]   Gage, *Hengrave*, p. 77.
[99]   Scarisbrick, *The Holy Life of Lady Warner*, p. 5.
[100] Ibid. p. 6.
[101] Ibid. pp. 8–10.
[102] Ibid. p. 17.

of Sister Clare of Jesus. An account of her life was written in 1691 by the Jesuit Edward Scarisbrick,[103] which gives us some idea of the community of Catholic and Protestant relations living at Hengrave in the 1640s and 1650s.

A curious feature of Trevor's desire to become a nun whilst at Hengrave is that neither she nor her father was a Catholic at the time. Much later, after her marriage to Sir John Warner, Trevor was surprised when Susan Hervey, supported by Sir Thomas, claimed that the Church of England taught the Real Presence of Christ in the Eucharist.[104] When Trevor confirmed that her father and stepmother were wrong, it marked the beginning of her conversion to Catholicism. Whether Sir Thomas and Lady Hanmer's misconceptions about the doctrine of the Church of England reflected the religious attitudes of the Hanmers or the Herveys (or both), their views were probably consciously adopted and denoted adherence to a High Church Laudian understanding of conformity. Certainly it would have been convenient for Susan Hervey, as Penelope's daughter-in-law living with the Catholic Gages, to gloss over doctrinal differences. It is somewhat remarkable that Trevor's Protestant father was content, at least for a time, for her to become a Catholic and a nun, and this hints strongly in favour of some sort of crypto-Catholicism on Sir Thomas Hanmer's part.

Penelope's third daughter, Penelope Gage, who had married Sir Henry Merry of Barton Blount in Derbyshire, seems to have been at Hengrave at some point in the 1640s, since in a letter to her grandmother Mary Kytson she referred to 'my eldest daughter which is at scoole at bery [i.e. Bury St Edmunds] and profiteth much in her learning'.[105] In July 1643 Penelope Gage was lying ill at Swaffham, but she was attended by a Catholic physician from Bury, Dr Richard Short, who may have been sent by her mother.[106] Penelope Gage had become separated from her husband and was unable to contact him, 'though we have sent manie letters'. Sir Henry was certainly a Royalist, and he eventually compounded £1,604 for his estates in 1655.[107] It is possible that he was either abroad or had joined the King at Oxford in 1643. In 1659 Mary Merry, daughter of Penelope Gage and Sir Henry Merry (and perhaps the same daughter who was at school in Bury), married

---

[103] On Edward Scarisbrick see G. Holt, 'Edward Scarisbrick (1639–1709): A Royal Preacher', *Recusant History* 23 (1996–97), pp. 159–65.

[104] Scarisbrick, *The Holy Life of Lady Warner*, p. 31.

[105] Penelope Gage to Mary Kytson, undated (1640s), CUL Hengrave MS 88/2/139.

[106] Penelope Darcy to Mary Kytson, 11 July 1643, CUL Hengrave MS 88/2/157.

[107] S. Glover, *The History of the County of Derby* (Derby, 1829), vol. 1, p. 84.

Thomas Jermyn (the future Earl of St Albans) on his return to England from exile in Paris,[108] thus securing another connection between the Jermyns and Gages. Penelope's social networking continued unabated in the 1640s and 1650s; she set up her daughter Ann's marriage to Sir Andrew Clifton during this period,[109] although the match was delayed by Penelope's financial difficulties in the summer of 1643.[110] Sir Andrew was dead by 1656 and Ann married her second husband, Henry Petre, the seventh son of William, 2nd Baron Petre.[111]

After Mary Hervey's death in 1654, Edward Gage took as his second wife Frances Aston of Tixhall in Staffordshire, daughter of Walter, 2nd Baron Aston of Forfar.[112] The first Lord Aston had been Charles I's ambassador to Spain and converted to Catholicism in 1623,[113] and the Astons remained a Catholic family. Frances Aston died in childbirth in 1660, but her son Francis Gage (1660–1729) survived, inheriting Packington Hall in Staffordshire from his mother. Penelope also settled the manor of Westley on Francis, but he sold it to Sir Thomas Hervey in 1693.[114] Edward Gage and Frances Aston's grandson, Devereux Gage, was a regular visitor to Hengrave in the 1730s (see Chapter 4) but the line of Packington Gages ended with him. The Astons were also connected with the Firle Gages through the marriage of the third Lord Aston (Sir Edward's brother-in-law) to Catherine, daughter of Sir Edward's brother, Sir Thomas Gage, 2nd Baronet of Firle.[115]

At the end of 1659 Edward was in London conducting business on behalf of his father-in-law Lord Aston, as well as his mother Penelope, when he was briefly caught up in the political turmoil that followed the dissolution of the Commonwealth and preceded the Restoration of Charles II. On the afternoon of 1 December, Edward was 'att a play' when he and everyone else there was taken by soldiers to St James's Palace, which the military had made its headquarters in its efforts to

---

[108] B. D. Henning, *The History of Parliament: The House of Commons 1660–1690* (London: Secker and Warburg, 1983), vol. 1, p. 651.

[109] Penelope Darcy to unknown recipient, undated, CUL Hengrave MS 88/2/172.

[110] Penelope Darcy to Mary Kytson, 7 July 1643, CUL Hengrave MS 88/2/156: 'It is true the concluding of the match is at a stay in respect of these distractions, yett it would much tr[o]ubble me if Nan should be hindred of the hopes of that preferment.'

[111] Gage, *Hengrave*, p. 240; Gage, *Thingoe*, p. 205.

[112] Gage, *Hengrave*, p. 24.

[113] A. J. Loomie, 'Aston, Walter, Baron Aston of Forfar' in *ODNB*, vol. 2, pp. 793–94.

[114] Gage, *Thingoe*, p. 90.

[115] J. Gillow, *A Biographical Dictionary of the English Catholics* (London: Burns and Oates, 1885–1902), vol. 1, pp. 80, 77.

exert influence on Richard Cromwell in the last days of his Protectorate. By the end of 1659 the Protectorate was over; Generals John Lambert and Charles Fleetwood had dissolved the Rump Parliament and set up the Committee of Safety. Soldiers regularly interrupted plays (particularly political satires) at this time,[116] and in October the Lord Mayor's Company had expressed concerns about performing its usual shows on Lord Mayor's Day.[117] The army's actions seem to have had more to do with preventing dissent than with enforcing Parliamentarian legislation against acting on stage. Edward gives no indication that he was actually in a theatre, and it was common for plays to be performed in alternative locations during the Commonwealth.[118] The play could have been considered a seditious gathering or, alternatively, the soldiers were looking for specific individuals among the crowd and decided to arrest everyone. Whoever they were looking for, it was not Edward Gage, who was released from prison before ten o'clock that night.[119]

Penelope Darcy's memory was cherished at Hengrave, and continues to be cherished at Firle Place, as the foundress of two branches of the Gage family. In the nineteenth century, visitors to Hengrave could see 'crystal ornaments' containing locks of her hair as well as her amber rosary and even her silver toasting fork.[120] Two paintings of Penelope are still to be found at Firle Place; a full-length portrait of her as a middle-aged woman wearing a violet gown hangs in the Great Hall, and a half-length portrait depicting her as a teenage girl hangs on the stairs. This latter portrait is identical to the engraving of a portrait at Hengrave included in John Gage's *The History and Antiquities of Hengrave*,[121] and it is either a copy or the original, bought by Viscount Gage in 1952. A further painting of Penelope was illustrated in Farrer's *Portraits in Suffolk Houses*.[122]

[116] S. Wiseman, *Drama and Politics in the English Civil War* (Cambridge: Cambridge University Press, 1998), p. 86.

[117] Ibid. p. 180.

[118] A small number of theatres were open in the late 1650s, including the Cockpit Theatre where musical masques defied the spirit if not the letter of the Parliamentarian ban, see E. A. Langhans, 'The Theatre' in D. P. Fiske (ed.), *The Cambridge Companion to English Restoration Theatre* (Cambridge: Cambridge University Press, 2000), p. 2.

[119] Edward Gage to Frances Aston, 1 December 1659, CUL Hengrave MS 88/3/61.

[120] CUL Hengrave MS 52.

[121] Gage, *Hengrave*, facing p. 224.

[122] E. Farrer, *Portraits in Suffolk Houses (West)* (London: B. Quaritch, 1908), p. 176.

The Gages and Catholic mission

At least one member of the Gage family was involved in the establish-ment of the first mission dedicated to serving East Anglia, the Jesuit College of the Holy Apostles. This was established in 1633 by Sir Francis Petre, 1st Baronet of Cranham in Essex (c.1605–58), whose wife was Elizabeth Gage (d.1655), Penelope's second daughter by Sir John Gage of Firle. In its early years, understandably given the inten-sity of persecution, the College had no permanent home and was a theoretical body, a *collegium inchoatum* consisting of the individual priests appointed to work in the area. Consequently, we have no way of knowing if or how Hengrave was served by a priest in the 1640s and 1650s. If it was, he was probably a Jesuit, but the absence of hiding places at Hengrave, a house that predated the Reformation, would have made it a dangerous place to visit at a volatile time. Michael Hodgetts, who based his view that 'there were undoubtedly hides at Hengrave' on the erroneous association of William Wright with the house, may be overconfident.[123] Furthermore, the absence of any reference in Scaris-brick's *Life of Lady Warner* to clerical influences on the aspiring nun during her period at Hengrave constitutes an argument of silence against the presence of a mission. The Protestant Sir William Hervey was, after all, the head of the household throughout the period.

Nevertheless, there were a number of clergy among Penelope's grand-children, the most famous of whom was surely Sir Edward Petre, 3rd Baronet of Cranham (c.1630–99), the second son of Sir Francis Petre and Elizabeth Gage, who was to become the most politically visible English Catholic priest of his generation as adviser and then Privy Coun-cillor to King James II.[124] The Petres took refuge at Hengrave in the 1640s and 1650s and Edward Petre may have spent some of his teenage years there.[125] Sir Francis's and Elizabeth's third son, Thomas Petre, also became a Jesuit; he was at the Venerable English College from 18 October 1658 to 23 May 1659, and took the alias Rivers from his great-grandmother Mary Kytson.[126] Edward Sulyard (alias Sutton), the son of Penelope's third daughter, Penelope Gage, and her second husband, Sir Edward Sulyard of Haughley, was admitted to the Venerable English College in Rome as a convictor on 25 November 1655, leaving on 4

---

[123]   M. Hodgetts, *Secret Hiding Places* (Dublin: Veritas, 1989), p. 55.
[124]   Foley, vol. 7:1, pp. 590–593; S. Handley, 'Petre, Sir Edward' in *ODNB*, vol. 43, pp. 706–7.
[125]   Dr Francis Gage to Penelope Darcy, 25 April 1650, CUL Hengrave MS 88/2/163.
[126]   Foley, vol. 5, p. 272.

March 1657 to study at St Omer.[127] However, rather than becoming a priest, Edward seems to have returned to England and married his first cousin, another Penelope Gage (Sir Edward Gage's eldest daughter) in the 1660s. Edward Sulyard's brother John (b.1634), on the other hand, who was at the Venerable English College from 11 October 1658 to 4 June 1659, was ordained as a secular priest.[128]

Conclusions

By the end of the 1650s, the Hengrave Gages had made marriage alliances with the Protestant Royalist gentry of the locality as well as with other Catholic families. Most notable was their triple alliance with the Protestant Jermyns of Rushbrooke through the first marriage of Sir William Hervey, Penelope's third husband, to Susan Jermyn; the marriage of Penelope's fourth son, Henry Gage of Harleston (d.1683), to Henrietta Jermyn;[129] and the marriage of Penelope's granddaughter Mary Merry to Thomas Jermyn. The Gages also contracted a double alliance with the Protestant Herveys of Ickworth through Penelope's marriage to Sir William Hervey and her third son Edward's marriage to Sir William's daughter by Susan Jermyn, Mary Hervey. The Gages allied with Catholic families through the marriage of Penelope's eldest daughter, Frances, to Sir William Tresham (d.1650) of Liveden in Northamptonshire, the marriages of Elizabeth and Ann Gage with two separate branches of the Petre family, and Edward's second marriage to

---

[127] Ibid. vol. 6, p. 393; vol. 4, p. 606.

[128] Foley, vol. 4, p. 606; D. A. Bellenger (ed.), *English and Welsh Priests 1558–1800* (Bath: Downside Abbey, 1984) (hereafter Bellenger), p. 112. In addition to these priests, Mother Bridget More, the first Prioress of the English Benedictine Nuns in Paris, has been described as granddaughter of 'Penelope Savage [sic], daughter of Earl Rivers' (*Miscellanea VII* (London: Catholic Record Society (hereafter CRS), 1911), p. 365). Bridget was in fact the sister of the mystic Helen Getrude More and her mother was Elizabeth Gage, daughter of Thomas Gage, younger brother of Sir John Gage of Firle, 1st Baronet and Elizabeth Guildford. Consequently, Penelope was related to the More family only by marriage; J. H. Anderson, 'More, Cressacre' in *ODNB*, vol. 39, p. 36.

[129] Henry Gage and Henrietta Jermyn were married by a magistrate 'at the Market Cross' in the parish of St James', Bury St Edmunds on 11 February 1655 (marriages were not required to take place in parish churches under the Presbyterian settlement of the Commonwealth): in S. H. A. Hervey (ed.), *Bury St. Edmunds, St. James Parish Registers, Marriages 1562–1800* (Woodbridge: G. Booth, 1916) (hereafter *St James Marriages*), p. 57. Henry Gage had a daughter, Mary, who became a nun and a son, John Gage of Princethorp, Norfolk (T. Wotton, *The English Baronetage* (London, 1727), vol. 1, p. 224).

Frances Aston of Tixhall in Staffordshire. Whereas the Gages' exogamous marriages to Protestants were local, they were prepared to go further afield to marry Catholics.

When Penelope Darcy died in 1660, it was something of a miracle that she was able to pass Hengrave on to her son Edward. Her mother's caprice and her partiality for the Savages, the spectre of popular violence and the Committee for Sequestrations had all threatened to come between her son and his inheritance. How Penelope secured Mary Kytson's favour we may never know, but Mary's decision not to give Hengrave to the Savages may have owed something to the Stour Valley Riots; Elizabeth Darcy's property could never be secure in Suffolk after what happened to Melford Hall. By her timely marriage to the influential Sir William Hervey, Penelope minimised the risk of an attack on her like the one that nearly killed her sister. Sir Harbottle Grimston's friendship with Mary Kytson and, apparently, the prospect of personal gain from her will, ultimately saved Hengrave from sequestration. However, the presence at Hengrave of the Parliamentarian informant Sir Thomas Hanmer might also have contributed to the lack of attention paid to the community there in the 1640s.

It is likely that Penelope Darcy did not face the same hostility as her sister on account of Bury's Janus-faced political character during the Civil War. The town lacked the critical concentration of fervent Puritans present in other towns. Some of Bury's townsfolk undoubtedly shared godly ideals and the town corporation was controlled by Parliamentarians. However, a significant component of the town's leading men remained Royalist in sympathy and attached to the Prayer Book; Thomas Stephens, the Master of the Bury Grammar School, attended secret Prayer Book services with his pupils throughout the Civil War and the Commonwealth period, and although Stephens was ejected in 1645, he was invited back two years later.[130] The schoolmaster, like the gentry, was indispensable, and the Parliamentarian authorities preferred to compromise with known Royalists rather than to surrender to chaos and lawlessness. Without doubt, the Gages were beneficiaries of such compromise.

---

[130] R. W. Elliot, *The Story of King Edward the Sixth School Bury St. Edmunds* (Bury St Edmunds, 1963), pp. 59–60.

2

'*BON TEMPS VIENDRA*': THE GAGES FROM RESTORATION TO REVOLUTION, 1660–88

The years after the Restoration saw Sir Edward Gage acquire a noble title, as well as becoming the wealthiest Catholic in Suffolk with the largest house in the county. Dividing his time between Hengrave, Bury St Edmunds and one of London's most fashionable addresses, Sir Edward could afford to give his sons a continental education. Having made a marriage alliance with the daughter of the Protestant Earl of Desmond, Sir Edward was eventually to have twelve children and become the patriarch of an even larger extended family, free from the fears of sequestration and persecution that had beset his childhood. In the 1670s the Gages were the neighbours of James, Duke of York and later sent a daughter to his court. However, at the end of the 1670s the Gages suffered the consequences of national panic in the Popish Plot scare; Sir Edward's son William and his family left the country, his younger son Francis was arrested, and Sir Edward himself was named when a priest who had ministered to the family in London was arrested and later confined to Newgate. These events seem to have left a lasting impression. While other local Catholics supported James II's efforts in 1687–88 to pack the Bury Corporation with Catholics and Dissenters in order to elect MPs supportive of toleration (an effort led by the Gages' relative Henry Jermyn, Lord Dover), Sir Edward Gage remained conspicuously silent. This stance may have bought him and his son a degree of immunity from the reprisals against Catholics that followed the landing of William of Orange in November 1688.

   J. C. H. Aveling suggested that Restoration Catholic families fell into three categories: they were either activist, passive or inclined to retreat into piety.[1] Sir Edward Gage was certainly a 'country' rather than a 'court' Catholic, as his reluctance to support Lord Dover demonstrated, and his first loyalty was to the local Catholic community rather than to abstract religious or political ideals. His translation work revealed a

---

[1]   Aveling, *The Handle and the Axe*, pp. 188–92.

Fig. 2. Sir Edward Gage, 1st Baronet (1626–1707), engraving from John Gage, *History and Antiquities of Hengrave* (1822) after an original portrait once at Hengrave Hall

deeply pious man, and an activist streak is detectable in his construction of a web of marriage alliances, which established the Gages – relative newcomers to Suffolk – as the county's leading Catholic family. However, political and financial advancement, except through the prestige of advantageous marriages, does not seem to have interested him, even when it became available in the reign of James II. In this sense, Sir Edward Gage does not fit neatly into any of Aveling's categories, yet he fulfilled aspects of them all.

Sir Edward Gage's baronetcy

Penelope Darcy's will, drawn up in 1656, seems to have been a conscious effort to distance herself from her mother Mary Kytson's vindictiveness and partiality. She took pains to defend her decision to pass all her lands, apart from the manors of Lackford and Fornham St Martin, to Edward Gage and demonstrated an awareness of the possibility of future brotherly strife:

> An earnest desire to raise another branch of my family, hath moved me to settle and assure my manors and hereditaments upon my said son, Edward, whereat, I desire my other sons to be no ways displeased with their said brother Edward, this being done without any sollicitation of his.[2]

In the event, dispute was delayed for another eighty years and, when it came, it concerned the codicil in which she bequeathed the manors of Stoneham and Beyton, together with lands in Coddenham, to her second son John Gage. When Penelope died in 1661 Edward was left in secure possession of the vast majority of his maternal inheritance, aided not least of all by the Restoration of Charles II and his connections to the Protestant Royalist Jermyn and Hervey families, both of whom received honours and public office under the new regime.

According to Sir Thomas Gage, 7th Baronet, Edward Gage was knighted soon after the Restoration. However, evidence for the reason why Sir Edward was created a baronet in 1662 is lacking, and Sir Thomas Gage's observation that we are dependent on the printed accounts of genealogists holds true today, just as it did in 1818.[3] According to an anecdote attributed to the genealogist Thomas Wotton (c.1695–1766), Charles II wanted to ennoble Henry Walrave Gage, the son of Colonel Sir Henry Gage, the heroic Governor of Oxford who fell in action at Cullum Bridge on 11 January 1645, 'as a recompence to the son, for the father's service to that Prince, in whose cause he lost his life'. Sir Henry Gage (1597–1645) was the son of Robert Gage of Haling in

2   SRO(B) 326/45.
3   CUL Hengrave MS 1/4, fol. 310.

Surrey, who in turn was the third son of Sir John Gage (d.1556), Comp-troller of the Household and Constable of the Tower to Mary I. Sir John was the grandfather of Sir John Gage, 1st Baronet of Firle and great-grandfather of Edward Gage of Hengrave, making Henry and Edward second cousins.[4]

Since Henry Walrave Gage had no son at the time, according to Kimber and Nicholson he 'procured the patent to be settled on Edward, his kinsman, a younger brother to Sir Thomas Gage, of Firle'.[5] Kimber and Nicholson, with their predilection for unsubstantiated anecdotes, cannot be taken at face value. Thomas Wotton noted only that Henry Walrave Gage 'resigned' his patent of baronetcy to Edward.[6] Henry Walrave Gage did have children (albeit not necessarily in 1662), but the fact that he was in the service of the Emperor in Flanders may have made it impolitic for Charles to award him an English baronetcy. Alternatively, the priest Dr Francis Gage (1621–82), Colonel Sir Henry Gage's half-brother, was close to Edward, and Francis could have been the agent by whose intervention the baronetcy was transferred from Henry to Edward. However, a patent of baronetcy, once granted, could not be applied to another individual and Wotton implied that the patent was granted first to Henry Walrave Gage, which was legally impos-sible. Although Edward's patent of baronetcy does survive amongst the Hengrave papers, it gives no clue as to the reason it was conferred on him.

Whatever the circumstances, Penelope Darcy's wishes for her son, 'to raise another branch of my family', were more than fulfilled when Edward was created a baronet on 15 June 1662. Through no merit of his own, but rather through the fame of a relative, Sir Edward came to preside over a newly ennobled branch of the Gages, a surprising destiny for the third son of Sir John Gage of Firle. However, Gordon Blackwood has observed that Charles granted baronetcies to Suffolk families across the political divide of the Civil War, with five ex-Parlia-mentarians and two ex-republicans receiving them as well as Royalists, while more ex-Parliamentarians than Royalists received knighthoods.[7] The purpose of Restoration baronetcies was to ensure the loyalty of the landed gentry in general to the King through personal indebtedness, rather than to honour specific individuals for their own achievements or, in Sir Edward's case, those of his relatives. Charles's distribution of honours looked to the future rather than to the past, and Edward may

---

4   On Sir Henry Gage see A. J. Loomie, 'Gage, Sir Henry' in *ODNB*, vol. 21, pp. 250–51.
5   Kimber and Nicholson, *The Baronetage of England*, vol. 2, p. 247.
6   H. Wotton, *The English Baronetage* (London, 1727), vol. 2, p. 222.
7   Blackwood, *Tudor and Stuart Suffolk*, p. 201.

simply have been a sufficiently wealthy and influential man in the right place at the right time.

Hengrave Hall at the Restoration

Shortly after Penelope's death, an inventory of the contents of Hengrave Hall was made by George Gage,[8] James Allington and Gregory Woods on 25 April 1661 (Appendix 2).[9] As well as giving a picture of Sir Edward's early household, his possessions and wealth, the inventory also gives some idea of the layout of Hengrave in the period. The inventory lists fifty individual rooms and their contents together with an estimated value for each one. Unfortunately, the compilers of the list mingled the ground floor and first floor rooms, making a reconstruction of Hengrave's interior from the inventory difficult. However, the inventory makes evident the extent of the reduction of the house from its original size by the demolition of the south court between the inner moat and the horse pond. In 1603, by comparison, the house had at least 121 rooms.[10] Furthermore, there are signs of significant internal changes to the remaining portion of the house; 'the longe gallerye over the dyning chamber' and 'the lower gallerye' mentioned in 1603 had certainly gone by 1661. They were probably subdivided into smaller rooms during the 1640s and 1650s when so many of the Gages' extended family were living at Hengrave.

By 1661, Sir Thomas Kytson's original chapel, with its Flemish stained glass, had become a bedroom, the Chapel Chamber (it would later have a mezzanine floor inserted to become two rooms).[11] In 1603 the chapel had been equipped with an altar, Bible and service book as well as 'one round cushion, w[i]th the picture of o[u]r ladye, wrought w[i]th gold'.[12] Keeping a chapel furnished for the rites of the Church of England may have served an important purpose for the Kytsons, since a conviction for recusancy on the basis of absence from divine service at the parish church might be contested by Catholics who could claim to have heard divine service in their own private chapels. By keeping a 'conformist' chapel the Kytsons had evidence, spurious or not, that

---

8   Probably George Gage of Raunds, second husband of Penelope's daughter Frances Gage.
9   CUL Hengrave MS 86.
10 Gage, *Hengrave*, p. 22.
11 The contents of the Chapel Chamber were 'One Posted Bedsted One ffeather Bedd One Boulster Two Blanketts One Quilt One Rugge [...] & Curtaines Three Chayers four Stooles a payer of Iron Dobirons a paier of Tonges a Suite of hangeings and Two Windowe Curtaines'. CUL Hengrave MS 86.
12 Gage, *Hengrave*, p. 32.

they heard the services of the Established Church. This practice may have continued up to the death of Elizabeth Cornwallis in 1628, but Penelope Darcy's known recusancy, as a member of the notorious Gage family, would probably have made such outward signs of conformity a redundant gesture. Although the Herveys were Protestants who could have made use of the chapel, the pressure for space in the house in the interregnum may have led to the chapel being reduced to a domestic bedchamber.

The only direct evidence for a possible Catholic chapel at Hengrave during the 1670s comes from a letter written by Sir Edward's eldest daughter, Mary Gage, to Thomas Halsall, the steward at Hengrave: 'I sup[p]ose you have received my father['s] orders by my brother concerning the chapel[.] I tould my lady what you desired me and asked if I should say any thing to you but she toul[d] me she would write her self.'[13] The Chapel Chamber was sometimes referred to simply as 'the Chapel', so it is possible that Mary was referring to the bedchamber, but this seems unlikely. If there was a Catholic chapel at Hengrave, it is most likely to have been located in the attic.[14] Naturally, an inventory would not have contained any reference to illegal articles at this time such as vestments and sacred vessels, but at the same time it was in the interests of owners to value their property accurately. Consequently, one way in which the location of a chapel or 'chapel stuff' could manifest itself was in the inflated value given to the contents of a particular room. In the 1661 inventory two rooms fall into this category. 'The Chamber in the Upper Matted Gallery' seems to have been located on the second floor, under the eaves, and was valued at £12, although all it contained was 'One Postedd Bedsted One Bedd Two Blanketts One Rugge One Boulster a suite of hangeings Two Stooles a payer of Dobirons a payer of Tonges & a ffire pann'. It is possible that the 'suite of hangeings' made up the value, but on the other hand the room was in a typical location for a secret chapel.

The other room that seems to have been overvalued was the 'Inward Chamber' next to 'The Chamber next the Chappell'. This chamber contained nothing particularly expensive, 'One Bedsted One ffeather Bedd One Boulster Two Blanketts One Kiverlett One Table and Two Stooles', and yet was valued at £15, making it one of the most valuable rooms in the house.[15] Because the attics were were constructed of timber rather than stone or brick, they were the only part of the house

13 Mary Gage to Thomas Halsall, undated (1670s), CUL Hengrave MS 88/2/175.
14 Michael Hodgetts, pers. comm.
15 Its value was matched by the Chapel Chamber and the Chamber over the Winter Parlour (£15) and exceeded only by the Grey Bedchamber (£20) and the Queen's Chamber (£30).

that could undergo significant architectural alterations without attracting attention. However, an attic chapel presented its own difficulties, as it rendered the fast dispersal of the congregation difficult in an emergency, such as the arrival of magistrates. Without an adequate escape route for the priest and faithful, the celebration of Mass at Hengrave would have been perilous. It is almost certain that a chapel existed somewhere in the house from the 1730s, when a priest said Mass there regularly, but the first chapel for whose location we have unequivocal evidence was established after 1791.[16] Sir Thomas Kytson the Elder's original chapel was not restored for worship until the early nineteenth century.

The 1661 inventory lacks the picturesque details to be found in the 1603 list, and it suggests that Penelope kept a somewhat Spartan household in comparison with her Kytson ancestors. Penelope had table silver worth £76,[17] a rather meagre collection that had probably been assembled since the end of the Civil War, when the compulsory seizure of silverware by the government to pay for the war effort was a common occurrence. The inventory mentions only nine 'pictures' in the Summer Parlour and there seem to have been few hangings and carpets; the most valuable items were beds. Penelope left behind £120 in ready money, £200 in 'Good Debts' and £250 'in Desperatt Debts', together with clothes worth £100. The agricultural assets listed give a snapshot of the estate's productivity.[18] The total value of Sir Edward's new estate was calculated at £1,367 3s 4d, although this did not include the land value of the Hengrave estate, nor indeed his other manors.

Sir Edward may have celebrated his inheritance of Hengrave and his baronetcy by commissioning a heraldic mural painting on the chimney breast in the ground floor room labelled as the 'Summer Dining Room' on John Gage the antiquary's groundplan of 1775,[19] which was probably the main dining room in the 1660s. The painting is a large armorial conceit 'in the midst of a species of Arabesque Ornament',[20] with the coat of arms of Gage quartered with St Clere, defaced by the coat of arms of Mary Kytson (Darcy quartered with Kytson) occupying the central position in a roundel. This is the full achievement of the arms of Sir Edward Gage, 1st Baronet, with the Badge of Ulster (the heraldic

---

[16] Edward Pugh to Sir Thomas Gage, 6th Baronet, 21 October 1802, CUL Hengrave MS 93/1/105.

[17] This included 24 plates, 2 tankards, 2 porringers, 30 spoons and 9 'salts', CUL Hengrave MS 86.

[18] The granary contained £14 worth of wheat, £9 of rye, £26 of barley; the estate had 20 'Milch cowes' worth £20, 10 bullocks worth £25, 15 'Steeres to ffatt' worth £50, 4 cart horses worth £10, 8 pigs worth £4 and 60 sheep worth £30.

[19] Gage, *Hengrave*, p. 18.

[20] CUL Hengrave MS 1/1, fol. 84.

emblem of a baronet) marking out his new status at the centre of the saltire gules of Gage. The presence of the Badge of Ulster would seem to date the painting to after 1662. Sir Edward's coat of arms is accompanied by Kytson impaled with Paget in the upper left-hand corner (representing the first marriage of Sir Thomas Kytson the Younger to Jane Paget) and Kytson impaled with Cornwallis, representing his second marriage to Elizabeth Cornwallis, Sir Edward's great-grandmother. In the bottom left-hand corner is a simplified version of Sir Edward's arms (Gage quartered with Darcy), and in the bottom right-hand corner the coat of arms of Penelope's third husband, Sir William Hervey; this, of course, was also the coat of arms of Sir Edward's first wife and the mother of his son and heir, Mary Hervey.

Within the pediment immediately below the central coat of arms are the arms of Elizabeth Cornwallis, the simplified arms of Kytson impaled with simplified Cornwallis. The strapwork decoration emanating from the central shield is inhabited by what John Gage the antiquary described as 'Gothique figures',[21] a satyr and a woman with a snail-like lower body, holding a baby swaddled entirely in red, and below that a vulture. The same scene is mirrored on either side of the central roundel, and is framed by fruit and vegetables (on the right-hand side a pair of scales) and, at the bottom of the picture, musical instruments such as bagpipes, lutes, viols and cornets and, on the right-hand side, an open book of music. The meaning of these conceits is unknown, but John Gage may have been right when he observed that the style of the painting was Jacobean; it is possible that the heraldry on an earlier painting was updated after 1662. The word IVSTITIA is inscribed above Sir Edward's coat of arms, and on the fireplace itself are gilded the words OBSTA PRINCIPIIS: POST FVMVM FLAMA, 'Resist the first beginnings: behind the smoke, flames'.

Although the precise meaning of the painting's obscure symbolism may now be irretrievable, the heraldic theme seems to be a celebration of Sir Edward's inheritance of Hengrave through the female line, hence the prominence of the coat of arms of Elizabeth Cornwallis. The juxtaposition of his arms with those of Hervey would seem to be an allusion to his marriage to Mary Hervey in 1648, for which this painting could have been completed, were it not for the Badge of Ulster in Sir Edward's coat of arms (although this, too, could have been painted on later). Mary Hervey died eight years before Sir Edward was created a baronet, on 13 July 1654.[22]

---

[21] CUL Hengrave MS 1/4, fol. 310 (note in the hand of John Gage).
[22] According to Farrer, *Portraits in Suffolk Houses (West)*, p. 206. A portrait of Mary Hervey still hangs at Ickworth Hall.

Fig. 3. Figurative painting above the dining-room fireplace at Hengrave Hall, probably to commemorate the marriage of Edward Gage and Mary Hervey in 1648 or Edward's baronetcy in 1662 (photograph by the author)

A possible clue to the intention of the painting, if not its precise meaning, can be found on the chimney breast of the room directly above the dining room, although it should be noted that the painting in this chamber looks fairly recent and is either a repainting of an original or an addition of the nineteenth or twentieth century. However, the fact that a pediment with three knops has been painted on to the chimney breast, mirroring the one in the dining room, suggests a connection. On the fireplace of the upper chamber, beneath the simple coat of arms of Kytson on the chimney breast, are the words FORTI ANIMO MALA FER NEC BIS MISER ESTO DOLORE NE CITRO VENTVRIS PRAE MORIARE BONIS, 'With a strong spirit bear ills, neither be wretched twice with grief lest thou diest before the good things to come'. The words *venturis ... bonis* in the inscription would seem to allude to the Gage family's French motto, 'Bon temps viendra' ('A good time will come').[23]

If this second painted inscription is genuinely seventeenth century, *venturis ... bonis* could well be a reference to the Restoration of Charles II, as well as the family motto, and *forti animo mala fer* would, in this case, be an exhortation to persevere through the difficult times of the Commonwealth.[24] Whatever the painting's true meaning, which we may never know, its heraldry celebrated the women through whom Sir Edward inherited Hengrave; his great-grandmother Elizabeth Cornwallis, his grandmother Mary Kytson and his mother Penelope Darcy.

The Gages at Hengrave, Bury and London

Blackwood estimated that Sir Edward Gage was the wealthiest Catholic in Suffolk in the reign of Charles II, with an annual income of around £2,000. This outstripped the Mannocks of Gifford's Hall, the Martins of Long Melford, the Sulyards of Haughley, the Tasburghs of Flixton and the Warners of Parham.[25] The gap in wealth between the Gages and other Suffolk Catholics may be one reason why Sir Edward's children allied with only one of these families by marriage, the Sulyards, in

---

[23] I am grateful to Michael Hodgetts for pointing out the superficial similarity of the two inscriptions at Hengrave to a passage from Ovid's *Remedia Amoris* (ll. 91–93): *principiis obsta, sero medicina paratur / cum mala per longas convaluere moras.* However, the resemblance of *mala per* to *mala fer* and *moras* ('you delay') to *moriari* ('die') is probably coincidental, since the meanings are so different.

[24] The word *iustitia* above Sir Edward's coat of arms recalls Royalist mottoes such as the *Fiat iustitia* on a Royalist banner captured at Marston Moor. See A. R. Young (ed.), *The English Emblem Tradition: Emblematic Flag Devices of the English Civil Wars 1642–1660* (Toronto: University of Toronto Press, 1995), p. xliii.

[25] Blackwood, *Tudor and Stuart Suffolk*, p. 230.

spite of his abundance of marriageable daughters. The potential financial returns on such marriages were not worth the outlay of dowries,
which were a continual worry for the seventeenth-century landed gentry,
whether Catholic or Protestant. Sir Edward was not only the wealthiest
Catholic; in 1674 Hengrave Hall was the largest single house in Suffolk,
with fifty-one hearths.[26] In addition, Sir Edward owned a house in the
North Ward of the parish of St James in Bury with seventeen hearths.[27]
This is almost certainly the house in Northgate Street, now divided into
numbers 9, 10 and 11, which the Rookwood Gages had refaced in brick
in the late eighteenth century.

An indenture of lease and release of 19 and 20 October 1675 between
Sir Edward and his son William gives a snapshot of the extent of the
family's lands at this time. The Gages owned the manors of Hengrave,
Flempton, Risby, Chevington, Fornham All Saints, Fornham St
Genevieve and the manor of Charmins, or Charmans, in the parish of
Risby, as well as several farms and windmills: 'the Grange' at Bury, the
former St Saviour's Hospital and Tollcott Farm on the Fornham road
(on the site of the present-day Tollgate public house) with eight acres
of meadow and a windmill, and a windmill on 'Shierhouse heath', just
to the south-east of the town. In addition, the Gages were in possession of the advowsons of Flempton-cum-Hengrave, Risby, Westley,
Fornham All Saints, Fornham St Genevieve, Chevington and Hargrave
and claimed nominal title to the entire Hundred of Lackford.[28] An
indenture of 1708 mentioned further parcels of land in the parishes
of Barrow, Lackford, Whepstead, Cavenham, Great and Little Horningsheath (Horringer), Great and Little Saxham, West Stow, 'Yalworth'
(Chelsworth?), Culford, Great and Little Livermere, Great Barton,
Timworth and Denham.[29]

Sir Edward Gage's ownership of St Saviour's Hospital and other
properties once belonging to the Abbey of St Edmund may have pricked
his conscience, as a Catholic, and he took steps to ensure that his title to
these lands was recognised not only under the law but also by the English
Benedictines. It is possible that Sir Edward, anticipating the possibility

---

[26] S. H. A. Hervey (ed.), *Suffolk in 1674, being the Hearth Tax Returns* (Woodbridge:
      G. Booth, 1905), p. 53.

[27] Ibid. p. 141.

[28] CUL Hengrave MS 1/4, fols 322–25. 'Hundred bailiffs' or 'hundred stewards' were
      appointed by the Abbey of St Edmund before the Reformation, and the Bacon family
      continued to claim stewardship of the entire Liberty of St Edmund into the seventeenth
      century. The Gage claim may have been a survival of a claim originally made by Sir
      Thomas Kytson the Elder to be Steward of the Hundred of Lackford, but such claims
      were virtually meaningless after 1606 when the Corporation of Bury St Edmunds
      received its first charter. See MacCulloch, *Suffolk and the Tudors*, pp. 87, 137–38.

[29] CUL Hengrave MS 1/4, fol. 336.

of a restoration of the monasteries under a Catholic monarchy, wanted to ensure that he retained or received compensation for his lands. John Gage described the evidence he discovered in the 'Benedictine Library' in London in 1824:

> By an Instrument in Writing dated 2 July 1661 Anselm Crowther, prior of the Church of Canterbury, and Provincial of the Benedictine Monks in England [sic],[30] in vertue of an alleged authority under Bulls of Pope Clement VIII. and Urban VIII, particularly the Bull Plantata,[31] confirmed to Sir Edward Gage of Hengrave Bart during the schism of England and for forty years afterward the possessions in Suffolk inherited by him parcel of the dissolved Monastery of St. Edmund on payment of forty pounds per ann[um].[32]

The idea of a restoration of Catholicism was not altogether absurd in the 1660s, and indeed it became increasingly likely as Charles II's brother, the Duke of York, converted to Catholicism in the early 1670s. The English Benedictines, unlike other Catholic religious orders in England, claimed direct legal continuity with their mediaeval predecessors, and therefore implicitly their property rights. However, after the accession of James II in 1685, anxious to avoid panic amongst Protestant landowners, the Benedictines completely and formally renounced their rights to their pre-Reformation lands. The Benedictine Philip Michael Ellis did this in a sermon preached before King James in the Catholic Chapel of the Palace of Whitehall on 13 December 1686.[33]

James's anxiety to allay fears that the monks would dispossess lay owners led him in 1685 to advise the English Benedictine monks of St Edmund's, Paris, who were offered the Abbey in Bury St Edmunds by its then owner, to decline it for this very reason.[34] It went to the Jesuits instead, which hardly did anything to assuage Protestant fears.

During the 1660s the Gages had sufficient surplus income to buy (or more probably rent) a house in London to which they paid regular visits, located in Southampton Buildings next to the Bull Inn, near Bloomsbury

---

[30] As titular Prior of Canterbury, Crowther was in fact only the Provincial of the monks in the South Province.

[31] The Bull *Plantata* of 1633 declared that all of the rights of the pre-Reformation monasteries devolved to the English Benedictine Congregation, a claim that aggravated the fears of both Protestant and Catholic owners of monastic property that the monks would seek to take back their lands in the event of a Catholic monarchy.

[32] CUL Hengrave MS 1/4, note in John Gage's hand facing fol. 319. The papers of the South Province of the English Benedictines were later transferred to Downside Abbey, but I have not been able to locate among them the original of the document paraphrased by John Gage.

[33] D. Lunn, *The English Benedictines 1540–1688* (London: Burns and Oates, 1980), p. 139.

[34] J. B. Mackinlay, *Saint Edmund, King and Martyr* (London: Art and Book Co., 1893), pp. 405–6.

market.[35] This was one of the most fashionable addresses in London; 'Southampton Buildings' was the beginnings of Southampton Square (now Bloomsbury Square), the Earl of Southampton's first building development in the area. The Gages' visits to London may have been purely for business and pleasure; on the other hand, well-timed absences from the county were an acknowledged means of avoiding presentation for recusancy at the quarter sessions.[36] Sir Edward's agent in London, Mr Enderby, received letters on his behalf at the Nag's Head in Holborn when he was out of town.[37]

While the Gages enjoyed London society, the Hengrave estate was managed by Sir Edward's steward, Thomas Halsall, who after one family journey was berated by the Baronet's teenage daughter Mary Gage for failing to ensure that her trunk followed her back to Hengrave.[38] While Sir Edward spent much of his time in London, William decided to live at Hengrave and his father grudgingly granted him an allowance of two hundred shillings a year, complaining that it was 'more than ever I was allowed my selfe till I had a settlement made upon me upon marriage'. However, Sir Edward evidently considered that he had spent quite enough on William: 'my intention is to be att no other kind of Charge concerning him whatsoever; if he finds the country to chargeable for this proportion, he knows he has a home here, where he will be att no expence except of cloaths & pockett money'.[39] Sir Edward himself was determined to enjoy the benefits of country life in the city, asking Halsall to instruct his gamekeeper to kill him a doe and send its meat up to his table in London.[40]

A few of Sir Edward's bills from the 1660s survive, and they are mainly for saddlery and ironware such as nails, harnesses, keys and bolts.[41] This pattern of expenditure might suggest a passion for riding and hunting, as well as bearing witness to the wear and tear occasioned by Sir Edward's journeys to London. Furthermore, it could be taken as indicative of expenditure on security, motivated either by concern that the bad times of the 1640s might return, or by Sir Edward's desire

---

35 For the address see Bridget Stanhope to Elizabeth Gage, undated (1660s), CUL Hengrave MS 88/3/58.

36 Glickman, *The English Catholic Community 1688–1745*, p. 59.

37 See Dr Francis Gage to Mr Enderby, 15 February 1668, CUL Hengrave MS 88/3/108: 'To my much hon. friend Mr Enderby at his lodgings at the naggs-head in Holbourn overagainst Giffords Buildings London.'

38 Mary Gage to Thomas Halsall, undated, CUL Hengrave MS 88/2/174, 88/2/175.

39 Sir Edward Gage to Thomas Halsall, undated (1660s), CUL Hengrave MS 88/2/179.

40 Sir Edward Gage to Thomas Halsall, undated (1660s), CUL Hengrave MS 88/2/178.

41 Sir Edward spent £11 14s 6d on saddlery and £14 7s 5d on ironware between February 1664 and September 1665; he received further bills for ironware in June 1665 (£5 4s 8d) and at Christmas the same year (£4 4s 10d), CUL Hengrave MS 93/1.

to restore Hengrave to some of its former magnificence. In 1665, Sir Edward also spent £32 8s on bricks, although there is no indication of what he was building. Sir Edward spent £50 on periwigs, a very large sum for the time that may indicate he was keen to keep up with the latest fashions in London.[42]

Sir Edward's second wife, Frances Aston, died in 1660 and his infant son Francis inherited Packington Hall in Staffordshire from his mother.[43] Until Francis attained his majority, the revenues of the estate were received by Sir Edward after the expenses of the estate had been accounted for, which included an allowance of £15 to Lady Aston, Sir Edward's mother-in-law 'for little ffrank Gage & his mayde for halfe a yeare' in 1661. Evidently Francis had been sent to live with his grand-mother at Tixhall, at Sir Edward's expense. In 1660 Sir Edward received £206 1s 2d from the Packington estate, but this fell to just £79 7s 7d in 1661, largely on account of outgoing expenses. By 1665, Sir Edward received little more than £19 from the Packington estate after expenses.[44]

Sir Edward's third wife, Anne Watkins, who bore him a son called Edward in 1662 or 1663,[45] seems not to have lived much longer than Frances Aston. With his fourth marriage, to Elizabeth Feilding (1639–89), second daughter of George, 1st Earl of Desmond by Bridget Stan-hope, Sir Edward made an impressive alliance with the Protestant aristocracy. The Feildings were not only Protestant; Basil Feilding, 2nd Earl of Denbigh (the Earl of Desmond's elder brother) had fought on the side of Parliament in the Civil War.[46] However, the family had successfully rehabilitated themselves as Royalists after the Restora-tion. Perhaps an alliance with the name of Gage, made famous by Sir Edward's cousin Henry's loyalty to the King, served their political purposes well. However, the Feildings had also become a family of local influence in Suffolk. In 1655, Elizabeth's father had acquired the manor of Euston from the recusant Edward Rookwood, who was ruined by an immense composition fine.[47] Sir Edward Gage's marriage to Elizabeth Feilding produced seven of his twelve children and it seems to have been based on genuine affection.[48] Elizabeth was fearful for the safety

[42] Sir Edward Gage to Thomas Halsall, undated (1670s), CUL Hengrave MS 88/2/179.

[43] The legal expenses associated with Frances Aston's will amounted to £72 2s 6d when the final bill was received on 7 May 1662, CUL Hengrave MS 92.

[44] CUL Hengrave MS 92.

[45] Foley, vol. 5, p. 525.

[46] A. Hughes, 'Feilding, Basil' in *ODNB*, vol. 19, pp. 238–41.

[47] Blackwood, *Tudor and Stuart Suffolk*, p. 198.

[48] Elizabeth did not receive her jointure by the marriage settlement until 1675, although she was certainly married to Sir Edward before this date; see W. Hervey (ed. J. Jackson

of her 'Dearest Dedre' when he was travelling, and was kept awake at night by imaginings of overturned coaches.[49]

Ironically, Sir Edward's youngest daughter, Basilia, who was named after her uncle, the Parliamentarian commander, became a maid of honour to Queen Mary of Modena and formed one of the family's links with the Stuart Royal Family.[50] The most important marriage alliances that the family made after the Restoration, however, involved Sir Edward's three eldest children by his first wife, Mary Hervey. William, his heir, married Mary Charlotte Bond, the only daughter of the Catholic Sir Thomas Bond, 1st Baronet of Peckham, Comptroller of the Household of Queen Henrietta Maria, in October 1675.[51] The Gages were doubly allied with the Bonds when Sir Edward's second daughter Mary (d.1719) married William Bond (d.1696),[52] a younger son of Sir Thomas Bond, who settled in Bury. Their marriage may have followed soon after Mary and Thomas's visit to the Continent in December 1678 as members of a party led by William Gage to escape persecution associated with the Popish Plot.[53] Sir Edward's eldest daughter Penelope continued the tradition of alliances with long-established local Catholic families by marrying her first cousin, Edward Sulyard of Haughley (her aunt and namesake Penelope Gage had married his father Sir Edward Sulyard in the 1630s).

Sir Edward was presented for recusancy at the Bury quarter sessions on 15 January 1674 and the Compton Census of 1676 recorded ten papists in the parish of Flempton-cum-Hengrave out of a total of one hundred communicants.[54] If this is an accurate figure, it would indicate that Sir Edward had no particular interest in employing Catholic servants, as some recusant families did. The largest concentration of papists to be found in the county outside Bury St Edmunds, which had a total of forty, was to be found in the parish of Stanningfield, which included the

---

Howard), *The Visitation of Suffolk* (London: Whittaker and Co., 1866–71), vol. 1, p. 105.

[49] Elizabeth Feilding to Sir Edward Gage, undated, CUL Hengrave MS 88/3/63.

[50] Basilia and her sister Catherine were painted by the Bury portrait artist Mary Beale (1632–97), probably in the 1680s, and their portraits were still at Hengrave in 1908; see Farrer, *Portraits in Suffolk Houses (West)*, pp. 173–74.

[51] Gage, *Thingoe*, p. 205. For Mary Charlotte's marriage settlement see SRO(B) 449/4/18. Sir Thomas Bond was created a baronet by Charles II while in exile at Brussels on 9 October 1658. G. E, Cockayne, *Complete Baronetage* (Exeter, 1900–09), vol. 3, p. 20.

[52] Mary Gage was buried at Hengrave on 28 February 1719 and William Bond was buried at Hengrave on 18 April 1696 (Gage, *Hengrave*, p. 77).

[53] *CSPD*, 1678, p. 618.

[54] SRO(B) 558/1; A. Whiteman and A. Clapinson (eds), *The Compton Census of 1676: A Critical Edition* (British Academy: London, 1986), p. 237.

Rookwoods' Coldham Hall (a total of sixteen).[55] In 1681 Sir Edward's name appeared again in *A List of the Names of Papist & reputed Papist in the County of Suffolk*,[56] alongside his brothers Henry Gage and John Gage of Stoneham.[57]

Joy Rowe has suggested that the thirty-five men and one woman listed in 1681, most but not all of them landed gentry, were individuals who had refused to swear the Oath of Allegiance, which included a repudiation of the doctrine of transubstantiation.[58] The list included two members of the Mannock family of Gifford's Hall; Sir Roger Martin of Melford Place; Sir Henry Bedingfield (probably of Coulsey Wood) and William Bedingfield of Redlingfield; three members of the Timperley family of Hintlesham; Richard Tasburgh of Flixton; Edward Sulyard of Haughley; Charles Yaxley of Yaxley; and two of the Daniels of Acton. Other names that appear in the list are less familiar and these individuals were not landed gentry in the traditional sense: John Rouse of 'Prison' (Preston?); Richard Milton of Ipswich; Christopher Gale and Richard Facon of 'Ottolt' (Occold?); Francis Brookworth and Robert Crow of 'Melle' (Mellis?); Nathaniel Thruston of Mickfield; John Hart of Hintlesham; Thomas Gutteridge, John Spicer and John Allen of Great Barton; Martin Cheney of Wickham Skeith; Margaret Whitewood of Wortham; William Pisbrow of Wetherden; Thomas Bullbrook of Woolpit; George Goodrick of Ashfield; and the Hammons of Great Feltham. It is notable that almost all of these Catholics were living in central and northern 'High Suffolk' or near Bury, rather than in the Stour Valley where the sole Catholics were gentry such as the Daniels, Mannocks and Martins.

The Compton Census of 1676, which recorded 167 recusants in the two parishes of St James and St Mary is not particularly useful, since it did not distinguish between Protestant Dissenters and Catholics. Recusants of either description constituted 4.5 per cent of the town's population and they were probably underestimated.[59] The hearth tax returns for 1674 yield a number of names that later make an appearance in the Benedictine mission register in the 1730s and 1740s. These include

---

55 Ibid. pp. 237–38.

56 'Popish Recusants in Suffolk', *East Anglian Notes and Queries* 1 (1885–86), pp. 345–46.

57 Henry Gage 'of Hengrave' drew up a will on 18 January 1684, in which he bequeathed £300 and a silver watch to his brother John; everything he else he bequeathed to Edward Cleast of St Giles in the Fields, Middlesex. The will was proved on 1 March 1684 (PROB 11/375).

58 J. Rowe, *The Story of Catholic Bury St. Edmunds, Coldham and Surrounding District* (Bury St Edmunds, 1981), p. 10.

59 D. Dymond, 'Suffolk and Compton Census of 1676', *Suffolk Review* 3 (1966), p. 115.

Adams, Balls,[60] Betts,[61] Bond,[62] Church,[63] Craske,[64] Frost,[65] King,[66] Mann,[67] Page,[68] Perry,[69] Rookwood[70] and Short,[71] as well as names associated with Catholicism elsewhere such as Hyldeyard,[72] Jernego (Jernegan?)[73] Jetter,[74] Stafford[75] and Teball (Theobald?)[76]. However, it is impossible to determine whether these families were Catholic in 1674; families drifted in and out of conformity and several (such as the Craskes and Betts) had both conformist and recusant branches. Furthermore, names such as Adams, Frost, King and Page were common and the families with these names extant in Bury in the 1670s may have been no relation to the Catholic families that appear from the 1730s onwards. Missing are the names of some of the stalwarts of the Catholic community from the 1730s, such as Birch, Brundle, Cranmer, Hunt, Horseman, Jellet, Larret and Merry; these families evidently arrived in the first half of the eighteenth century.

Educating the future

Sir Edward's second son by his first wife Mary Hervey, John Gage the Elder (1651–1728),[77] studied Humanities at the Jesuit College at St Omer before being professed as a Jesuit on 7 July 1670 at Watten. John was ordained on 1 April 1679 and sent to Bruges to minister to English

---

60 Hervey (ed.), *Suffolk in 1674*, pp. 54, 55, 60.
61 Ibid. pp. 56, 60, 63.
62 Ibid. pp. 53 (Henry Bonds), 55, (John Bond), 57 (Laurence Bond).
63 Ibid. p. 60.
64 Ibid. pp. 52, 58.
65 Ibid. pp. 56, 59, 60, 62.
66 Ibid. pp. 59, 60, 62, 63.
67 Ibid. pp. 61, 62, 64.
68 Ibid. pp. 53, 55, 56, 63.
69 Ibid. p. 60.
70 Ibid. pp. 52 (Ambrose Rookwood, seven hearths), 54 ('Mrs Wrookwood', seven hearths).
71 Ibid. pp. 54 (Dr Perry Short, seven hearths; Dr Short Junior, seven hearths).
72 Walter Hyldeyard appeared in the January 1674 list of recusants (SRO(B) 558/1) and owned a house with eleven hearths in the parish of St Mary in the same year (Hervey (ed.), *Suffolk in 1674*, p. 56).
73 The Jernegans or Jerninghams of Costessey were among the leading Catholic families of Norfolk. A 'Widow Jernego' shared a house with three hearths in 1674 (Hervey (ed.), *Suffolk in 1674*, p. 58).
74 Ibid. p. 58.
75 Ibid. p. 56.
76 Ibid. p. 60.
77 So called here to distinguish him from John Gage the Younger SJ (1720–90), also a Jesuit missionary in the College of the Holy Apostles.

exiles fleeing the Popish Plot scare in 1681. He was appointed Spiritual Coadjutor in 1684 and sent on the English mission, attached to the College of the Holy Apostles (the Jesuits' East Anglian mission) from 1685.[78] Although John Gage the antiquary did not recognise John Gage the Elder as the son of Sir Edward and Mary Hervey it is not possible, given his age, that John Gage was the son of Sir Edward and Elizabeth Feilding. He was certainly a Hengrave Gage, as he was described as 'a native of Suffolk', and there was only one Suffolk branch of the Gages in 1651 (John Gage the Elder's contribution to the College of the Holy Apostles will be addressed in Chapter 3). On the other hand, Geoffrey Holt's identification of the George Gage who was educated at St Omer between 1690 and 1694 as being the eldest son of Sir Edward and Elizabeth Feilding is plausible.[79]

Sir Edward was sufficiently concerned for the education of his eldest son and heir, William, that he engaged the secular priest Dr Francis Gage, who had studied at the Sorbonne, to arrange his continental education. Francis Gage was a son of John Gage of Haling by his second wife, Anne Barnes, and thus a half-brother of Colonel Sir Henry Gage, the hero of Cullum Bridge. Both of his brothers, George and Thomas, were also priests. Francis had considerable experience as a tutor, having been appointed to teach Thomas Arundel in 1648. Francis gained a Doctorate of Divinity from the Sorbonne in 1654 before returning to England, where he was appointed Archdeacon of Essex, under the jurisdiction of Vicar Apostolic Richard Smith, and thereafter the Chapter of the English Secular Clergy. In 1659–61 he was in Rome as agent of the English clergy until his return to England; in November 1667 he went back to Paris as tutor to Philip Draycot of Painsley, Staffordshire.[80] In January 1668 Sir Edward contacted him about taking on William Gage as well, and sent Francis some money. The priest was frank in his reply to Enderby: 'Really I think S[i]r Edward ought to spend one hundred at least upon his sonne; or if his occasions will not allow it, I conceive he would doe better to breed him in some place more out of the eye of the world.'[81]

Sir Edward, who seems to have underestimated the cost of living in Paris (there is no evidence that he ever went abroad himself), complied with the request for more money and William arrived in February. If the idea of sending William to Paris was that he would receive a Sorbonne

[78] Foley, vol. 7:1, p. 282.
[79] G. Holt (ed.), *St. Omers and Bruges Colleges, 1593–1773: A Biographical Dictionary* (London: CRS, 1979), p. 109.
[80] C. Dodd, *The Church History of England* (Brussels, 1742), vol. 3, pp. 295–97; T. Cooper (rev. D. Milburn), 'Gage, Francis' in *ODNB*, vol. 21, p. 249.
[81] Dr Francis Gage to Mr Enderby, 18 January 1668, CUL Hengrave MS 88/3/109.

education, he may have been enrolled at St Gregory's College, the English College set up by John Betham and Miles Pinkney in 1667 to replace the pre-Civil War Arras College (1611–35) to prepare English clergy for the Sorbonne. The college would later become notorious as a centre of English Jansenism, a movement in which another Bury Catholic, Dr Richard Short, was heavily implicated.[82] The only other English school for young men in Paris at the time was the Benedictine St Edmund's, but it seems unlikely that William would have attended a Benedictine school under the tutelage of the secular Francis Gage.[83] If William was in Paris for his higher studies, he may already have completed his 'Humanities' at the English College in Douai, but there is no record of him being there. At any rate, William comes across as somewhat hapless in Francis Gage's letters to Enderby. Gage had to find lodgings for William, but when he did, William 'tooke such a dislike to the place, that no persuasion could prevaile w[i]th him to continue any longer in it'. Gage added that 'this resolution of his father [to send William to Paris] comes very seasonable to the young mans inclination: who indeed is so nice and shiftlesse, that he can live no where, without a great helpe and assistance'.[84]

Francis Gage realised that William would need a great deal of care and attention, but in his letter to Sir Edward he sought to create the impression that the young man was independent: '[I] desire it may not be knowne that I have any care of him, more than as a friend'. Francis's letters to Sir Edward were designed to reassure the Baronet concerning William's welfare. However, Francis Gage's chief concern was to ensure he had sufficient funds from Sir Edward to look after William. Earlier he had complained to Enderby that the £100 Sir Edward had set aside was woefully insufficient,[85] and by the end of his letter to Sir Edward he had outlined annual expenses for William that amounted to nine hundred Louis d'Or.[86] Indeed, Francis was so insistent on spending money on a completely new set of furniture, for instance, that it is possible that he was taking advantage of Sir Edward's seemingly limitless financial resources. Francis explained that it was expected William would go to 'our English Court', in other words the court of the Dowager Queen

---

[82] Glickman, *The English Catholic Community 1688–1745*, p. 176; F. Young, *English Catholics and the Supernatural, 1553–1829* (Farnham: Ashgate, 2013), p. 60.

[83] Having said this, the survival of a painting of Dr Francis Gage at Douai Abbey, the successor to St Edmund's, suggests that there could have been a connection.

[84] Dr Francis Gage to Mr Enderby, 15 February 1668, CUL Hengrave MS 88/3/108.

[85] Dr Francis Gage to Mr Enderby, 18 January 1668, CUL Hengrave MS 88/3/109.

[86] These included William's pension, his chambers, an extra charge for having rooms on the first floor, his manservant's wages and his fees; it did not include clothes and other costs.

Fig. 4. Dr Francis Gage (1621–82), tutor to Sir William Gage, 2nd Baronet
(reproduced by kind permission of Douai Abbey, Woolhampton)

Mother, Henrietta Maria, 'w[hi]ch the queene doth expect of all the
English that live in town, at least some times'.[87]
    Although Francis Gage made frequent references to Philip Draycot in
his personal journal, William Gage merited only one mention in 1669:
'In sept[ember] w[illiam] Gage fell ill of the small pox.'[88] William made

---

[87] Dr Francis Gage to Sir Edward Gage, 4 March 1668, CUL Hengrave MS 88/2/181.
[88] Journal of Dr Francis Gage, 1621–77, fol. 473, Archives of the Archbishop of
      Westminster, Correspondence of the Vicars Apostolic, vol. XXXIV, N125.

a complete recovery, however,[89] and it is very likely that William met his future wife, Mary Charlotte Bond, at the Queen Mother's court in Paris. Mary's father, Sir Thomas Bond, 1st Baronet of Peckham, was Comptroller of the Household to the Queen Mother and his daughter was brought up in the household of Henrietta, Duchess of Orléans, the youngest daughter of Charles I. A painting at Hengrave by Van Dyck showed Mary presenting a bouquet of flowers to the Duchess.[90] After William and Mary's marriage in 1675, Mary's French mother, the daughter of Charles Peliot, Baron de la Garde, came to live at Hengrave where she died in 1696. Through this match the Gages of Hengrave were linked to an English émigré community in Paris first established during the Civil War, a community that provided an opportunity for advancement that Catholics were denied in England; it also foreshadowed the court of James II and Mary of Modena at Saint-Germain-en-Laye. It was through circumstances such as these that English Catholics came to be tied by an 'umbilical cord' to the Continent.[91]

The Bonds were a gallicised family who were fluent in French, and one of them either wrote or copied into manuscript directions for confession ('Conduite pour la Confession'), which appear in the 1872 catalogue of Hengrave Hall's library but do not seem to have found their way into the Hengrave manuscripts.[92] Another French manuscript, 'Testament de l'âme chrestienne', does survive and was meticulously hand-illuminated by Thomas Bond for his mother, Marie Peliot, in 1683; it was probably copied from one or more books of devotion in French.[93]

The only other one of Sir Edward's sons to show an interest in the priesthood was Edward, his only son by Anne Watkins, his third wife, who made this declaration at the English College, Rome, on 15 July 1685:

> My name is Edward Gage. I am son of Edward Gage, of Suffolk. My mother's name was Watkins. I was born in 1662 or 1663, and educated at Douay. My parents and other connections are well born & wealthy, and all

[89] Bridget Stanhope to Elizabeth Feilding, December 1669, CUL Hengrave MS 88/3/58.

[90] Gage, *Hengrave*, n. p. 243; *A Catalogue of the Whole of the Very Interesting and Historical Contents of Hengrave Hall, Bury St Edmunds* (London: Hampton and Sons, 1897) (hereafter *Catalogue*), p. 47.

[91] Marshall and Scott, *Catholic Gentry in English Society*, p. 15. There is no evidence for Norman Scarfe's assertion that Sir William Gage, 2nd Baronet was responsible for introducing the Reine-Claude plum or 'greengage' into England (F. de Rochefoucauld (trans. and ed. N. Scarfe), *A Frenchman's Year in Suffolk* (Woodbridge: SRS, 1988), n. p. 35).

[92] CUL Hengrave MS 52.

[93] CUL Hengrave MS 57. The MS was given by Thomas Bond's daughter Judith to her nephew Charles Jermyn Bond in 1749 (see Chapter 5) and acquired by John Gage the antiquary in 1807.

are Catholics. I have four brothers & four sisters. I was always Catholic, & have suffered nothing for my faith, but my parents have suffered much. I promise to enter the priesthood, & return to England to help in the salvation of souls, should Superiors see fit.[94]

Unfortunately, Edward does not seem to have had his half-brother John's staying power, and he left the English College without taking the missionary oath on 31 August 1686, although he remained in Rome.[95] However, Edward did not disappear from history entirely after his unsuccessful attempt at entering the priesthood; he was living in Bury in 1700 when he gave his consent to Gage's Estate Act (see Chapter 3).[96]

Learning and devotion

Sir Edward Gage was fluent in French and he maintained an interest in French devotional works, at least two of which he translated; one of these translations was published in 1694. His library gives us some insight into his religious and intellectual interests. The handwritten library catalogues compiled in the early nineteenth century by Sir Thomas Gage, 7th Baronet contain a number of books published before 1707, although in the absence of a contemporary catalogue we cannot be sure that all of these books were actually purchased in Sir Edward's lifetime. They could have been old books later acquired by the family.[97]

In the area of liturgy and devotions, the library at Hengrave contained two copies of the *Missale Romanum* (1605 and 1615), two copies of the *Office of the Blessed Virgin Mary* in Latin (1591 and 1680),[98] three copies of the *Breviarium Romanum* (1622, 1624 and 1669) and one of the *Rituale Romanum* (1619). Sir Edward owned an English translation of the *Confessions* of St Augustine (1679); a mystical treatise by Luis de Granada (1582);[99] a translation of St Francis de Sales's *Introduction to a Devout Life* (1648), popular with both Catholics and Protestants;[100] and, unsurprisingly since it concerned the history of his own family, Edward Scarisbrick's *Life of Lady Warner* (1691).[101]

---

94   Foley, vol. 5, p. 525.
95   Foley, vol. 6, p. 436.
96   Various eds, *The Manuscripts of the House of Lords* (London, 1887–1977) (hereafter *Lords MSS*) 1699–1702, vol. 4, p. 83.
97   CUL Hengrave MSS 50, 52.
98   *Catalogue*, pp. 94, 99.
99   Ibid. p. 94.
100   On the significance of the writings of St Francis de Sales in the English Catholic community see Glickman, *The English Catholic Community 1688–1745*, pp. 66–67.
101   *Catalogue*, p. 95.

Three tracts of the Jacobean era by the Jesuit Robert Parsons that may have been collected by Penelope or her son featured in the library: *A Review of Ten Public Disputations ... under K. Edward & Qu. Mary* (St Omer, 1604) and Parsons's *Answere to the fifth part of Reportes lately set forth by Syr Edward Cook* (St Omer, 1606) sought to discredit the Reformation and defend the continuity of the Catholic Church in England, while *A Treatise tending to Mitigation Towards Catholic Subjects in England* (St Omer, 1607) defended Catholic loyalty to the Crown. A later work of apologetics was R. Caron's *Vindication of the Roman Catholicks of the English Nation* (London, 1660), which also defended Catholics against accusations of disloyalty.

Works of catechesis and church history included a five-volume translation of the French Jesuit Nicolas Caussin's *The Holy Court* (London, 1650); Nicolas Talon's *Holy History* (London, 1653) (a commentary on the Old Testament); and *A Declaration of the Principal Pointes of Christian Doctrine* (Paris, 1647), otherwise known as the 'Tournay Catechism', since it was produced by the clergy of the College de Tournai and was given to English priests by Cardinal Richelieu between the dissolution of Arras College and the establishment of St Gregory's. Sir Edward also owned a copy of Battista Platina's lives of the popes in Italian, *Delle Vite dei Pontefici* (1685).

Sir Edward took advantage of the explosion of Catholic printing during the reign of James II by acquiring a copy of the English translation of Toussaint Bridoul's 1672 tract *The School of the Eucharist Established* (London, 1687) as well as T. W. Gent's translation of Henry VIII's *Assertion of the Seven Sacraments* (London, 1687) and John Barclay's *Defence of the Most Holy Sacrament of the Eucharist* (London, 1688). These were all works published in the hope of refuting Edward Stillingfleet's accusations of 'bread worship' and idolatry against Catholics.[102] The Protestant side of the controversy was represented by copies of John Tillotson's *Discourse against Transubstantiation* (Dublin, 1686) and Peter Manby's *Reformed Catechism* (London, 1687) as well as Gilbert Burnet's anti-Catholic tracts. John Gother's *Good Advice to the Pulpits* (London, 1687), printed by the Catholic printer Henry Hills, was intended to persuade Protestant preachers not to condemn James II's policy of toleration.

Sir Edward's library even contained non-Catholic commentary, such as Theophilus Dorrington's *Observations Concerning the Present State of Religion in the Romish Church* (London, 1699) and *Jovian: Or, an Answer to Julian the Apostate* (London, 1683), a defence of

---

[102]   On this controversy see A. B. Gardiner, 'Defenders of the Mystery', *Recusant History* 30 (2010), pp. 241–60.

the High Tory doctrine of passive obedience by George Hickes, then Vicar of All Hallows, Barking and a Prebendary of Worcester. Hickes went on to lead the nonjuring Jacobite Church of England after the 1688 Revolution. In a similar vein was *Dissenters Sayings* (London, 1681) by the High Tory propagandist Sir Roger L'Estrange. Thomas Vincent's eschatological work *The Only Deliverer from Wrath to Come* (London, 1671) is a more surprising addition to the library, whilst it is understandable that the Gages should want to have a copy of *Directions to Churchwardens* (London, 1704) by the Archdeacon of Suffolk, Humphrey Prideaux, since it partly concerned the implementation of laws and penalties against Catholics and was written by a clergyman with local authority.

One work whose presence in the library is suggestive of the Gages' relationship with Paris and with the court of Henrietta Maria was *Exercises d'une âme Royale* (Paris, 1655) by Cyprien de Gamages, who was a chaplain to the Dowager Queen and was present in 1649 when Thomas Jermyn, her Master of the Horse and later 1st Baron St Edmundsbury, arrived at the Louvre with news of the execution of King Charles I.[103] Another was the pamphlet *Impeachment and Articles of Complaint against Father Phillips the Queenes Confessor* (London, 1641), detailing the allegations against Henrietta Maria's Scottish Oratorian chaplain, Robert Phillip. Although the Gages never went into exile in Paris, the Parisian educations of Sir Thomas Gage of Firle in the 1630s and William Gage in the 1660s, together with William's marriage to the daughter of Sir Thomas Bond, the Comptroller of the Queen's Household, suggests that Paris was the Gages' continental spiritual home from home. However, Sir Edward's Jesuit devotions indicate that he and his family did not follow St Gregory's, its principal John Betham and other English Catholics associated with Paris and the Sorbonne towards Jansenism and Anglo-Gallicanism. The Jesuits were the greatest enemy of both movements.

A partiality for French Jesuit spirituality is suggested by a copy of Jean Croisset's *A Spiritual Retreat for One Day in Every Month* (Paris, 1700) in Sir Edward's library. We know from a manuscript in his own hand that Sir Edward's personal devotional life was nourished by the works of the Pontoise Jesuit Michel Boutauld. Between 1677 and 1680 Sir Edward made a translation of the second volume of Boutauld's *Les conseils de la sagesse, ou le recueil des maximes de Salomon les plus necessaires à l'homme pour se conduire sagement*,[104] calling it 'A

---

103 Hervey (ed.), *Rushbrook Parish Registers with Jermyn and Davers Annals*, pp. 259–60.

104 Boutauld's book was first published in Paris in 1677, and the first English translation by 'E. S.' (dedicated to Queen Catherine of Braganza) appeared in 1680 as *The*

Collection of Such Maximes of Solomon as are most Proper to Guide us to the Felicity of Both the Present and the Future Life with Reflections upon the Maximes'.[105] Sir Edward's translation, running to sixty-two pages, was presumably for his own use and that of his family, and consisted of a series of Latin quotations from the 'Wisdom Books' of the Catholic Old Testament, each one followed by a 'Paraphrase' and a 'Reflection'. Given that we have no evidence that Sir Edward received a continental education,[106] he apparently taught himself French and thought it worth translating Boutauld's work as an act of piety. The tone of the book is a kind of 'Christian stoicism' that certainly corresponds to the literature of moral perfection that Glickman associates with later English recusants.[107] Boutauld's work, along with Luis de Granada, Francis de Sales and Scarisbrick's *Life of Lady Warner*, was identified by Patricia Brückmann as a standard spiritual work accessible to most educated English Catholics.[108]

Following Sir Edward's retirement from the running of the Hengrave estate after the Revolution, he went a step further than merely translating a work of devotion. His translation of apocryphal 'Essays' attributed to the French grandee Nicolas Fouquet appeared in print in 1694, prefaced by a letter addressed to 'Lady Hanmer'. Lady Hanmer was Sir Edward's sister-in-law Susan Hervey, the widow of Sir Thomas Hanmer. In the letter, Sir Edward referred to a recent visit Lady Hanmer had paid to Hengrave when he lent her the French original of the translation he now presented. Most remarkably, however, Sir Edward made a less-than-veiled allusion to his desire that Lady Hanmer would consider converting to Catholicism:

> If you find in places of this Volume, when you converse farther with it, a Spirit of Devotion, I hope you will take notice in what Perswasion it was written, and examine, whether you ever met with any thing truly of that kind, which has been written out of that Perswasion: And I wish, Madam, you may make such an advantageous Observation here as I could desire.[109]

Counsels of Wisdom or, A Collection of the Maxims of Solomon; Most Necessary for a Man towards the Gaining of Wisdom: With Reflexions upon the Maxims. Sir Edward presumably made his own translation before that of 'E. S.' became available.

[105] CUL Hengrave MS 56.

[106] On the contrary, the surviving letters would seem to confirm that Edward was in England throughout the 1640s and 1650s, although it is possible that he was abroad in the late 1630s in his early teenage years.

[107] Glickman, *The English Catholic Community 1688–1745*, pp. 66–67.

[108] P. Brückmann, 'Virgins Visited by Angel Powers: *The Rape of the Lock*, Platonick Love, Sylphs, and some Mysticks' in G. S. Rousseau and P. Rogers (eds), *The Enduring Legacy: Alexander Pope Tercentenary Essays* (Cambridge: Cambridge University Press, 1988), p. 11.

[109] N. Fouquet (attrib., trans. E. Gage), *Essays suppos'd to be written by Monsieur*

Translations of devotional literature written by Catholics ('written out of that Perswasion') were widespread in the second half of the seventeenth century, and were avidly read by Protestants. Free from overt doctrinal content, they could serve as a 'Trojan horse' for Catholicism that rendered Protestant readers sympathetic to the idea that Catholics were as capable of true devotion as anyone else.[110] If Edward Scarisbrick's account of Trevor Hanmer is to be believed, Susan Hervey was already a crypto-Catholic who believed in the real presence of Christ in the Sacrament in the 1640s, so she may have been receptive to Sir Edward's gentle proselytism.[111] Certainly, the letter is evidence of a genuine and earnest desire to convert others on Sir Edward's part. Indeed, religion may have become his chief preoccupation in the 1680s; this would explain why he showed no inclination to politics in James II's reign and sold most of his lands to his son in the early 1690s. Although by no means a prolific author, Sir Edward Gage played a small part in the transmission of French devotional literature to England – and, through his library, his translation work and the education and marriage of his son, he was intellectually and spiritually tied to France, and to Paris in particular.

The Gages and the Popish Plot

Although the Gages seem to have largely escaped the effects of recusancy legislation in the 1660s, the onset of the Popish Plot threatened all Catholics, even those as discreet as the Gages. Sir Edward Gage seems to have been a keen observer of political life, and among the Hengrave manuscripts is a detailed report of proceedings in Parliament sent to Sir Francis Mannock in March 1678 in Sir Edward's hand.[112] The first attention the Gages received from the authorities after Titus Oates's 'disclosure' of the Plot in September 1678 was on 4 December, when a London informant reported to the Privy Council that he saw John Naylor, a 'reputed Popish priest', baptise a child at the Green Dragon in Great Queen Street, 'and that he was reputed to be priest to Sir Edward Gage'. Nailor admitted to being a papist but denied that he was Sir

---

Fouquet: being reflections upon such maxims of Solmon as are most proper to guide us to the felicity of both the present and the future life (London, 1694), prefatory letter.

[110] See, for instance, the argument for the value of Catholic literature in George Hickes's preface to *Devotions in the Way of Ancient Offices* (London, 1701), pp. xix–xx.

[111] Scarisbrick, *The Holy Life of Lady Warner*, p. 31.

[112] Sir Edward Gage to Sir Francis Mannock, 13 March 1678, CUL Hengrave MS 88/2/182.

Edward's chaplain.[113] A search of the Green Dragon was conducted and 'books and beads' were found; the only action taken was to hand these over to the Bishop of London.

There was only one priest in England at the time using the alias Naylor, the Benedictine Roger Jerome Hesketh.[114] Hesketh was born at Whitehill in Lancashire and professed at St Gregory's, Douai on 21 September 1639. He was appointed Procurator of the Northern Province of the English Benedictine mission in 1657, then returned to France to act as confessor to the English Blue Nuns in Paris from 1675–78. He was in England, in the South Province, in 1678 and his association with Sir Edward may have owed something to the fact that the Baronet was a benefactor to the English Benedictines, through his £40 annuity to them described above. It is likely that Hesketh was saying Mass at Sir Edward's house near Bloomsbury Market and was seen by the informant. Although no further action was taken on this particular informant's testimony, the climate was such that having been brought to the attention of the authorities once, Hesketh was soon arrested again and this time confined to Newgate for fifteen months.[115] On his release he returned to Douai where he was elected Prior of St Gregory's in 1681; he died on 21 September 1693.

What happened to Hesketh was probably sufficient motivation for Sir Edward to leave London. His son and heir William went even further when he obtained a pass from the Secretary of State to go abroad on 12 December 1678 with his wife Mary Charlotte Bond, his mother-in-law Lady Bond, his brother-in-law William Bond, his sister Mary Gage and a certain 'Mistress Anne Owen'. The party took eight male and seven female servants with them.[116] Everyone who left the country was required to swear not to consort with the King's enemies, visit Rome, enter a foreign seminary or place his children there.[117] William's was one of the thirty-four parties of Catholic aristocrats and gentry who left the country before the end of 1678.[118]

---

113   *Lords MSS* 1678–88, p. 20.

114   A. Allanson (ed. A Cranmer and S. Goodwill), *Biography of the English Benedictines* (Ampleforth: Ampleforth Abbey, 1999), pp. 115–16; Bellenger, pp. 71, 221; H. N. Birt, *Obit Book of the English Benedictines, 1600–1912* (Edinburgh: Mercat Press, 1913), p. 61. Hesketh also used the name James Baker.

115   Birt, *Obit Book of the English Benedictines, 1600–1912*, p. 61; Lunn, *The English Benedictines 1540–1688*, p. 130.

116   *CSPD* 1678, p. 618.

117   Ibid. pp. 618–19. It is not necessarily the case, as Blackwood, *Tudor and Stuart Suffolk*, p. 235 suggests, that William went abroad for his own safety.

118   J. P. Kenyon, *The Popish Plot* (London: Penguin, 1974), pp. 257–58.

William's half-brother Francis Gage of Packington, Sir Edward's only son by his second wife Frances Aston, was less circumspect. In January 1679 he was brought before the Privy Council for being in London in defiance of the King's proclamations of 30 October and 6 November 1678 commanding Catholics to leave London and forbidding them to travel more than five miles from their homes.[119] Francis was also accused of slandering Stephen Dugdale, Lord Aston's steward, who was arrested in December 1678 and retained as a key government informant. On the basis of Dugdale's allegations, Sir Edward's father-in-law, Lord Aston, was confined to the Tower of London in January as one of the supposed 'Staffordshire plotters'.[120] Given that Francis Gage was Lord Aston's grandson, he may have been in London with Dugdale on the same business for Lord Aston when the former was arrested, and he could not have been best pleased when Dugdale turned against his grandfather. However, the accusations against Francis came to nothing, and he was granted a pass to leave the country in March.[121]

The Gages and James II

Following the passage of the first Test Act in June 1673, the Catholic heir to the throne, James, Duke of York, was deprived of his official appointments and suddenly found himself at leisure. As John Callow has observed, James used hunting as an opportunity to escape his troubles,[122] and by 1674 he had bought the lease of the Culford estate from the owner Frederick, 1st Baron Cornwallis of Eye. Culford was relatively close to Newmarket and offered good hunting on the edge of Breckland. However, it was also adjacent to Hengrave Park, on the north side of the River Lark. It is unclear how much use James made of his new estate. Although Culford's occupier was listed as 'the Duke of Yorke' in the hearth tax returns of 1674, the property was then empty.[123] However, Sir Robert Carr wrote to Joseph Williamson on 21 March 1675 that: 'The Duke is gone to Culford.'[124]

The local belief that James was present at the wedding of William Gage to Mary Charlotte Bond in October 1675 is not, therefore, implausible but no documentary evidence confirms it. Another local belief relates that the Rector of Culford's daughter, Elizabeth Norridge, threw

119   Ibid. p. 258.
120   Ibid. p. 256.
121   *Lords MSS* 1678–88, vol. 13, p. 480.
122   J. Callow, *James II: The Triumph and the Tragedy* (London: Sutton, 2005), p. 36.
123   Hervey (ed.), *Suffolk in 1674*, p. 88. Culford was listed as having twenty-nine hearths.
124   *CSPD*, 1675–76, p. 32.

herself from a window of Culford Hall in May 1674 when she was left alone with King Charles II, who had ridden over from West Stow to join his brother.[125] The Gages' Catholicism, together with the celebrated loyalty of Sir Edward's cousin to the House of Stuart, could have made them the recipients of a visit from the heir to the throne during this period, but it remains speculation unsupported by evidence.

A more than passing connection between the Gages and the Duke of York is suggested by the survival at Hengrave of a painting of James, which could not be dispersed in 1897, 1952 or 2005 because it is embedded in the panelling of what was then the Gatehouse Chamber (now known as the Oriel Chamber), the room directly above the main entrance to the Hall over the moat. This was the only room in the house whose original panelling survived Hengrave's period of dereliction in the late eighteenth century and the restorations of Sir John Wood. Judging from James's age in the painting it was probably completed in the 1670s. In 1897 a further portrait of James II by the King's court painter William Wissing was sold,[126] and in 1908 there were two portraits of the King at Hengrave.[127] However, whether James gave one or more of these portraits to Sir Edward as a present, or Sir Edward commissioned them to commemorate James's visit, we have no way of knowing.

If James was not acquainted with the Gages before his accession, after 1685 the rapid rise at court of Sir Edward's nephew, the Jesuit Edward Petre, had the potential to place the family at the centre of power. Petre may have been involved with the upbringing of James's illegitimate children at the time he was arrested for involvement in the Popish Plot. Scheduled to be tried with Lord Aston, he was released because there was only one witness for the trial, Aston's steward Stephen Dugdale (the same witness Petre's cousin Francis Gage had been arrested for slandering). However, in 1685 (presumably for services rendered to the Duke of York) Petre was appointed Dean of the new Catholic Chapel Royal at Whitehall.[128]

John Miller has pointed out that Petre's status in the English Province of the Society of Jesus was 'lowly', and he owed his success at court to his own personal charm, James's regard for him, and the Earl of Sunderland's desire to manipulate him for his own ends.[129] Although he did not formally become a member of the Privy Council until 1688, Petre was a member of the 'secret Council' of Catholics that surrounded James

125   G. Storey, 'Culford Hall, Near Bury St. Edmunds' in *People and Places: An East Anglian Miscellany* (Lavenham: Dalton, 1973), p. 144.

126   *Catalogue*, p. 42.

127   Farrer, *Portraits in Suffolk Houses (West)*, p. 177.

128   S. Handley, 'Petre, Sir Edward' in *ODNB*, vol. 43, pp. 906–7.

129   J. Miller, *James II*, 3rd edn (New Haven, CT: Yale University Press, 2000), p. 149.

from the summer of 1686. Historians' assessment of Petre's importance has varied. While Jock Haswell insisted that 'James consulted [Petre] on most things and usually took his advice – particularly on matters connected with religion',[130] Miller believed that historians from Lord Macaulay onwards, keen to portray James as a weak monarch manipulated by unscrupulous Jesuits, had generally overestimated Petre's influence.[131] Nevertheless, as Miller writes, 'his [James's] influence and lack of political sense made him a powerful if unreliable instrument which could be manipulated by cleverer men'.[132]

James was damning of Petre in his own memoirs, while recognising that he was a mere tool in Sunderland's hands:

> [Sunderland] saw the King had a personal kindness for that Father, which he endeavour'd to highten by the huge commendation he gave of his abilities; his Majesty was charm'd, to find a Person he afected so much, extoll'd at that rate by one he knew to be no ill judg of capacitys, while Father Petre himself, (who was indeed a plausible but weak man, and had only the art by an abundance of words to put a Gloss upon a weak and shallow judgment) was the more easily dazled with the dust which this cunning Statesman cast in his eyes, so he took him for an unfain'd friend.[133]

Although Miller attributed the papal embassy of Roger Palmer, Earl of Castlemaine to procure a bishropric for Petre to the priest's 'pestering' of the King,[134] it is evident from James's memoirs that it was the King's personal affection for Petre, coupled with Sunderland's scheming, which led to the request being made so persistently. In November 1685 Pope Innocent XI agreed to make the Queen's unsuitable uncle Rinaldo d'Este a cardinal in order to 'soften the blow' of refusing to make Petre a bishop, presumably considering Rinaldo a lesser evil than the elevation of an obscure English Jesuit. In June 1687 James asked the Pope for a cardinal's hat for Petre instead, and when this was refused, Petre (or Sunderland, as the actions of the two men were not necessarily separable) blamed Cardinal Howard for the Pope's refusal and James made Rinaldo Cardinal Protector of England in Howard's place.[135]

Petre was in essence a courtier-priest whose influence derived from his ability to charm the King, but whatever he was in reality, in the

---

130   J. Haswell, *James II: Soldier and Sailor* (London: Hamilton, 1972), p. 253.

131   Miller, *James II*, pp. 149–50. For Macaulay, '[Petre] bore, perhaps, the largest part in the ruin of the House of Stuart'. T. B. Macaulay, *The History of England* (London: Penguin, 1968), p. 139.

132   Miller, *James II*, pp. 149–50.

133   J. S. Clarke, *The Life of James the Second King of England* (London, 1816), vol. 2, p. 76.

134   Miller, *James II*, p. 149.

135   Ibid. p. 153.

popular imagination of Protestant England he was the archetype of the sinister, manipulative Jesuit. It was widely rumoured that the King intended to make him Archbishop of York.[136] Knowing this, Sunderland exploited Petre in the knowledge that if he spoke and acted through him, Petre would attract all of the blame and divert attention from his own schemes.[137] However, by 1687 Sunderland had realised that the bold toleration policy would not work, yet Petre and the 'extremists' in James's court, led by the Earl of Melfort, had the power to remove him from office; Sunderland was locked into advancing a policy that, according to Miller, he took every opportunity to advise James against.[138] Petre's formal appointments as Clerk of the Closet and Privy Councillor in November 1687, an effort by James to compensate him for the elusive cardinal's hat, made no difference to his power but were disastrous for the image of the regime.[139]

At the end of November 1688 Petre fled England, apparently for Rome, but he did accompany James II to Ireland in March 1689. Petre's eyesight was failing and, offended by a sermon delivered by the philosopher Michael Moore in Christ Church Cathedral, Dublin in 1690 on the verse 'If the blind lead the blind, both shall fall into the ditch' (Matthew 15:14), he persuaded James to banish Moore from the city.[140] Liam Chambers suggests that Petre's antipathy to Moore was connected to the Jesuits' desire to take control of Trinity College, of which Moore was provost.[141] At any rate, the internal squabbles of the Jacobite regime in Dublin were ended with William of Orange's victory at the Boyne in July 1690, and Petre returned to the Continent. He was eventually appointed Rector of the Jesuit College at St Omer before dying at Watten in 1699.[142] Unlike Melfort, he did not follow the Jacobite court to Saint-Germain-en-Laye.

Edward Petre was not the only relation of the Gage family to be a member of James's court. Sir Edward's second daughter by Elizabeth Feilding (and his eleventh and youngest child), Basilia, became a maid of honour to Mary of Modena; it is unclear whether this took place before the 1688 Revolution or whether Basilia went to Saint-Germain-en-Laye. When Basilia left the Queen's service, the Queen gave her a

---

[136] Ibid. p. 171.
[137] Clarke, *The Life of James the Second King of England*, vol. 2, p. 77.
[138] Miller, *James II*, pp. 174–75.
[139] Ibid. p. 181.
[140] J. Ware (ed. W. Harris), *The whole works of Sir James Ware concerning Ireland* (Dublin, 1764), vol. 2, p. 289.
[141] L. Chambers, *Michael Moore c.1639–1726: Provost of Trinity, Rector of Paris* (Four Courts: Dublin, 2005), p. 60.
[142] Handley, 'Petre, Sir Edward', p. 907.

carriage clock that had belonged to the King, and this was treasured by the Gages. A brass plaque on the clock bore the inscription:

> This clock belonged to King James II., and was given by Mary d'Este the Queen to her Maid of Honour Basilea Gage, the youngest daughter of Sir Edward Gage, Baronet, of Hengrave, and his wife Lady Elizabeth Gage, daughter of George Feilding, Earl of Desmond, K.B., brother of Basil Feilding, second Earl of Denbigh. Basilea Gage by her will bequeathed to her brother Sir William Gage, the second Baronet, her dear mistress the Queen's clock.[143]

Since Basilia outlived her brother William (she was still living in 1733),[144] the inscription is inaccurate and the Sir William to whom she bequeathed the clock was probably her nephew, Sir William Gage, 4th Baronet.

In spite of their family connections with the court of James II, Sir Edward himself kept his distance from the local project to give Catholics greater influence in public life. In Suffolk, James dismissed four justices of the peace (JPs) and replaced all four of them with Catholics: Sir William Mannock of Gifford's Hall, Ambrose Rookwood of Stanningfield, Edward Sulyard of Haughley and Richard Tasburgh of Flixton.[145] Sir Edward was an obvious choice to join the ranks of the new Catholic JPs, but he either refused the appointment or James's agents knew better than to ask him.

Henry Jermyn, Lord Dover (1636–1708), whose niece Merelina Jermyn became William Gage's second wife after the 1688 Revolution, was tasked by a committee of the Privy Council in October 1687 with ensuring that sympathetic MPs were elected for Bury St Edmunds in the election of 1688. Edward Petre sat on the same committee.[146] Dover was the second son of the Royalist Thomas Jermyn of Rushbrooke, the Jermyn who took refuge in Paris at the court of Henrietta Maria. He was thus related to the Gages by marriage several times over. His aunt, Susan Jermyn, was the first wife of Sir William Hervey, and so his Hervey cousins were brought up at Hengrave. However, Dover was not one of the Jermyns visited so often by the Herveys and Gages at Rushbrooke during the 1640s and 1650s; instead he spent his later childhood and teenage years on the Continent, returning to England in 1660.[147] This was when his elder brother Thomas, Lord Jermyn married Mary

143   For the inscription see *Catalogue*, pp. 21–22.
144   According to John Alexius Jones, 'Mrs Bas. Gage' dined with the Bonds on 9 June 1733 (CUL Hengrave MS 69).
145   Blackwood, *Tudor and Stuart Suffolk*, p. 241.
146   Handley, 'Petre, Sir Edward', p. 906. On this committee see Miller, *James II*, pp. 179–80.
147   Hervey (ed.), *Rushbrook Parish Registers with Jermyn and Davers Annals*, p. 310.

Merry (as his second wife), the daughter of Sir Edward Gage's sister Penelope. In 1655 a further link was forged when Dover's sister Henrietta married Sir Edward's younger brother, Henry Gage of Harleston.

After a disreputable career at the court of Charles II, from which he was eventually ejected for his affair with the King's mistress, Lady Castlemaine, Dover was ennobled by James II on 13 May 1685, not long after his coronation. Dover converted to Catholicism at some time in the 1670s,[148] and he was close to the King, who apparently wanted to use Bury St Edmunds, where a Jermyn would have most influence, as one of the testing grounds for his plan to pack Parliament with Dissenters and Catholics who would support toleration and the repeal of the Penal Laws against Catholics. This goal was easier to achieve in Bury than in some other towns, since it was among those that had received new charters from Charles II in 1684, limiting the electoral franchise to the mayor, twelve aldermen and twenty-four common councilmen and allowing the members of the Corporation to be removed from office and appointed directly by the King in Council.[149] All that needed to be done in order to elect two Dissenters as MPs for the town was to purge the Corporation of anyone who gave the wrong answers to three questions about their support for legalised toleration, and pack it with James's supporters.[150]

Knowing that the MPs recommended by the Jermyns had always been elected by the Corporation,[151] Dover was confident that he could manipulate the body. However, after it produced a lacklustre 'loyal address' to the King, Dover decided to adopt more heavy-handed tactics. He tendered the 'three questions' to the Corporation, and having received unsatisfactory answers he removed Mayor Richard Pryme, as well as a number of aldermen and common councilmen in January 1688. By March, Dover had replaced Pryme with John Stafford, a Catholic silk mercer. Dover's side of his subsequent correspondence with Stafford survives. Dover was determined that local Catholics should be appointed to the Corporation, mentioning in particular 'the two Doctor Shorts'.[152]

The Short family was a sprawling dynasty of medical doctors who did a great deal to maintain the vitality of Bury's Catholic commu-

---

[148] Ibid. p. 318.

[149] Bury was one of only nineteen boroughs with such a charter (P. Bishop, *The Sacred and Profane History of Bury St. Edmunds* (London: Unicorn, 1998), p. 69).

[150] Miller, *James II*, p. 178.

[151] Hervey (ed.), *Rushbrook Parish Registers with Jermyn and Davers Annals*, p. 320.

[152] Henry Jermyn to John Stafford, 22 March 1688, SRO(B) E2/41/5 fo. 37. On Dover's campaign in Bury see P. E. Murrell, 'Bury St. Edmunds and the Campaign to pack Parliament, 1687–8', *Bulletin of the Institute of Historical Research* 54 (1981), pp. 188–206; Young, '"An Horrid Popish Plot": The Failure of Catholic Aspirations in Bury St. Edmunds, 1685–88, pp. 210–13.

nity from the late sixteenth century, when the Shorts first appear in Bury parish registers, until well into the eighteenth century.[153] The Shorts were not so much 'Catholic gentry doctors' – Catholic gentry who became doctors because it was one of the few professions open to recusants[154] – but rather a Catholic family that had come from nothing by bettering itself through the medical profession. They seem to have defied Aveling's generalisation that Catholic gentry doctors were not well-respected, perhaps because they did not truly belong to that category.[155] For centuries, the Royal College of Physicians had accepted doctors trained abroad at great institutions like the Universities of Padua and Montpellier (indeed, such foreign training was admired), and consequently it imposed no religious tests as a matter of course. This provided a loophole for English Catholics who were able to train in Catholic universities and then practise at home.

The elder of the two doctors mentioned by Dover was Dr Richard Short (1641/2–1708), perhaps the most controversial figure ever to emerge from Bury's Catholic community. Charles Dodd erroneously reported that Richard was born in London,[156] and this assertion has also crept into the subsequent work of Ruth Clark and Eamon Duffy. He was in fact born in Bury St Edmunds and baptised in St James's church on 7 January 1642.[157] Richard Short's father (also Dr Richard Short) had been a doctor in Bury and an active Royalist pamphleteer who seems to have reverted to his family's ancestral Catholicism by the 1650s, while his uncle was the 'scandalous minister' William Short, Rector of Euston.[158] The younger of the doctors was Dr Thomas Short, the grandson of Richard's uncle, William, the Rector of Euston. Thomas's father, Dr Thomas Short (d.1685) achieved fame as Charles II's personal physician. The younger Thomas Short was married to Ursula Daniel, daughter of John Daniel of Acton, who became the focus of anti-Catholic conspiracy theories on the collapse of James's regime.[159]

---

153 For an account of the Shorts see Young, 'The Shorts of Bury St Edmunds', pp. 188–94.
154 An example of a 'Catholic gentry doctor' was Dr Henry Huddlestone, the brother of Francis Huddlestone of Sawston, who later married into the Gages.
155 Aveling, *The Handle and the Axe*, pp. 268–69.
156 Dodd, *The Church History of England*, vol. 3, p. 460.
157 S. H. A. Hervey (ed.), *Bury St. Edmunds, St. James Parish Registers, Baptisms 1558–1800* (Bury St Edmunds: Paul and Mathew, 1915) (hereafter *St James Baptisms*), p. 125.
158 Young, 'The Shorts of Bury St Edmunds', p. 191.
159 A. J. B. 'A "Gunpowder Plot" at Bury St. Edmund's' (late nineteenth-century newspaper cutting) in J. C. Ford, *Mayors and Aldermen of Bury St. Edmund's 1302–1896*, pp. 94–95 (SRO(B) 942.64 BUR). The original printed version of this letter, prefaced by a letter from 'E. N.' to a 'Right Reverend Father in God' (possibly Bishop

This Thomas Short and his brother Francis both had sons who became Dominican friars, one of them even rising to become Provincial of the English Dominicans (see Chapter 5).

In addition to the Shorts, the Rookwoods of Coldham Hall became involved in Dover's scheme and Ambrose Rookwood of Stanningfield and Henry Audley, an Essex gentleman, took seats on the Corporation.[160] These were the only Catholics who could be induced to take part. The Gages' reluctance to participate may have owed something to Thomas Hervey of Ickworth's opposition to Dover in his role as Assistant Justice of the Liberty of St Edmund.[161] Thomas Hervey was the son of Sir William Hervey, Sir Edward Gage's stepfather, and had been brought up at Hengrave. Whatever the truth, Dover's attempt to divide and rule on confessional grounds was alien to the spirit of the Suffolk gentry, for whom ties of kinship were of greater importance than religious convictions. An enthusiastic convert who had spent much of his life in France rather than a culturally English Catholic, Dover belonged, along with Melfort, to the 'extremist' section of James's court that envisaged a mirror image of the absolutist Bourbon monarchy.

A cause divided: Jesuits and Jansenists

The Catholic community in Bury St Edmunds, galvanised though it may have been by the possibility of toleration in 1685, was not as united as it seemed. The strain between two political visions of English Catholicism threatened to destroy the unity of the national community, and some of the key players in this struggle were associated with Bury. On the one hand, Jesuits such as Petre believed that James II should seek to imitate Louis XIV's conspicuous orthodoxy and obedience to the Holy See, while on the other, English Catholics inspired by the Gallican movement in France and often labelled as 'Jansenists' (whatever their specific theological leanings) thought that Catholic toleration could only gain popular acceptance if the English Church repudiated the Jesuits and, by implication, the authority of Rome itself. One of the leading 'Anglo-Gallicans', and perhaps the leading English Jansenist, was the younger Dr Richard Short.

The Jesuit mission had dominated Catholic East Anglia since at least the establishment of the College of the Holy Apostles in 1633, and as early as 1589 the Rookwoods' home at Coldham Hall was the de facto

Compton of London, an enthusiastic supporter of the Revolution) is to be found in Oxford University, Bodleian Library, Tanner MS 28, fol. 273. I am grateful to Dr John Sutton for alerting me to this reference.

160   Henry Jermyn to John Stafford, 23 August 1688, SRO(B) E2/41/5 fo. 44.

161   Henry Jermyn to John Stafford, 31 May 1688, SRO(B) E2/41/5 fo. 44.

headquarters of the Jesuit mission in England,[162] a role it resumed in the late eighteenth century. Sir Edward Gage, apart from his kinship with Edward Petre, had a Jesuit son and, as we have seen, was attracted primarily to French Jesuit spirituality. John Stafford, Bury's new Catholic mayor, had a brother in the College of the Holy Apostles. The Short family, by contrast, had strong anti-Jesuit tendencies.

In a letter written by Richard Short in 1679, just after he was excluded from the Royal College of Physicians for his refusal to take the sacrament (even though he had already taken the Oath of Supremacy),[163] he blamed the Jesuits for his misfortunes. Short declared that 'the factious and ambitious principles of the Jesuits ... were the true cause of all prejudices against us: and ... such as could clear themselves absolutely from those doctrines and dependencies might live quietly provided they liv'd privately and aim'd at no public preferments'. Short proposed that, instead of penal laws that punished all Catholics without distinction, a religious test should be imposed that only those who held 'Jesuitical' opinions on the deposing power of the Pope would be unable to take. He resented the fact that honest men suffered for principles to which they did not subscribe, while 'the Jesuits have more ways of escape, more friends to protect them and more arts to avoid the Laws'.[164]

Charles Dodd, himself an ardent opponent of the Jesuits, described Richard Short as a 'Jansenist without restriction',[165] and it is true that Short became very friendly with Catholics in the Diocese of Utrecht, which was in schism with Rome (ostensibly over a canonical issue, but essentially over papal authority).[166] Short wrote to a Dutch bookseller, Van Rhyn, that the English Church was 'in a cowardly manner given over to the Jesuits at their discretion; she has never had the heart to shake off her chains. Ignorance flourishes here almost as much as in Goa, and if the Sorbonne flutters its eyes at a few priests it does not cure them of timidity. Our ills seem to be without remedy.'[167] Although Short wrote this in 1706, long after his participation in the failed Bury

---

162   J. Gerard, *The Autobiography of an Elizabethan* (London: Longmans, Green and Co., 1951), pp. 24–31.

163   In 1679 Charles II issued letters patent requiring the Royal College of Physicians to administer the Oaths of Obedience and Supremacy to its fellows (H. J. Cook, *The Decline of the Old Medical Regime in Stuart London* (Ithaca, NY: Cornell University Press, 1986), p. 192).

164   Richard Short's letter is quoted in D. Krook, *John Sergeant and his Circle: A Study of Three Seventeenth-Century Aristotelians* (Leiden: Brill, 1993), pp. 161–62.

165   C. Dodd, *The Secret Policy of the English Society of Jesus* (London, 1715), p. 267.

166   R. Clark, *Strangers and Sojourners at Port Royal* (Cambridge: Cambridge University Press, 1932), pp. 164–65.

167   Quoted in Clark, *Strangers and Sojourners at Port Royal*, pp. 165–66 (my translation of the original French).

Corporation experiment, at least some of the bitterness he felt against the English Jesuits must have dated from this period.

Short made contact with Pasquier Quesnel, the spiritual figurehead of the Jansenist movement who was then living in exile in Holland, and corresponded with Quesnel until his death. Short sent money to Quesnel, began to translate his *Réflexions Morales* into English and, in August 1708, even invited Quesnel to come and live with him. It is likely that Short was in Bury (rather than London) at the time,[168] since he was buried in St Mary's churchyard on 14 December 1708.[169] However, Quesnel declined Short's invitation to come to England[170] – it is intriguing to imagine what would have happened if he had accepted – and Bury St Edmunds had become the centre of the Jansenist movement.

Short was passionate in his beliefs; in the words of Eamon Duffy, 'Wherever he went, among the poor, among his patients, among friends, he talked endlessly of the love of God insulted by Jesuit casuists, peddlars of cheap grace.'[171] Before his death, Short also corresponded with a canon of Utrecht named Van Erkel, who viewed the status of the secular clergy in England as similar to that of the clergy of Utrecht, whose authority was disputed by the regulars (especially the Jesuits). Short wrote a condemnation of *The Secret Policy of the Jansenists* by Etienne de Champs, denouncing it as a 'slandering libel' put about by the Jesuits,[172] and the Jansenist label seems to have been applied to other members of the family as well. In 1707 a Catholic convert, Richard Gomeldon, accused Richard's nephew Thomas Short of being a Jansenist.[173]

Richard Short did not live to see Quesnel officially condemned by the papal bull *Unigenitus* in 1713, and his translation of Quesnel remained unpublished on the orders of Bishop Bonaventure Gifford.[174] Had the book made it into print, then Short would probably be a much better known figure, since Quesnel was popular among English Protestants as well as Catholics. The later career of Richard Short raises the question of why, in 1688, he apparently abandoned the conviction he

---

[168]   E. Duffy, 'A Rub-up for Old Soares; Jesuits, Jansenists, and the English Secular Clergy, 1705–1715', *Journal of Ecclesiastical History* 28 (1977), p. 304.

[169]   Estcourt and Payne (eds), *The English Catholic Non-Jurors of 1715*, p. 265.

[170]   Clark, *Strangers and Sojourners at Port Royal*, p. 167.

[171]   Duffy, 'A Rub-up for Old Soares', p. 304. On the chaos caused by Short in London's Catholic community see idem, pp. 303–7.

[172]   Clark, *Strangers and Sojourners at Port Royal*, p. 170.

[173]   *The Old Brotherhood of the English Secular Clergy: Catalogue of Part of the Archives* (London: Catholic Record Society, 1968), p. 34.

[174]   Duffy, 'A Rub-up for Old Soares', p. 307.

had expressed in 1679 that English Catholics should not seek political office, and joined the Bury Corporation, an institution under the sway of a mayor who might be expected to favour the Jesuits.

Perhaps Short believed that he could influence the direction of Catholic revival from the inside. There is no direct evidence of theological conflict among Catholics in Bury during James II's reign, but there is one puzzling fact that may be related to the antipathy of some Catholics to the Jesuits. We know that an effort was made in 1685 to allow the Bury Grammar School, of which Thomas Short was an alumnus, to admit the sons of recusants.[175] Since the number of Catholic children in the town was still small, and the new Jesuit school in the Old Abbot's Palace was surely capable of educating them all, it seems odd that there was a parallel effort to allow the admission of recusants to the grammar school – unless there was a section of the Catholic community, led by the Shorts, that opposed the Jesuits and wanted to protect Catholic children from Jesuit influence. As late as 1761, when the Jesuit mission in Bury had already been re-established for six years, the Shorts were still maintaining their own Dominican chaplain (see Chapter 5).

It is possible that, if the Gages stood (as seems likely) on the pro-Jesuit side of the divide in English Catholicism, they did not want to be involved with the Shorts. On the other hand, the ties that bound the Shorts to other Suffolk Catholics may have been stronger than any abstruse theological disagreements. Richard Short's father treated Sir Edward Gage's sister Penelope during the Civil War, and the younger Richard Short and his brother Peregrine witnessed the will of Robert Rookwood in 1673.[176] If the Catholic community was divided by politics it was united by faith, and even politics proved to be a unifying force in the 1680s.

Revolution and retribution

The Gages' ties to the Jermyns were strong, and Sir Edward's younger brother Henry Gage borrowed a large sum of money (£1,400) from Dover's brother Thomas Jermyn, Earl of St Albans, in 1673.[177] However, they did not prove strong enough for the family to involve itself in local or national politics during the brief window of opportunity that James's reign presented to Catholics. That window closed abruptly in November 1688, as news of Prince William of Orange's landing spread to East Anglia. Already in October, Stafford and the other Catholics

175   Elliot, *The Story of King Edward the Sixth School Bury St. Edmunds*, p. 71.
176   CUL Hengrave MS 76/2/1.
177   CUL Hengrave MS 88/3/60.

on the Bury Corporation had been forced to step down, as James tried to reverse his constitutional changes in an effort to retain the nation's favour. However, by the end of November mobs throughout the country were burning, ransacking and demolishing Catholic chapels, including at Bury. One correspondent wrote:

> The news of peoples going over to the P[rince] of O[range] dayly encreases, so th[a]t wee deem there will not be much bloodshed. the people are everywhere in a strange ferment, & as much as can be shew their anger ag[ains]t the P[apist]s ... at Bury the Mass house in the Abby Yard was pull[e]d down and all the furniture carryed away plate and all. it was defended by one prittyman who kill[e]d 3 of the Company and is since fled[,] his Mothers house being the Corner Taverne in the Market place is likewise pulled down.[178]

'Prityman' was probably a son of Thomas Prettyman, a Bury tradesman who issued halfpenny trade tokens in 1667 and whose widow, Martha, was a cousin of Mayor John Stafford and still living in Bury in 1695 (see Chapter 3). It seems likely that the statement that Prettyman killed three men is an exaggeration, since there is no evidence of a manhunt or an inquest into the deaths of the three men. A fight in the Abbey yard may well have become inflated into a deadly struggle in the telling. However, there is corroboration of the attack on Prettyman's mother's house in a contemporary newssheet, which reported that the mob 'plundered a Lady's House, she escaping with great difficulty; as also the House of an Alderman and another eminent Person, with two others that were Roman Catholicks'.[179] The two Catholics may well have been the Shorts, but Richard had already left for the Continent at this point anyway.[180]

The semi-organised mob-violence of the winter of 1688 bears comparison with the Stour Valley riots of the 1640s, and in 1688, as then, the mob walked considerable distances in order to wreak havoc. Henry Jermyn, Lord Dover suffered the worst consequences of his political efforts when his house at Cheveley was ransacked and the chapel pulled down by a mob from Bury and Cambridge that gathered on Newmarket

---

178 Unknown correspondent to Edmund Bohun, 30 November 1688, CUL Add. MS 4403/27. The destruction of the chapel was also recorded by Narcissus Luttrell, *A Brief Historical Relation of State Affairs from September 1678 to April 1714* (Oxford: Oxford University Press, 1857), vol. 1, p. 483. I am grateful to Dr John Sutton for alerting me to the letter to Edmund Bohun, which shows that I was in error to argue that the chapel did not meet a violent end (Young, '"An Horrid Popish Plot": The Failure of Catholic Aspirations in Bury St. Edmunds, 1685–88, p. 217).

179 *The London Mercury or Orange Intelligence* (31 December 1688–3 January 1689).

180 Young, '"An Horrid Popish Plot": The Failure of Catholic Aspirations in Bury St. Edmunds, 1685–88, p. 221.

Heath on 12 December.[181] A second riot seems to have broken out in Bury in December, and another newssheet reported on 22 December that the rabble 'began to plunder the Houses of some Papists', but that Sir John Cordel had raised two troops of horse (120 men) in order 'to appease them'.[182] Sir Robert Davers of Rushbrooke took control of the situation in Bury and put looters in gaol. Stolen goods were restored, and the local gentry demonstrated, as they had in 1642, that they valued order and the security of property above Protestant triumphalism.

There is no evidence that the Gages suffered any kind of reprisals in November or December 1688, although Hengrave was in easy walking distance from Bury for an angry mob. Nor is there any evidence of steps that Sir Edward Gage may have put in place to ensure that his house was not targeted. However, there is likewise no surviving evidence of an attack on Coldham Hall, the home of the Rookwoods, who were certainly much more intimately involved with James's regime. Perhaps the Gages were just lucky, or perhaps the leaders of the mob, whoever they were, appreciated the Gages' political neutrality. Whatever the truth, in spite of the Gages' noninvolvement in politics, the evaporation of James's plans for toleration must have come as a disappointment to them, and 1688 marked the end of what had been, barring the unpleasantness of the Popish Plot, a period of prosperity and security for the family.

Conclusions

Sir Edward Gage benefitted from Charles II's desire to reconstitute the landed gentry of counties such as Suffolk and strengthen their ties to the Crown with the award of new titles. He was apparently the beneficiary of the King's attention on account of his famous cousin Sir Henry Gage, but this story cannot be confirmed. Sir Edward consolidated and made grand once more the estates he had inherited from his mother Penelope Darcy. After a series of brief marriages cut short by death, his alliance with Elizabeth Feilding, the daughter of the Protestant peer the Earl of Desmond, endured and produced the majority of his children.

Sir Edward's numerous offspring secured the continuance of his lineage but his interests were not only the domestic ones of a country squire. He insisted that his eldest son receive a Sorbonne education, and both he and his household were strongly influenced by French piety; French Jesuit authors predominated in Sir Edward's library and his heir married a wife with a French mother. Through his daughter-

---

[181] *The Universal Intelligence* 3 (15–18 December 1688).
[182] *The London Mercury or Moderate Intelligencer* 5 (24–27 December 1688).

in-law and his Jermyn relatives the Baronet was linked with the court of the Dowager Queen and he sent his daughter to the court of Queen Mary d'Este. He translated and published French devotional works and became increasingly preoccupied with religion as he grew older. Yet Sir Edward cannot be caricatured as an inward-looking provincial recusant; rather, he was tied to the Continent without ever, to our knowledge, having left England.

Nevertheless, when the opportunity to advance himself politically arrived, Sir Edward and the rest of his family apparently refused it. There is no evidence that he had any involvement in the events of 1687–88 when Henry Jermyn, Lord Dover attempted to gain control of the Bury Corporation; nor is there any evidence that he or his property suffered violence thereafter. Apart from his son Francis's brief encounter with magistrates in 1679, Sir Edward was relatively unscathed by the Popish Plot scare as well. However, he had handed over control and ownership of most of his lands to his son William as early as 1693 and seems to have been happy to surrender his responsibility.

Little evidence survives on the wider Catholic community in the Bury area for this period but there seems little reason to suppose, in line with Gordon Blackwood, that 'Catholics in urban Bury were as much under gentry domination as Catholics in rural Suffolk'[183] in the Restoration period. Indeed, the opposite would seem to have been the case. It was two urban families, the Shorts and the Staffords, who took up the cause of toleration for Catholics in the reign of James II, and the influence of the Gages on the local community may have been diminished by frequent absences in London. Nevertheless, the Gages remained throughout the period the wealthy and symbolic leaders of the Catholic community in the western half of the county.

---

[183]   Blackwood, *Tudor and Stuart Suffolk*, p. 231.

3

REVOLUTION AND RECOVERY, 1688–1727

In the aftermath of the 1688 Revolution English Catholics faced an onslaught of punitive legislation. It began with the double land tax (1692) and the Popery Act (1698). Under the latter Act, any adult who refused to take the Oath of Allegiance was disqualified from inheriting or purchasing land; it also provided that land bequeathed to such a person should pass to their Protestant next of kin. Anti-Catholic legislation was popular, and a simple yet blunt means of penalising Jacobite sympathisers, whilst also punishing loyalist Catholics. More laws followed the Jacobite rising of 1715. The Papists Act of that year appointed commissioners to enquire into Catholics' estates with a view to confiscating two-thirds of them, and the Papists' Estates Act of 1716 permitted two JPs to tender the Oaths of Allegiance and Supremacy, as well as an Oath of Abjuration of the Pretender, to any Catholic they chose, as well as obliging Catholic landowners to register their estates with all future conveyances and wills.[1]

Catholics throughout England reacted to this barrage of legislation in a variety of different ways, and Peter Marshall and Geoffrey Scott aptly sum up the historical caricature of Catholics after 1714, 'retreating as backwoodsmen or vainly battling against the tide by striving to preserve their hold over native Catholicism through sustaining or creating households of the faith comprising their own tenants'.[2] Aveling saw this period as nothing less than 'the death of Catholic aristocracy'.[3] It is certainly true that Catholics faced unprecedented challenges, yet for the Gages and other Bury Catholics this was not so much the beginning of a terminal decline as an opportunity to recover and regroup before the Benedictine mission revitalised the local community in the 1730s.

Exile was one option that some Catholics took up in response to severe penal laws, although it tended to confirm an individual's allegiance to the Jacobite cause and could easily lead to forfeiture of an

---

[1] Rowe, 'The 1767 Census of Papists in the Diocese of Norwich', pp. 188–89.
[2] Marshall and Scott, *Catholic Gentry in English Society*, p. 18.
[3] Aveling, *The Handle and the Axe*, p. 253.

estate.[4] Apostasy or conformity was another possibility; attendance at the services of the Established Church theoretically removed immediately all recusancy penalties and opened up the possibility of holding public office. However, the legal processes to obtain exemption from double land tax were protracted and complex, since the tax was fixed on the land, not the person who owned it. Furthermore, after 1750 competition for government office was intense, and conversion was no guarantee of preferment.[5] Nevertheless, this was the route taken by a group of Sussex gentry that included Sir William Gage, 7th Baronet of Firle, in 1715. Sir William began a parliamentary career in 1723 and his Protestant successor was a viscount.[6] Yet conformity remained the exception rather than the rule for long-standing recusant families; it created its own challenges, potentially excluding an individual from the social web of Catholic families, whilst offering no guarantee of acceptance in the Protestant community. In East Anglia the Catholic gentry largely stood firm.

Catholics who stayed in England had no prospect of political advancement, and consequently they had time on their hands to manage their estates shrewdly, set up advantageous marriage alliances and cultivate good relations with their Protestant neighbours. Many took great pride in the miniature 'fiefdoms' over which they presided,[7] which may well have been better managed than the neglected estates of busy Protestant office-holders. Some consciously strove to imitate the 'improvements' wrought to their homes and parks by Protestant neighbours,[8] although such aspirations would not affect Hengrave until the 1770s. Apart from religious commitment and heartfelt belief, the importance of what Joy Rowe calls 'a deeply rooted counter-culture of scepticism' among English Catholics should not be underestimated.[9] The long life of the Jacobite movement is evidence enough that some Catholics actively craved exclusion and nonconformity. Families such as the Gages of Hengrave and the Throckmortons of Coughton, who were politically loyalist by instinct, had become inured to repression by the early eighteenth century and were 'habituated to their circumstances'.[10]

---

[4]   One Suffolk example was Henry Timperley, who mortgaged Hintlesham Hall in 1720 and 'went abroad and died in some convent' (Ryan and Redstone, *Timperley of Hintlesham*, p. 86).

[5]   Aveling, *The Handle and the Axe*, p. 263.

[6]   Glickman, *The English Catholic Community 1688–1745*, p. 59.

[7]   Ibid. pp. 59–64.

[8]   Aveling, *The Handle and the Axe*, p. 271.

[9]   Rowe, '"The Lopped Tree": The Re-formation of the Suffolk Catholic Community', p. 191.

[10] G. Scott, 'The Throckmortons at Home and Abroad, 1680–1800', p. 171.

It should come as no surprise, therefore, that the Gages remained committed recusants in the early eighteenth century. The advantages of church papistry and occasional conformity had evaporated in a society where a family's historic confessional identity was public knowledge. However, the eighteenth century was also a time when confessional identity mattered less to some in the establishment than ever before, and consequently anti-Catholic legislation was unevenly enforced (if at all) in some areas. It certainly cannot be assumed that all Catholics suffered under all the laws all the time; the severity of their execution depended on individual sheriffs and magistrates, and perhaps to an even greater extent on the families that dominated local politics. In West Suffolk the Herveys of Ickworth and the Jermyns of Rushbrooke fulfilled this role, and both were on friendly terms with the Gages; in the case of the Jermyns, the web of family connections was overwhelming. Nevertheless, the Gages evidently did not escape all penalties, especially after the Jacobite rising of 1715; Sir William Gage unsuccessfully petitioned against the Papists Act 1716 and was forced to sell two manors and two advowsons shortly thereafter.

Also in 1716 Sir William's eldest son died, which might well have put the estate in further peril. However, the strength of character of Thomas Gage's widow, Delariviere D'Ewes, seems to have ensured that Sir William's grandson, Sir Thomas Gage, 3rd Baronet, was well advised and the estate well managed. Sir William's second marriage to Merelina Jermyn (1673–1727), the widow of Sir Thomas Spring, brought him into alliance with two important Protestant families, and the attraction of Merelina's beautiful and marriageable daughters brought the Gages into the centre of Bury's polite society.[11] At the same time, Catholic life in Bury was revitalised by the migration of a branch of the Lancashire Tyldesley family to Fornham St Genevieve, a village close to Hengrave. By the time of Sir William's death in 1727 local Catholics had recovered, both numerically and socially, from the low point of the Revolution. Evidence in the Hengrave manuscripts for the last years of the seventeenth century is slim; either the practice of keeping household letters begun by Margaret Donnington finally lapsed or they have been lost. No personal correspondence of members of the Gage family exists from the period, but a number of other sources are available that allow the family's financial and social circumstances to be glimpsed in this crucial period of transition and survival.

---

[11] Farrer, *Portraits in Suffolk Houses (West)*, p. 196 recorded and illustrated a portrait of Merelina then at Hunston Hall. There was also one at Hengrave purchased by Sir John Wood in 1904, ibid. p. 175.

The end of the first Jesuit mission

By the end of 1688 the Suffolk gentry, both Catholic and Protestant, were chastened by new evidence of the terrifying power of the mob and the consequences of anti-Catholic hysteria. The Bury Corporation had reverted to the Charter of 1668 after the problems caused by the 1684 Charter, and the Jesuits had been forced to abandon their college in the old Abbot's Palace, even though they continued their ministry in the locality under the patronage of the Burton family of Beyton. Apart from the chapel, which was pulled down in 1688, the Abbot's Palace was left intact and the Jesuits made attempts to recover their property, even after it became impossible and unwise for them to keep open their public school. In 1689 the annual accounts of the College of the Holy Apostles recorded that £1 1s 6d was spent 'Securing goods at Bury'. The Jesuits never seem to have given up the hope of salvaging something, and as late as 1728 Charles Shireburne, the Superior of the English Jesuits, was in Bury 'to inquire about books and other effects, left there ever since the demolition of that school'.[12]

Surviving seventeenth-century chalices associated with the College of the Holy Apostles may be evidence of the Jesuits' success in recovering their property,[13] along with the composition of the Rookwood family's library at Coldham Hall. According to a 1737 inventory made by Elizabeth Rookwood,[14] Coldham's library contained 476 books of particular relevance to the Catholic community, 259 of which (54 per cent) were printed before 1688. Only eighty-six books were published after 1700, suggesting that the Coldham Library was a largely static collection. Although these books may always have been at Coldham, it is also possible that the Rookwoods' extraordinary library, which contained 1,889 books in total, was at least partly the surviving library of the College of the Holy Apostles.

We know from the autobiography of the Carmelite nun Catharine Burton, who described life in her father's household at Beyton immediately after the Revolution, that the Jesuits of the College of the Holy Apostles spent a lot of time at the Burtons' home after the abandonment of the Abbot's Palace. Catharine was ill throughout much of her youth, and she recalled that 'Mass was said every day in my room when

---

[12] Foley, vol. 5, p. 538.

[13] These include a chalice from the Martin D'Arcy Collection in Loyola University Museum of Art in Chicago with a gilded cup of traditional pre-Reformation 'rose chalice' design donated to the College by Elizabeth Rookwood in 1684, as well as chalices at Georgetown University and Stonyhurst donated by William, 4th Lord Petre.

[14] CUL Hengrave MS 77/2, fols 28–56.

the priest was at home',[15] suggesting that at least one priest lived at Beyton. That priest may have been Francis Rockley (alias Ireland), who was Catharine's confessor from 1688–91.[16] In 1690 Catharine's father, Thomas Burton, invited Lewis Sabran to visit his sick daughter, and in 1691 she was visited by William Collins,[17] who was to be the decisive spiritual influence on her choice to become a nun; evidently Jesuits were still moving freely in West Suffolk.

Catharine's miraculous cure in May 1691 attracted the attention of Catholics and Protestants alike. Apart from the theological opposition of the Rector of Beyton, Richard Nesling, the Protestant response was sympathetic: 'The longer I stayed the more came to visit me, and though the parson of the place had declared from the pulpit, not long before, that miracles were ceased, yet the Protestants themselves looked on my cure as miraculous.'[18] Catharine left England to enter the Carmelite convent at Antwerp in November 1691; her father died on 8 January 1695, and in the same year Nathaniel Stafford (brother of the deposed Mayor), who had been Vice-Rector of the College of the Holy Apostles, returned to St Omer.[19] Burton's death may have been the catalyst for the final abandonment of the Bury area as the base of operations for the College.

From the mid-1690s the geographical focus of the College of the Holy Apostles seems to have shifted south to the patronage of the Daniels of Acton and the Mannocks of Gifford's Hall. However, the Gages remained involved in the College through Sir William's younger brother John Gage the Elder, who became an increasingly influential figure and in old age rose to become Superior of the College. John Gage was born in 1651 and it is likely that he was the second son of Sir Edward Gage and Mary Hervey. The suggestions of Sir Thomas Gage, 7th Baronet that he was either the youngest son of Sir Edward Gage and Elizabeth Feilding or a son of George Gage of Raunds and Frances Tresham are impossible and unlikely respectively.[20] John Gage was much too old to be a son of Elizabeth Feilding. The George Gage of Raunds was a Protestant (even if his wife was not), and John Gage was elsewhere described as originating in Suffolk. John Gage trained at St Omer until his profession as a Jesuit on 7 September 1670. John spent the next eight years studying philosophy and theology at Liege and was

---

[15] T. Hunter, *An English Carmelite: The Life of Catharine Burton, Mary Xaveria of the Angels, of the English Teresian Convent at Antwerp* (London, 1876), p. 61

[16] Ibid. pp. 89–90. Rockley was in Bury as early as 1687, see Foley, vol. 1, p. 662.

[17] Hunter, *An English* Carmelite, pp. 65–66.

[18] Ibid. 83–84.

[19] Beyton Parish Registers SRO(B) FL 528/4/1; Foley, vol. 1, p. 729.

[20] CUL Hengrave MS 1/4, fol. 317.

ordained a priest on 1 April 1679.[21] He was sent to serve the gathering of English exiles forced to flee the country by the Popish Plot scare, first at Ghent in 1679 and then at Bruges in 1680; the exiles to whom he ministered may have included his brother.[22] The following year, in 1681, John Gage the Elder was sent to the Jesuit College of St Thomas of Canterbury (covering Kent and south-east England). He took the alias of Lewis, although it is unclear why he chose this surname; priests' aliases were often drawn from the names of their relatives.

John Gage the Elder served in the College of the Holy Apostles from 1683–87, which included the period when the College acquired a permanent home in the old Abbot's Palace. Thereafter, Gage's periods of ministry in the College were sporadic, presumably interrupted by visits abroad. He was back in Suffolk in 1689, then again from 1691–93, 1696–1701 and finally from 1703 until his death in 1729. From 1725–27 he served as Rector of the College, dying at Great Waldingfield on 12 January 1729.[23] However, John Gage was buried at Hengrave five days later, which is a strong indication of his close relationship to Sir Edward.[24] In a list of 'Addresses of the Stations in England served by the Jesuit fathers, 1727–1734', 'Mr Lewis' was to be found 'at Mrs Daniel's in Shaddow Street, Great Warningfield near Sudbury, Suffolk'.[25] On his death, John Gage's body was brought back to Hengrave to rest with his ancestors; he was buried in the church on 17 January 1729.[26]

The Jesuits did not entirely abandon the Bury area, and there was a Jesuit mission at Coldham Hall served by Henry Rookwood up to his death in 1730, at the age of seventy-one.[27] However, Rookwood would have lived at Coldham alongside the Benedictine Francis Howard, who arrived there in 1717.[28] In the 1730s, whether through Jesuit inactivity or a preference for the Benedictines among the Catholic gentry, the monks supplanted the Society of Jesus as the dominant missionary influence in West Suffolk. As Glickman has shown, the Catholic mission could be riven with internal politics; in 1725 the Mannocks were campaigning for the rights of chaplains and patrons against the claims of the vicars

---

[21] G. Holt, *St. Omers and Bruges Colleges, 1593–1773: A Biographical Dictionary* (London: CRS, 1979), p. 109.

[22] *CSPD*, 1678, p. 618.

[23] Foley, vol. 5, p. 514; G. Holt (ed.), *The English Jesuits 1650–1829: A Biographical Dictionary* (London: CRS, 1984), p. 97.

[24] CUL Hengrave MS 1/4, fol. 317.

[25] *Miscellanea VIII* (London: CRS, 1913), p. 176.

[26] Gage, *Hengrave*, p. 77.

[27] *Miscellanea VIII* (1913), p. 175. Henry Rookwood was the uncle of Elizabeth Rookwood, the wife of John Rookwood Gage.

[28] Birt, *Obit Book of the English Benedictines, 1600–1912*, p. 101.

apostolic.[29] In many cases, the conflict between patrons and the vicars apostolic was personal and financial, but it could also have an ideological dimension. The Mannocks were Jacobite in sympathy, while Vicar Apostolic John Talbot Stonor was not; and where Jacobites were often the champions of the power of lay patrons, the vicars apostolic could be seen as agents of a papacy from which Jacobites were increasingly alienated.[30] While the evidence points to the Gages' apolitical or even loyalist sympathies, they cannot have been immune to the politicisation of missionary activity, especially when Hengrave did not have a mission of its own and Sir William Gage exercised no direct clerical patronage. In 1720, when Bishop Stonor conducted the confirmation ceremony for Sir William's grandsons, it took place somewhere in Bury rather than at Hengrave.[31]

Bury's Catholics in 1695

On 1 June 1695 Samuel Oxborough, Dalton Simonds, Henry Willis and Robert Haward began to take down the names of all inhabitants of the parish of St James, Bury St Edmunds for the purposes of assessing them for a new tax on marriages, births and burials in order to help fund the ongoing war with France.[32] Only the assessment for St James survives but it amounts to a full census of the parish, albeit the ages and professions of the individuals listed were not recorded. Of the 138 surnames of Bury Catholics that occur in the five eighteenth-century sources available, forty-one of the names also occur in the 1695 assessement, although this is hardly surprising, as many of them are relatively common surnames. It is impossible to assume without evidence that any of these families were Catholic in 1695, quite apart from the fact that in many cases a surname was represented by several families and several social ranks.[33] A good example of this is the Craske family. The assessors were evidently instructed during or after their work to list as a 'gentleman' anyone who had an income of more than £50 a year, since a number of individuals were initially recorded as 'gent.'; this

---

[29] Glickman, *The English Catholic Community 1688–1745*, p. 216.

[30] Ibid. pp. 169–71.

[31] Benedictine mission register for Hengrave and Bury St Edmunds kept by Dom Francis Howard, 1734–51 (Downside Abbey MSS) (hereafter *Hengrave Register*).

[32] SRO(B) 508/1.

[33] The surnames in 1695 that later occur as those of Catholic families are: Adams, Allen, Annis, Baker, Balls, Bennet, Betts, Bond, Burton, Christmas, Clarke, Cocksedge, Cooper, Craske, Crispe, Curtis, Frost, Gallant, Gibbon, Godfrey, Goodrich, Green, Hunt, King, Kenyon, Lambe, Mann, Moore, Mount, Murrell, Page, Parker, Perry, Prettyman, Rutter, Short, Simpson, Sparke, Steward, Thorpe, Tillott, Vincent.

Fig. 5. The Gage family's townhouse in Bury St Edmunds, now the Farmers' Club at numbers 9, 10 and 11 Northgate Street (photograph by the author)

was then crossed out and '50 l. p[er]. an[num].' written instead. This was the fate of William Craske, living with his wife Elizabeth and two servants on the north side of Eastgate Street; Henry Craske next door, living with just one servant, evidently had an even smaller income. John Craske, who was living with his wife Susan and their four daughters in the Buttermarket, did manage to qualify as a gentleman, while an Ann Craske was a servant in the household of Thomas Macro on the east side of the Great Market (in today's Cupola House).

For a small number of those whose names occur in the 1695 assessment we have independent evidence that they were Catholics, and in this case the document illuminates their domestic circumstances at this time as well as where they were living. In the thirty-second house recorded in Risbygate Street were living Richard Short, gentleman, with his wife Mary and children Henry, Charlotte and Maximilian and two servants. This was probably the same house in the 'High Ward' of Risbygate Street that was recorded as having seven hearths and belonging to Peregrine 'Perry' Short and 'Doctor Short jun.' in 1674.[34] I have previously identified 'Doctor Short jun.' as the younger Dr Richard Short (b.1641) who

---

[34] Hervey (ed.), *Suffolk in 1674*, p. 54.

served on the Bury Corporation before the 1688 Revolution.[35] However, he was certainly out of the country in 1695, so the Richard Short who occupied the house on Risbygate Street in 1695 was probably his son.

In the eighth house listed in Cotton Lane we find William Bond, his wife Mary Gage and their children Mary, Charlotte and William, together with four servants.[36] William Bond's household is listed as the third house before the Grammar School, which was not in Cotton Lane but on Northgate Street, raising the possibility that William Bond was in fact living in the Gage family townhouse (now numbers 9, 10 and 11 Northgate Street). This would explain why the Gages do not feature in the assessment in spite of their townhouse being within the parish of St James. It may be, therefore, that Sir Edward permitted his eldest daughter to live with her family in the townhouse. It certainly never formed part of her marriage settlement, however, as it was not inherited by her children but passed back into the Gage family's ownership, probably on her death in 1719 or beforehand.

Not far away, on the north side of Eastgate Street, Thomas Bond was living with his wife Henrietta Maria Jermyn and their children Henrietta, Thomas, 'Sharly' (Charlie?), Henry and Hannah, as well as four servants. Two children, Mary Charlotte and Judith, had yet to be born at this point. Since Thomas Bond's eldest son Thomas died in infancy, this house on Eastgate Street was inherited by his second son Henry, and its chapel was one of the centres of Catholic life in Bury from at least the 1730s until the completion of John Gage the Younger's chapel in 1762. Unfortunately, road-widening in the 1920s led to the demolition of the entire north side of Eastgate Street up to the Fox public house, so no trace of the Bonds' home or their chapel remains.

Six doors up from Thomas Macro on the east side of the Great Market, Ann Prittyman, widow, was living with Martha Prittyman and three servants. This was probably the same Martha Prettyman who was recorded as holding property at Fornham St Genevieve in 1715; she was a cousin of the former mayor, John Stafford, and his Jesuit brother Nathaniel, and may have been the widow of the 'Prityman' who valiantly defended the Mass House in 1688. Stafford himself was no longer to be found in the Cook Row, where his mercer's shop had once been located, although he was still very much alive in 1695. The partial nature of the evidence, being as it is only an assessment for the parish of St James, makes it impossible to trace what all of Bury's known Catholics were doing in 1695.

---

35 Young, 'The Shorts of Bury St Edmunds', p. 190.
36 William and Mary Bond's eldest son, Henry, was buried at Hengrave on 15 October 1689 (Gage, *Hengrave*, p. 77).

Sir William Gage and his children

Sir Edward Gage's fourth wife, Elizabeth Feilding, died in 1689 and he married for the fifth and last time, to Bridget Feilding, the widow of a certain Mr Slaughter, who may have been Elizabeth's sister.[37] Mr Slaughter was a noted benefactor to St Bonaventure's, the English Franciscan house at Douai.[38] However, Sir Edward withdrew from the management and even the ownership of the Gage family estates in 1706. By an indenture of 24 October that year, Sir Edward vouched to his son and to his grandson Thomas Gage, who had just come of age, the entirety of the estates.[39] Nevertheless, Sir Edward Gage was impressively long-lived, and Sir William would have been over fifty-five years old when he inherited the baronetcy in January 1707. In his will of 28 June 1706, written at his house in Bloomsbury Square, Sir Edward bequeathed £600 each to his sons John and James, £20 to Henry, £80 to George, and appointed his youngest daughter, Basilia, as his executrix and residuary legatee.[40] By 1706 Sir Edward's estates were already under William's control, and consequently his only bequests were in ready money. In contrast to the impression Sir Edward gave of his son as 'nice and shiftlesse' in the 1660s, and as a financially demanding burden in the 1670s, Sir William seems to have dealt astutely with the financial challenges brought about by the new government's punitive measures against Catholics. His strategies included mortgaging parts of the estate, selling off a legacy, and aligning himself with loyalist Catholics to petition Parliament for an easing of the penal laws.

A nineteenth-century guide to Hengrave Hall and its contents listed three paintings of Sir William, the first (on the stairs) depicting him 'as a boy'. Another portrait in the dining room, which was reproduced by J. Linnell for Sir Thomas Gage and photographed by Edmund Farrer for his *Portraits in Suffolk Houses*, was painted by A. R. de Charas in 1688 and depicted the future baronet in armour,[41] a rather surprising pose given that Sir William never served in any military capacity. The portrait

---

[37] Gage, *Thingoe*, p. 209. 'The Hon. Lady Bridget Gage' was buried at Flempton on 11 August 1702, SRO(B) FL571/2. The Earl of Desmond's third daughter, Bridget, married Sir Lawrence Parsons, an Irish landowner ('Illustrative Memoir of the Right Honourable Lady Emily Feilding', *La Belle Assemblée* 2:11 (1825), p. 188).

[38] T. Hermans, *The Franciscans in England 1600–1850* (London, 1898), pp. 92–93.

[39] CUL Hengrave MS 1/4, fol. 335.

[40] CUL Hengrave MS 1/3, fol. 318.

[41] Farrer, *Portraits in Suffolk Houses (West)*, p. 175. Another portrait of Sir William was to be found at Coldham Hall in 1908, which presumably originally hung at Hengrave, ibid. pp. 323–24. For an earlier list of the portraits at Hengrave see CUL Hengrave MS 1/1, fols 90–93.

may have been intended to assimilate him to the military prowess of his famous relative, the Civil War hero Colonel Henry Gage. Alternatively, it may allude to Sir William's life on the Continent, first in Paris at the court of Henrietta Maria and again at the time of the Popish Plot scare (the portrait may even have been painted in France). A third portrait (on the stairs) seems to have been an amateur attempt by Sir William's half-brother Henry; it depicted Sir William at the age of fifty-three and bore the legend 'Hen. Gage fecit 1708'.[42]

By his first wife, Mary Charlotte Bond, Sir William had three sons and seven daughters. Sir William's eldest son Thomas (1684–1716) continued the Gage tradition of marriage alliances with the Jermyns when he married Delariviere D'Ewes, daughter of Sir Simonds D'Ewes, 3rd Baronet of Stowlangtoft and Delariviere, a daughter of Thomas Jermyn, 1st Baron St Edmundsbury. The D'Ewes family, who had migrated from Guelderland in the reign of Henry VIII, originally made their fortune in printing, and Delariviere's grandfather, Sir Simonds D'Ewes, 1st Baronet, was a Presbyterian and a Parliamentarian during the Civil War, as well as a celebrated antiquary and collector of books.[43] Thomas and Delariviere's first son, later Sir Thomas Gage, 3rd Baronet, was born on 25 September 1712.[44]

Evidence suggests that Sir William's relationship with his eldest son was clouded with financial disputes. In 1712 Sir William drew up proposals for a marriage settlement for Thomas and Delariviere, according to which he agreed 'to convey 400l per ann. to trustees to the use of Mr Gage for life with power to make a jointure of 250l … the 400l to be settled upon the issue male of that Marriage [i.e. with Delariviere D'Ewes]'. However, either Thomas or his lawyers turned down the proposal, insisting that Thomas receive income from rents to the value of £500 rather than £400 from Michaelmas 1712. Sir William's attorney advised him that he might actually be better off in the long run if he accepted his son's proposal, especially if Thomas predeceased him.[45] On 2 May 1715 Sir William drew up his will, which left his entire estate not to Thomas, but to his second wife Merelina Spring.[46] A 'family settlement' was drawn up on 16 and 17 August 1715 investing the Gage estates in trustees and apportioning the revenues of those

---

42 'Catalogue of Books, Manuscripts and Pictures at Hengrave Hall' (1872), CUL Hengrave MS 52. Sir William's age is evidently an error as he could not have been fifty-three in 1708 if his mother died in 1654.

43 See J. M. Blatchly, 'D'Ewes, Sir Simonds' in *ODNB*, vol. 16, pp. 1–4.

44 CUL Hengrave MS 1/4, fol. 341.

45 Thomas Hollens to Sir William Gage, 12 November 1713, CUL Hengrave MS 76/2/28.

46 PROB 11/615. In the event, Merelina's death shortly after her husband meant that her powers as executrix passed to her eldest son, Sir William Spring.

estates between Sir William's sons.[47] The dispute between father and
son may or may not have been resolved. With Thomas's early death on
1 March 1716 the issue became a dead letter.[48]

Sir William's second son, William, died in infancy; his third son,
John (1688–1728) enjoyed a Parisian education of some sort, which
gained him the distinction of being chosen as a Page of Honour to Louis
XIV, a story repeated by Sir Thomas Gage, 7th Baronet on the authority
of 'Mrs Maxwell of Munches'.[49] Although the circumstances of this
connection with the French court are unknown, Sir William's own visits
to the court of Queen Henrietta Maria may have opened the way to
his son's position at Louis's court. On 7 January 1718 a clandestine
marriage, celebrated by the missionary priest in Bury, Hugh Owen, took
place between John Gage and Elizabeth Rookwood. It was witnessed
by John's sister Henrietta Gage (d.1757) and a Catholic labourer, Nicholas Horsman.[50] Sir Thomas Gage, 7th Baronet described John as 'an
intimate Friend of Mr Rookwood's, and often on hunting parties at
Coldham', and the marriage was an obvious dynastic choice. However,
Thomas Rookwood had been determined that his daughter should marry
a baronet, and he was not best pleased when her pregnancy forced her
to reveal the secret marriage. Elizabeth was a woman of 'strong principles, a superior Understanding, and a highly cultivated Mind'.[51] She
had lived much of her life on the Continent, owing to her father's exile
at Bruges. It is likely that she left England with him when she was five
years old (in 1688), and she did not return until she was twenty-one.
Both John and Elizabeth belonged to the English Catholic expatriate
community as much as the Suffolk gentry.

The Rookwoods were a controversial family of committed recusants. Elizabeth was the great-great-granddaughter of the Gunpowder
Plotter Ambrose Rookwood (1578–1606). Her uncle, another Ambrose
(1664–96), joined the court of James II at Saint-Germain-en-Laye as
a member of the King's bodyguard. As a brigadier, Ambrose returned
to England in 1696 in order to participate in Sir George Barclay's
conspiracy to assassinate William of Orange. Ambrose Rookwood was

---

[47] CUL Hengrave MS 1/4, fol. 313.
[48] Estcourt and Payne (eds), *The English Catholic Non-Jurors of 1715*, p. 255. For
      Thomas Gage's memorial inscription in Hengrave church see Gage, *Thingoe*, p. 236.
[49] CUL Hengrave MS 1/4, fol. 348.
[50] Sir Thomas Gage, 7th Baronet pasted the original certificate of marriage into the
      Rookwood family genealogy (CUL Hengrave MS 76/1). A 'James Horsman, labourer'
      was recorded as a popish nonjuror in 1745 (SRO(B) D8/1/3 bundle 2) and numerous
      members of the Horsman family appear in the Benedictine mission register of 1734–
      51, the Jesuit mission register (from 1756) and the Returns of Papists of 1767.
[51] CUL Hengrave MS 1/4, fol. 348.

tried and convicted of high treason and executed at Tyburn on 29 April 1696, the second of his family to die a traitor's death in a century.[52] In 1704 Thomas Rookwood finally returned to England, violating the Act of Banishment against him, but he does not seem to have suffered any legal consequences from this act.[53]

The extent of tolerance for local Catholics is demonstrated by the petition submitted to Queen Anne by Thomas Rookwood's Protestant friends and neighbours against his exile on 20 January 1703. The petitioners testifying to Rookwood's good character and loyalty were Thomas Hanmer, Simonds D'Ewes of Stowlangtoft, Robert Davers of Rushbrooke, John Poley of Boxted, Thomas Robinson, Bartholomew Young, James Harvey, John Risby, William Rowett and Thomas Macro. The presence of Thomas Hanmer and Sir Simonds D'Ewes in this list is suggestive of the Gages' influence: D'Ewes's daughters Delariviere, Mary, Merelina and Henrietta were all married to Catholic gentlemen, and Thomas Hanmer was the Gages' distant cousin, with no other local connections.

The petitioners insisted that Thomas Rookwood's continued exile would: 'Fatally and inevitably involve him in great Debts, inextricable Law Suits, intirely ruine his Estate, and finally disable him from paying his just Debts, and consequently redound to many of yo[u]r good Subjects irrecoverable Loss and Detriment'.[54] It was typical of the Suffolk gentry to join ranks to protect their own, whatever their religion. Robert Davers of Rushbrooke, a signatory of the 1702 petition, had opposed the Catholics in their attempt to seize control of the Bury Corporation in 1688, but when the mob attacked the houses of the gentry he led the restoration of law and order in the town and ensured that all stolen property was returned. Likewise, John Risby had been removed as a JP under James II (presumably for adherence to High Tory principles) but evidently bore no ill will to Catholics.[55] The welfare of the Rookwood estates in the interconnected web of land ownership outweighed such abstract issues as Thomas Rookwood's religion and his presence in this or that foreign country.

Either the Rookwoods' politically explosive history or their frequent periods on the Continent ensured that the marriage of John Gage and Elizabeth Rookwood was the only alliance between the two wealthiest Catholic families in the Bury area. Like the Gages, the Rookwoods maintained a townhouse in Bury; they also supported a chaplain from

---

52 J. Bernardi, *A Short History of the Life of Major John Bernardi* (London, 1729), pp. 86–92; K. Hopkins, 'Rookwood, Ambrose' in *ODNB* vol. 47, pp. 700–1.

53 *CSPD* May 1704–October 1705, p. 117.

54 CUL Hengrave MS 76/2/21.

55 Blackwood, *Tudor and Stuart Suffolk*, p. 241.

at least 1691.[56] John and Elizabeth's marriage turned out to be most significant for both families, since on the extinction of the senior line of Hengrave Gages in 1767, John Gage's son Thomas Rookwood Gage inherited the baronetcy. However, there were also financial benefits to the marriage, since Elizabeth Rookwood was not only Thomas Rookwood's sole heiress but also the heiress of her mother, Tamworth Martin, the only daughter of Sir Roger Martin of Long Melford.

The certificate of John Gage and Elizabeth Rookwood's Catholic marriage on 7 January 1718 is the earliest written record we have of the mission at Bury and comes from an era before the keeping of registers was considered necessary. It is likely that certificates such as this one were retained by individual families, although whether similar documents were produced in order to prove Catholic baptism is unknown. A record that a canonical marriage had taken place according to the rites of the Church could be important in the event of annulment; it was especially important in this case, as the marriage was clandestine. The fact that a simple labourer, Nicholas Horsman, could be called upon to witness the marriage of the third son of Sir William Gage is an indication of the extent to which penal-era Catholicism crossed social boundaries.

Sir William's daughter Julia is mentioned only in the text of an Act of Parliament of 1700 (see below) and she may have died before attaining her majority. Charlotte married the Protestant Fitznun Lambe of Troston and Lackford,[57] and her eldest son John Lambe of Frimley married Ann Pooley, daughter of John Pooley of Badley.[58] Ann Pooley would later get involved in a legal dispute with the Gages. Two of Sir William's daughters married doctors. His sixth daughter Mary Laelia (d.1770) married the Catholic Dr Henry Huddlestone of Durham, the younger brother of Francis Huddlestone of Sawston in Cambridgeshire,[59] while Catherine (d.1733) married Dr Henry Sorrel of Bury St Edmunds (probably a Protestant) at Nowton on 1 December 1730.[60] Three of Sir William's daughters died unmarried, with only one of them becoming a nun; since this often required a dowry, it may be that Sir William's resources did not extend to Henrietta (d.1757) and Anne (d.1760). Sir William made

---

[56] The Jesuit Henry Rookwood was at Coldham from this date (Holt (ed.), *The English Jesuits 1650–1829*), pp. 214–15).

[57] Charlotte was living as a widow in Bury in 1745, SRO(B) D8/1/3 bundle 2.

[58] CUL Hengrave MS 1/4, fol. 325.

[59] Gage, *Thingoe*, pp. 205, 209. Mary was living in Bury as a widow with her daughter Laelia in 1745, SRO(B) D8/1/3 bundle 2.

[60] Gage, *Thingoe*, p. 205. For the memorial inscription to Catherine Sorrel in St Mary's Church see Tymms, *An Architectural and Historical Account of the Church of St. Mary, Bury St. Edmunds*, p. 201.

Charles, Lord Talbot (son of the Earl of Shrewsbury), the trustee of the portions he assigned to his children in his will.[61]

Sir William's daughter Penelope (1687–1772) entered the convent of the English Augustinian Canonesses at Bruges, taking the name of Sister Stanislaus. She was professed in 1712 and served as subprioress for twenty years before her death.[62] When she died, on 27 October 1772, the community's annals recorded that: 'She seemed never to have lost her first fervour, was remarkably humble and meek, and in the latter years of her life gave herself much to prayer and solitude … her virtue made us much regret the loss of so great an example of religious perfection.'[63] Penelope was not the only member of the family to join the Augustinian Canonesses; John Gage the antiquary noted that Catherine Gage, 'Daughter to a younger Brother of Sir William Gage', was professed as Sister Mary Xaveria in 1740 and died in 1763, 'much lamented for her amiable qualitys'.[64] The Gages' family link with a continental convent, through Penelope Stanislaus Gage, would later prove momentous, since it contributed to the willingness of Sir Thomas Rookwood Gage, 6th Baronet to lend Hengrave to the English canonesses of Bruges when they were fleeing the French revolutionary army in 1794. The then prioress, Mother Mary More, described Hengrave as 'the nursery of our dear Sister Stanislaus Gage'.[65]

On the death of Sir William's first wife Mary Charlotte Bond in April 1707,[66] he stayed with family tradition by marrying a Jermyn. Merelina Jermyn (d.1727) was the sister of Delariviere Jermyn who married Sir Simonds D'Ewes and became the mother-in-law of Sir William's son, Thomas. In the absence of a brother, Delariviere and Merelina were Lord Jermyn's co-heiresses and, on his death in 1708, the co-heiresses of Henry Jermyn, Lord Dover as well.[67] Merelina's first husband, Sir Thomas Spring of Pakenham, whom she married in 1691, died in 1704 leaving her with three sons and six daughters, who came to live at Hengrave with the Gages after her marriage to Sir William. Her eldest daughter Merelina (1695–1761) married Thomas Discipline of Bury St

[61] CUL Hengrave MS 1/4, fol. 327.

[62] Memorandum in the hand of John Gage the antiquary, CUL Hengrave MS 21/1/199.

[63] C. S. Durrant, *A Link Between Flemish Mystics and English Martyrs* (London: Burns and Oates, 1925), p. 374.

[64] Memorandum in the hand of John Gage the antiquary, CUL Hengrave MS 21/1/199. Mary Xaveria was the same name taken by the Carmelite Catharine Burton who was such an influence on Sir William's niece Mary Charlotte Bond.

[65] Durrant, *A Link Between Flemish Mystics and English Martyrs*, p. 374.

[66] Mary Charlotte Bond was buried at Hengrave on 18 April 1707 (CUL Hengrave MS 1/4, fol. 327; Gage, *Hengrave*, p. 77).

[67] Gage, *Thingoe*, p. 210.

Edmunds (d.1704),[68] while her daughter Mary (1698–1763) became the toast of the locality for her beauty and accomplishments.

It is hard to determine the financial impact of the double alliance the Gages made with the Jermyn sisters, since much of Delariviere's wealth passed to the D'Ewes family and much of Merelina's passed to her daughters by Sir Thomas Spring. Sir Thomas Gage, 7th Baronet observed that 'his Family and her Family were nearly equal, and a separate Establishment was kept up for each'.[69] This is hardly suggestive of a great deal of affection between Sir William and Merelina. However, the social credit of being allied by marriage to the families of Jermyn, Spring and D'Ewes may have outweighed the promise of material gain. Merelina Jermyn was Sir William's first cousin (her mother Mary Merry was the daughter of his aunt, Penelope Gage). In addition, her first husband Sir Thomas Spring was a distant cousin of the Gages through his connections to the Kytsons of Hengrave. Merelina was part of the Gages' social circle well before her marriage to Sir William. A letter written to John Hervey by his wife on 25 October 1697 portrayed a social life consisting of late-night whist parties and early morning hunts:

> The four [Jermyn] sisters have been here this afternoon and, (as they never come unattended), brought with them Mr. Ga—,[70] Mr. Down—, and Mr. Bo—.[71] Part of them staid and playd whish til this moment, which is past eleven a'clock, tho' they are to hunt tomorrow morning.[72]

During the 1720s Mary Spring, Merelina Jermyn's second daughter by Sir Thomas Spring, attracted the romantic attention of Major Richardson Pack, a Suffolk man who initially went up to St John's College, Oxford and then trained at the Middle Temple before deciding that he preferred the army to the law. He served in the War of the Spanish Succession, and was commanding a company of foot in March 1705. In 1707 he fathered an illegitimate daughter, then returned to farm near Ipswich. In 1714 he was called up to serve in the army again, this time to suppress the Jacobite rising. He was in Scotland for three years, during which time he married Mary Campbell, although they were estranged not long afterwards.[73] In 1720 the newly demobilised Major Pack bought the old Abbot's Palace that the Jesuits had vacated in 1688, although he soon passed it on to Sir Jermyn Davers, who had pulled it down (presumably to sell the materials) by 1728, destroying one of the few Abbey build-

---

[68] *St James Burials*, p. 205.

[69] CUL Hengrave MS 1/4, fol. 335.

[70] William Gage.

[71] Thomas Bond the husband of Henrietta Jermyn.

[72] Hervey (ed.), *Rushbrook Parish Registers with Jermyn and Davers Annals*, p. 309.

[73] J. M. Blatchly, 'Pack, Richardson' in *ODNB*, vol. 42, pp. 305–6.

ings that survived the Dissolution and obliterating all remaining traces of the Jesuit College.[74]

In 1724 Pack bought Northgate House in Northgate Street (later the home of Norah Lofts), just a few doors down from the Gages' townhouse in the same street, and it was at this time that he became a frequent visitor to Hengrave. In 1725 he published a collection of poems containing his 'Bury Toasts', verses addressed to Merelina Jermyn's daughters Mary ('Molly') and Delariviere ('Dilly') and even Merelina herself – perhaps surprising given his sometimes lurid lines on her daughter (Appendix 3).[75] A number of these poems were set in 'the Hide Wood', which Pack described as 'A Celebrated Wood near Hengrove-Hall [sic] in Suffolk, the Seat of Sir William Gage'.[76] The Hyde Wood still exists, close to the boundary between the parishes of Hengrave and Risby. Pack either recalled or imagined a series of amorous encounters and dialogues with Mary Spring or 'Caelia'. In one of them, 'Writ on a Seat in the Glade of the Hide', Pack seems to play deliberately on the Catholicism of the Gages (which Mary Spring may have shared) with his use of the vocabulary of Catholic theology ('Pray for the soul', 'state of grace' and 'Purgatory'):

> Pray for the Soul of One in Love,
> That often Haunts this Gloomy Grove.
> The Wretch was in a State of Grace,
> Whilst He cou'd View Bright Caelia's Charms;
> For Paradise is in her Face,
> And Heaven, I trust, is in her Arms.
> But from That Goddess far Remov'd,
> He hovers between Hope and Fear;
> And Death-like Absence having Prov'd
> Now Mourns in Purgatory Here.[77]

In his 'Extempore Epistle to Mrs. Merelina Spring' Pack wrote, 'More greedily your Lines I Learn, / Than … / Lady's Chaplain crams his Belly/ With Whipt cream, Marmalade, or Jelly', although whether this was personal satire directed against a Catholic chaplain at Hengrave or simply an established stereotype is unclear. Pack evoked a happy family life at Hengrave when he concluded his poem:

> Commend me then in short to all,
> Who Live and Laugh at Hengrave-Hall,

---

[74] R. Yates, *The History and Antiquities of the Abbey of St. Edmund's Bury* (Bury St Edmunds, 1805), p. 68.

[75] R. Pack, *Poems on Several Occasions* (London, 1725), pp. 29–67.

[76] Ibid. p. 35.

[77] 'Writ on a Seat in the Glade of the Hide' in ibid. p. 43.

From little Dilly sly and sleek,
To Molly with her Dimpled Cheek.

In 1727 Pack was recalled to Scotland, where he died the following year. The fact that as ardent a servant of the Hanoverian monarchy as Richardson Pack could enjoy himself so much at Hengrave testifies to the Gages' normal status in polite Protestant society. There is no evidence to suggest that Mary Spring responded to Pack's advances (he remained, in any case, a married man), and on 27 January 1726 she married at Hengrave Dr John Symonds (1696–1757), a clergyman who held in plurality the livings of Rushbrooke, Little Whelnetham, Horringer and Nowton and enjoyed the patronage of the Davers family.[78] In 1742 Symonds was elected incumbent of St Mary's Church in Bury St Edmunds.[79] Mary and John's first three sons died in infancy, but their fourth son, John Symonds (1730–1807), became Professor of Modern History at Cambridge and left a lasting legacy in the form of Robert Adam's Palladian mansion, St Edmund's Hill (now called Moreton Hall), which he built on the lands of Eldoe Farm, inherited from his mother as part of Lord Jermyn's legacy.[80] Mary died in Bury in 1763 and was buried in Pakenham church.

Sir William does not seem to have shared his father's interest in religious controversy, and only a handful of religious works were added to Hengrave's library after Sir Edward's death. *The Annals of the Church* by Ambrose Burgis (London, 1712) was a work on early church history, while William Darell's *The Case Review'd* (St Omer, 1715) was a Catholic response to an anti-Catholic pamphlet by Charles Leslie. *A Catholick Answer to Barrett's Sermon* (1724) was, likewise, a reply to an anti-Catholic sermon preached by Serenus Barrett, curate of Midhurst in Sussex, while the anonymous tract *Pax Vobis* (1717) was a work of Protestant controversy. An interest in the House of Stuart, if not political Jacobitism, is suggested by the fact that the library at Hengrave contained a copy of *Memoirs of the Chevalier de St. George* (London, 1712), containing a biography of James II.[81]

[78] Gage, *Hengrave*, p. 77; S. H. A. Hervey (ed.), *Horringer Parish Registers* (Woodbridge: G. Booth, 1900), p. 349.

[79] Tymms, *An Architectural and Historical Account of the Church of St. Mary, Bury St. Edmunds*, p. 130.

[80] Hervey (ed.), *Rushbrook Parish Registers with Jermyn and Davers Annals*, p. 115.

[81] CUL Hengrave MS 52.

The financial aftermath of the 1688 Revolution

William Gage responded to the financial threats against his lands in the aftermath of the Revolution by embracing an enterprising spirit, first evidenced by the agreement he entered into with Henry Ashley, the proprietor of the Mildenhall-to-Bury navigation, on 11 March 1694. Ashley made the Bourne (or Lark) River navigable between Mildenhall and Bury. At that time the river was already navigable between Mildenhall and King's Lynn, and Ashley's works allowed coal from Newcastle to be shipped to Lynn and then taken directly by barge to Bury. Through an agreement with Ashley, William gained exemption from tolls for the transport of coal, fuel, corn, fodder and 'materials for building and reparations to be used in or about Hengrave hall'. A subsequent Act of Parliament, which became law in 1702, contained a clause enabling the Lord of the Manor of Hengrave and his tenants to convey hay, manure and other produce toll-free.[82] As Bury's population grew and the need for fuel increased, William Gage had the opportunity to acquire a new source of income through the sale of his toll-free produce to others. Whilst William's engagement with canal-building may have fallen short of the 'proto-industrial experimentation' of cash-strapped Catholic families in northern England,[83] it demonstrated an interest in inventive financial management.

An indication of the financial straits in which the Gage family found itself after the Revolution can be found in two private Acts of Parliament for which William Gage petitioned in the 1690s. By 1695, he had purchased much of the estate from his father, and the fact that this was done by means of trustees, rather than by William himself, suggests that it was a safety measure to protect the land from the danger of sequestration. In 1700 'An Act for further preventing the Growth of Popery' limited the ability of Catholics to inherit land and provided that it should pass to the nearest Protestant relative, but the Gages notably avoided the impact of this law.[84] Furthermore, Sir Edward may have considered it safer for his lands to be held in his son's name, since William presumably had fewer (if any) convictions for recusancy against him, and it is always possible that Sir Edward had been involved in James II's regime in ways that history has not recorded.

In 1695 William Gage petitioned the House of Lords for 'an Act to enable Trustees of William Gage, Esq., to raise money by a mortgage of part of his Estate for the preservation of the timber growing thereon'.

---

[82] Gage, *Hengrave*, p. 3.
[83] Glickman, *The English Catholic Community 1688–1745*, p. 61.
[84] Ryan and Redstone, *Timperley of Hintlesham*, p. 108.

In other words, William knew that without taking out a mortgage on part of his estate he would have to sell the timber. William Covell of Horringer, then steward at Hengrave,[85] testified that the timber growing at Hengrave was worth £1,000, not including the Hyde Wood, which was worth a further £1,000. The timber at Chevington and Barrow was worth £8,000, and that on 'the Chevington farms' a further £1,000. In addition, the timber growing at Hargrave, 'Tisby' [sic], Feldington and 'Oxastrind' was worth £1,500. It was in William's interests for Covell to inflate these figures; even so, they demonstrate the tremendous value of mature timber as a financial asset, making a total of £12,500. The Gage's Estate Act was given the royal assent on 8 February 1695, and by it William Gage saved both Hengrave's ancient parkland and the Hyde Wood, which remain to this day.[86] In 1712 the extent of Hengrave Great Park was still about five hundred acres (it had halved in size by 1838), and it extended into the neighbouring parish of Fornham All Saints.[87]

Timber was again an issue in 1713, when Sir William seems to have accused a tenant, Mr Hamond, of cutting down more than he was entitled to during the lifetime of Sir Edward Gage. Sir William's attorney, Thomas Hollens, argued that he should drop the matter, on the grounds that the state of timber on the estate was now healthy, and that without Hamond's investment of £3,000 over the course of the time he had lived on the Gages' lands, a number of farms would have fallen into disrepair, since Sir Edward did little to maintain them. Hollens also reminded Sir William that at the time that Hamond was despoiling the trees Sir William could not have been certain that he would inherit his father's property.[88]

In addition to mortgaging part of the estate in 1695, William raised money through the sale of his mother-in-law's jewels and relieved his brother-in-law, Sir Henry Bond, 2nd Baronet of Peckham of the obligation of repaying his debts to his mother's estate. On her death in 1696, the French-born Lady Bond (Marie Peliot), who had lived at Hengrave since 1675, left a problematic will that could only be resolved by an Act of Parliament. This did not happen until 1700, presumably because Parliament had more pressing business. Lady Bond had bequeathed 'several

---

[85] The first mention of Covell is in the will of Penelope Gage (Gage, *Thingoe*, p. 208); he is also mentioned in a letter from Mary Gage to Thomas Halsall, probably written in the 1670s, CUL Hengrave MS 88/2/175, and it is likely that he succeeded Halsall as steward.

[86] *Lords MSS* 1693–1695, vol. 1, pp. 504–5.

[87] Gage, *Thingoe*, p. 213.

[88] Thomas Hollens to Sir William Gage, 12 November 1713, CUL Hengrave MS 76/2/28.

jewels' to William's daughter Julia, then a child, as well as £8,000 to be divided between her daughter Mary Charlotte Bond (William's wife) and her son Thomas Bond. Julia could not inherit the jewels until she attained her majority at the age of eighteen, and the £8,000 could not be realised; most of it was due as a debt to his mother from Sir Henry Bond, who was unable to pay. Without an Act of Parliament, the jewels could not be sold and payment of the £8,000 to Lady Bond's children could not be waived. The Act was given the royal assent on 8 February 1700.[89]

The parties required to give their consent to 'Gage's Estate Act' were all those with an interest in the case as beneficiaries of Lady Bond's will, namely Sir Edward Gage, Mary Charlotte Bond, Henry Jermyn, Lord Dover,[90] William Bond of Bury St Edmunds,[91] Edward Gage of Bury St Edmunds,[92] Penelope Sulyard,[93] Mary Bond,[94] William Hanmer of Flintshire, Susan Hanmer,[95] Francis Gage of Packington,[96] and Charles Gage.[97] Even after so long, the Hanmer family remained involved with the Gages, at least financially.

Obtaining a private Act of Parliament was no easy thing in the eighteenth century, when the business of Parliament was constantly expanding and limited time was available to debate private bills. The fact that William Gage, a Catholic who did not even have the right to vote, managed to secure two such acts within five years is a sign that he enjoyed influence in Parliament. By far the most likely source of such influence was William Hanmer, who was himself named in Gage's Estate Act, and was MP for Flintshire at the time. The Gages were, if not part of the establishment, certainly hovering at its fringes in the early eighteenth century. On 4 June 1716 Sir William Gage joined eight other Catholic peers, baronets and landed gentlemen in petitioning the House

---

[89] *Lords MSS* 1699–1702, vol. 4, p. 83.

[90] Dover had returned to England from his poverty at the Court of Saint-Germain-en-Laye and reclaimed his estate at Cheveley, having petitioned King William III in February 1692, see Hervey (ed.), *Rushbrook Parish Registers with Jermyn and Davers Annals*, p. 331.

[91] Husband of Sir Edward's second daughter, Mary Gage.

[92] Presumably Sir Edward's son by Anne Watkins, who attempted to enter the English College, Rome in 1685.

[93] Sir Edward's eldest daughter, widow of Edward Sulyard of Haughley.

[94] Sir Edward's second daughter, Mary Gage.

[95] Possibly Sir Edward's stepsister Susan Hervey, widow of Sir Thomas Hanmer, although she would have been in her seventies or eighties by 1700.

[96] Sir Edward's only son by Frances Aston.

[97] A son of Sir Edward by Elizabeth Feilding.

of Lords against part of the proposed Papists' Estates Act.[98] It seems to have been the last part of the Act (obliging Catholic landowners to register their estates with all future conveyances and wills) that the petitioners were mainly concerned about. Several of the nine petitioners were associated, then and later, with a Hanoverian loyalist grouping that emerged among eighteenth-century Catholics. In 1727 Thomas Belassis, 2nd Viscount Fauconberg and Henry Browne, 5th Viscount Montague met with Prime Minister Robert Walpole in the hope of securing a form of the Oath of Allegiance acceptable to Catholics.[99] Thomas Stonor was the elder brother of John Talbot Stonor, Bishop of Thespia, who led the campaign for a Catholic oath,[100] and Sir William Goring would later conform to the Church of England.[101]

In 1716 Sir William Gage chose to align himself with a group of Catholic peers and gentlemen who were politically conformist by instinct, although the desire to distance himself from fervent Jacobites at a dangerous time could also have motivated Sir William to join the petitioners. At any rate, they were unsuccessful, and it was as a consequence of cumulative anti-Catholic legislation that Sir William was forced to mortgage the manor, park and hall of Hengrave, the manor and advowson of Chevington and the manor of Risby to the Earl of Sunderland and Francis Godolphin.[102] Later he sold the manor of Chevington and the advowsons of Chevington and Hargrave to Dudley North,[103] followed by the manor of Lackford in 1717.[104] In the same year he apparently gave up the Bear Inn in Bury, which he had owned since 1705.[105] In 1715 his son Thomas sold the manor of Little Whelnetham to Sir Robert Davers of Rushbrooke.[106] As Sir Thomas Gage, 7th Baronet later noted: 'The pressure of the penal laws against Catholics was a primary cause of distress, and was the consequence [sic] of the sale of considerable parts of the Gage Estate.'[107] The Gages could at least take consolation in the fact that they were not alone in their predicament. Consolidation of estates and a reduction in the number of houses the Catholic gentry

---

98   *Lords MSS* 1714–18, vol. 12, p. 290. The other petitioners were Viscount Montague, Viscount Fauconberg, Lord George Howard, the Hon. Marmaduke Langdale, Sir William Goring, Sir Henry Bedingfield, Thomas Stonor and Henry Nevill.

99   Glickman, *The English Catholic Community 1688–1745*, p. 147.

100   Ibid. p. 122.

101   Ibid. p. 58.

102   CUL Hengrave MS 1/4, fol. 336.

103   SRO(B) FL550/11/7; Gage, *Thingoe*, p. 328; CUL Hengrave MS 1/4, fol. 338.

104   Gage, *Hengrave*, p. 9.

105   SRO(B) 744/2/22.

106   SRO(B) HA 507/2/372.

107   CUL Hengrave MS 1/4, fol. 336.

were able to maintain led to a shortage of mass centres as the eighteenth century drew on. According to Rowe, only the Jetters in Lothingland and the Tasburghs at Flixton were supporting chaplaincies that also served the local area in the early years of the eighteenth century,[108] and Flixton was in any case an independently funded Benedictine mission by this period, rather than a gentry chaplaincy.[109]

In the midst of financial gloom, close family relationships brought rewards in the form of legacies and marriage alliances. Sir William's childless first cousin, John Gage of Harleston, by his will of 15 June 1718 left his whole estate to the Baronet. The will gives us some idea of the web of Gage relations at the time, mentioning Sir William's son John, Francis Gage of Packington, Edward Gage of Whittlebury in Northamptonshire and his son George,[110] George and Henry Gage (the sons of Sir Edward Gage), Penelope Sulyard, Mary Bond and Basilia Gage, Elizabeth (daughter of Penelope Sulyard and the testator's executrix), Elizabeth Gage (daughter of Frances Gage[111] and George Gage of Raunds).[112] Furthermore, the marriage of Sir William's son John to Elizabeth Rookwood brought financial rewards, since she was sole heiress not only of the Rookwoods of Stanningfield but also of the Martins of Long Melford.[113]

Sir William Gage seems to have enjoyed a relationship of friendly rivalry with John Hervey, 1st Earl Bristol, whose father Sir Thomas Hervey was Sir Edward Gage's stepbrother. Whereas the Gages' lands were primarily located to the north of the Bury to Cambridge road (now the A14), those of the Herveys were to the south, centred on their seat at Ickworth. The Gage and Hervey lands converged at Westley, the first parish on the west side of Bury. The Gages owned the manor of Westley and Sextons Farm. Another manor in the parish, Downhams, was part of the settlement of Francis Gage of Packington, which he sold to the Herveys in 1693.[114] However, it made little sense for the Herveys to farm one manor and not the others, and by 1715 they were renting the manor of Westley from the Gages. The fact that Sir William's lands

---

[108] Rowe, '"The Lopped Tree": The Re-formation of the Suffolk Catholic Community', pp. 184–85. The Bedingfields and Wingfields were also forced to consolidate their properties.

[109] On the Tasburghs of Flixton see F. Young, 'The Tasburghs of Flixton and Catholicism in North-east Suffolk, 1642–1767', *PSIAH* 42 (2012), pp. 455–70.

[110] This is presumably the same Edward Gage who tried to become a priest at the English College in 1685.

[111] Sir William's aunt, the widow of Sir Thomas Tresham.

[112] J. O. Payne, *Records of the English Catholics of 1715: Compiled Wholly from Original Documents* (Burns and Oates: London, 1889), pp. 64–65.

[113] CUL Hengrave MS 76/1.

[114] CUL Hengrave MS 1/4, fol. 313.

were owned not by him but by his trustees, gave rise to problems of communication. In July 1715 Sir William sold two manors to the Earl of Bristol, which became the occasion for an argument about the value of the rents on the estate. Sir Thomas Hanmer, one of Sir William's trustees, wrote to Edmund Howard demanding answers. Howard, who seems to have been either a friend or agent of Sir William, was present at Ickworth on the day of the sale. Howard was able to offer Hanmer some reassurances.[115] Difficulties continued at Westley, however, and on 14 October 1719 Hervey wrote to his wife:

> I was obliged to meet Sir W. Gage at Westley to terminate all differences between our tenants there, (wherin I have made many more concessions than I should have mett with had he been in my place,) he went for Bury, where he lay at my house, & rode post for London this morning.[116]

A paper in the Hengrave manuscripts details: 'The particulars that S[i]r W[illia]m Gage insists upon to be his Right in westley wherein he is obstructed by the Earl of Bristol tenant.'[117] The document largely concerned Sir William's desire to defend ancient land rights and usages (such as common pasture) that the Earl, as tenant of the manor, was denying his subtenants. The question of whether a tenant (or even a landowner) had the right to infringe upon customary rights was a vexed one throughout the eighteenth century. Doubtless, from the Herveys' point of view, Sir William's insistence on respecting custom was a hindrance to efficient farming.

In 1716 Hervey had been involved in restoring an officer's commission to 'Captain Gage', 'on the account of his father's forsaking him, & all his other friends abandoning him ever since he forsook the errors of the Church of Rome'. Hervey described Captain Gage as 'my relation', which could suggest that he was a member of the Hengrave branch of the family, perhaps a son of one of Sir William's half-brothers. Whatever the Captain's identity, Hervey's words and actions were an indication of the affinity he still felt with the family into which his grandfather had married in 1642.[118]

Sir William Gage's good relationship with Hervey, an important Whig politician, would have been a valuable asset in avoiding fines and other unwelcome attention. However, the relationship of the two men

---

[115]   Edmund Howard to Sir Thomas Hanmer, 2 August 1715, CUL Hengrave MS 88/4/27.

[116]   S. H. A. Hervey (ed.), *Letter-Books of John Hervey, First Earl of Bristol* (Wells: E. Jackson, 1894), vol. 2, p. 93.

[117]   CUL Hengrave MS 92.

[118]   Hervey (ed.), *Letter-Books of John Hervey, First Earl of Bristol*, vol. 2, pp. 38–39. This was probably the same Captain Gage who, according to Robert Harland, 'stands a fair Chance of being brought to Boards End for carrying his wife to sea with him' (Robert Harland to Sir William Gage, 7 November 1742, CUL Hengrave 88/4/44).

was delicate. In November 1725 Sir William wrote to the Earl, rather reproachfully, about 'a very unfaire push made att me by a countryman of ours mr Guidotts kinsman, which you and [Lord Godolphin] putt by with mr Guidott'. He reassured the Earl that: 'I alwaise lookd upon that matter as an effect of the gentelmans vanity and temper … rather than as a memento that I was backword in my rewards.' The nature of the 'push' is unclear – it could have been anything from a lawsuit about property to an attempt to inform on Sir William for having Mass said in his house. However, Sir William pointedly reminded the Earl at the end of the letter that he was his 'near Kinsman'.[119]

Catholic settlers: the Bonds, Burtons and Tyldesleys in Suffolk

From the 1670s onwards, the Bonds were the Catholic family with whom the Gages allied themselves most closely, first by William Gage's marriage to Mary Charlotte Bond and then by Mary Gage's marriage to William Bond of Bury St Edmunds. The decision of two sons of Sir Thomas Bond, 1st Baronet of Peckham to settle in Bury may have been motivated by their marriages to members of the local gentry, although the context of these marriages was the court of Queen Henrietta Maria in Paris rather than Suffolk society. It seems likely that William Gage met Mary Charlotte during his stay in Paris in the late 1660s, when he certainly visited the Dowager Queen.[120] Mary Charlotte's brothers, Thomas and William, followed her to Bury. Thomas married Henrietta Jermyn, the sister of Lord Jermyn and Henry Jermyn, Lord Dover. However, since Lord Jermyn and Sir Thomas Bond had both served Henrietta Maria, as Master of Horse and Comptroller of the Household respectively, the likelihood is that the match between Henrietta and Thomas had its origins in Paris. Likewise, Mary Gage went abroad with William Bond during the Popish Plot scare and the couple were married not long afterwards.

In the case of the Gages, Bonds and Jermyns, English Catholic continental society mirrored the geographical proximity of the families in Suffolk.[121] Thomas Bond and Henrietta Jermyn's daughter Mary Charlotte (not to be confused with the wife of William Gage) became the mistress of her father's household after her mother's early death, and later the Revolution may have forced the family to move to Bruges.

---

119 Sir William Gage to John Hervey, 1st Earl of Bristol, 22 November 1725, BL Add. MS 61457, fol. 182.

120 Francis Gage to Sir Edward Gage, 4 March 1668, CUL Hengrave MS 88/2/181.

121 The extent to which English enclaves on the Continent mirrored English life and society has been observed by Glickman, *The English Catholic Community 1688–1745*, pp. 76–77.

Here, Mary Charlotte contemplated becoming a canoness of St Augustine at the English Convent, but on visiting Antwerp, where her brother Henry was studying and had contracted smallpox, she came across the English Carmelite Convent, where she met Catharine Burton of Beyton, now Mary Xaveria of the Angels. Catharine prophesied that Mary Charlotte would become a Carmelite, even though she initially joined the Augustinian canonesses, a prophecy that came true in 1713. Mary Charlotte (now Teresa Joseph of the Sacred Heart) was elected Prioress of Antwerp Convent in 1730 and died in 1735.[122]

Mary Charlotte Bond's special connection with Catharine Burton may well have been personal and social as well as spiritual; both women belonged to the Catholic gentry living around Bury St Edmunds and had shared in the struggles of Suffolk's Catholic community. However, the Bonds, like the Burtons, were newcomers to the area, in contrast to the Gages, who in spite of their Sussex ancestors, still represented the continuity of the Kytson lineage. Unlike the aristocratic Gages, with their knightly ancestors, the Bonds were originally a London merchant family,[123] and the Burtons were Yorkshire yeomen. The early eighteenth century saw the arrival of another Catholic family in the locality, the Tyldesleys from Lancashire.

The Tyldesleys were a family notorious for their Jacobitism. They raised a regiment of dragoons for James II in 1689 and fought in the risings of 1715 and 1745.[124] However, they had numerous branches and the one that settled at Fornham St Genevieve, the village that lay on the river between Hengrave and Bury, does not seem to have been particularly militant. Indeed, it may have been in order to escape the attention Catholics received in Lancashire that the Fornham Tyldesleys settled in Suffolk, a testament to the relative tolerance that Catholics experienced in the area. According to Joseph Gillow and Richard Trappes-Lomax, the Suffolk Tyldesleys descended from the Tyldesleys of Stanzacre, on the basis that John Tyldesley of Fornham (d.1723) sold Stanzacre early in the eighteenth century.[125]

[122] N. Hallett, *Lives of Spirit: English Carmelite Self-Writing of the Early Modern Period* (Aldershot: Ashgate, 2007), pp. 101–3.

[123] Sir Thomas Bond's grandfather George Bond was Lord Mayor of London in 1587 and the family originated from Buckland in Somerset; see J. Burke, *A Genealogical and Heraldic History of the Commoners of Great Britain and Ireland* (London, 1836), vol. 1, p. 241.

[124] Glickman, *The English Catholic Community 1688–1745*, pp. 47, 261; Estcourt and Payne (eds), *The English Catholic Non-Jurors of 1715*, p. 155.

[125] J. Gillow and R. Trappes-Lomax (eds), *The Diary of the 'Blue Nuns'* (London: CRS, 1910), p. 426.

John Tyldesley of Fornham St Genevieve married Catherine Stafford (d.1712), daughter of the John Stafford who was Mayor of Bury under James II, and they had a son and two daughters.[126] It was presumably through the influence or under the protection of the Tyldesleys that the Observant Franciscan Anthony Tyldesley came to Suffolk. There seems to be little basis for Joy Rowe's assertion that he was 'the son of a Bury family'.[127] Anthony was born in 1686 and trained at St Bonaventure's Friary at Douai before being professed in 1703.[128] He was ordained in 1710 and left for England in 1714.[129] According to the Franciscan necrology he was 'Lancastriensis', i.e. born in Lancashire.[130] Rowe thought that he was a chaplain at Gifford's Hall,[131] but he may have spent some time in Bury, as he was buried in St Mary's churchyard four years later, on 24 July 1718.[132] Unfortunately, our knowledge of the Suffolk Tyldesleys is marred by the loss of the parish registers of Fornham St Genevieve, which were destroyed by fire, along with the church, in 1782.

Catholic incomers of middling social status such as the Burtons and Tyldesleys, together with Bury's long-established Short family, formed a foundation for the small but resilient community of 'plebeian' Catholics in Bury that endured throughout the eighteenth century. The Staffords' cousins, the Prettymans, owned land in Fornham St Genevieve;[133] so did the Shorts, some of whom were buried in the church there.[134] Fornham's attractiveness to Catholics may have been a combination of its proximity to Bury and its closeness to the Gages' Hengrave estate, which it bordered. The marriage of John Tyldesley to Catherine Stafford demonstrated that newcomers were prepared to marry into Bury families, while the Staffords had formed an alliance with the influential Pret-

---

[126] John (d.1729), Elizabeth (d.1727) and Mary (d.1728), according to Estcourt and Payne (eds), *The English Catholic Non-Jurors of 1715*, pp. 258–59. The Katherine Tildesley buried in St James's churchyard on 8 September 1718 may also have been a daughter (see *St James Burials*, p. 227). John Tyldesley the Younger had two daughters, Frances and Bridget, and his will was proved on 1 April 1735, see Payne, *Records of the English Catholics of 1715*, p. 66.

[127] Rowe, *The Story of Catholic Bury St. Edmunds, Coldham and Surrounding District*, p. 11.

[128] Bellenger, p. 117.

[129] J. Moorman, *The Franciscans in England* (London: Mowbray, 1974), p. 310.

[130] R. Trappes Lomax (ed.), *Franciscana* (London: CRS, 1922), p. 293.

[131] Rowe, *The Story of Catholic Bury St. Edmunds, Coldham and Surrounding District*, p. 11.

[132] Trappes-Lomax, *Franciscana*, p. 293; J. Lunn, *The Tyldesleys of Lancashire: The Rise and Fall of a Great Patrician Family* (Astley: privately published, 1966), p. 172.

[133] Estcourt and Payne (eds), *The English Catholic Non-Jurors of 1715*, pp. 258–59.

[134] Ibid. p. 259.

tymans, and the Shorts (appropriately enough for a medical family) had allied themselves with the Cressener family who ran an apothecary's shop in the town.[135]

The flourishing network of Catholic families of the 'middling sort' in Bury St Edmunds and the possible existence of an urban mission patronised by the Shorts raises questions about the extent of the Gages' involvement in Catholic missionary activity in the early eighteenth century, not to mention the assumptions about 'seigneurial Catholicism' that have characterised some analyses of the East Anglian situation. The Gages certainly did not dominate Suffolk Catholicism in the early eighteenth century; if they did exercise missionary patronage at all it was probably to the Jesuits through Sir William's brother John Gage the Elder. It is likely that the Gages' involvement, like the Rookwoods' patronage of the Benedictines, ran in parallel with the missionary activity of Bury's plebeian Catholics rather than coming into conflict with it. In the absence of any surviving registers from before 1734, it is impossible to say with certainty whether gentry families such as the Gages, Bonds and Rookwoods worshipped separately or together with their social inferiors. The balance of probability is that, as in the 1730s, the town-dwelling Bond family formed a social bridge between the Gages and other local Catholics, who were prepared to receive the ministry of any clergy who happened to be on hand.

Suffolk papists in 1715

In the aftermath of the Jacobite rising of 1715 against the government of King George I, Parliament passed 'An Act to oblige Papists to register their names, and Real Estates'. The resulting list of those unable in conscience to swear the Oath of Allegiance provides a snapshot of English Catholicism at the beginning of the Georgian era, and the information it contains on the Gages and their neighbours is no less revealing. The list was first published in 1745, but an earlier list, sometimes containing slightly different valuations, was printed for the House of Commons in 1719.[136] Sir William Gage declared the annual value of his manor of Fornham All Saints as £169 1s 2d, while his daughter-in-law Delariviere D'Ewes, the widow of his eldest son Thomas, declared a 'jointure estate' at Fornham All Saints to the value of £253. John

---

135   Young, 'The Shorts of Bury St Edmunds', p. 191.
136   *The Report to the Honourable the House of Commons ... of the Commissioners ... Appointed to Execute the several Trusts and Powers ... contained in Two several Acts of Parliament* (London, 1719), p. 17.

Gage of Harleston, son of Sir William's uncle Henry, held the manor of Harleston to the value of £184 13s 1d,[137] as well as two houses in Arlington Street, London.[138]

Henry Bond, the son of Thomas Bond and Henrietta Jermyn who studied at Antwerp, was living at a house in Bury worth £20 a year, while Sir William's sister Penelope, widow of Edward Sulyard, was living in the parish of St Andrew's, Holborn and declared the annual value of her estate at Wetherden as £375 5s.[139] Her son Edward Sulyard held the manor of Haughley in fee tail for £116 6s 4d. Outside of the Gages' relatives, we find Thomas Burton, the brother of the nun Catharine, holding two freehold messuages in Beyton including the Bull Inn, valued at £52, as well as the enterprising Bury tailor George Birch, who let out his house in Westgate Street into four tenements worth a total of £17 20s.[140] Martha Prettyman of Bury St Edmunds held a tenement at Fornham St Genevieve worth £3 8s, and John Tyldesley's 'life estate' at Fornham was valued at £32. Peregrine Short held farms in St James's parish while Thomas Short rented a house from him, and Dr Henry Short rented three meadows, amounting to a total of £25.[141] Thomas Rookwood of Stanningfield's Suffolk lands were valued at £522 10s and his Essex holdings at £98.[142]

The records of the nonjurors of 1715 give us a snapshot of the wealthier members of Bury's Catholic community whilst leaving aside the Catholics with little or no property who were counted as nonjurors in 1745. However, they do reveal that Delariviere D'Ewes had converted to Catholicism by 1715. It was not uncommon for Catholic wives to retain their religion on marriage to Protestant husbands, and vice versa; none of the properties of Sir William's wife Merelina were listed, indicating that she remained a Protestant.

Conclusions

Although the period between the 1688 Revolution and the arrival of the Benedictine mission in the Bury area is a comparatively dark one for which we are forced to rely on an odd assortment of evidence, the picture that emerges is of a family prepared to adapt in order to survive.

[137] Estcourt and Payne (eds), *The English Catholic Non-Jurors of 1715*, p. 255. The 1719 list valued Sir William's estate at £699 1s 2d.

[138] Ibid. p. 171.

[139] Ibid. p. 256.

[140] Ibid. p. 257. The Birch family appears in the list of nonjurors of 1745 as well, SRO(B) D8/1/3 bundle 2.

[141] Ibid. pp. 258–59.

[142] *The Report to the Honourable the House of Commons* (London, 1719), pp. 7, 17.

Sir William Gage's second marriage to Merelina Jermyn, the widow of Sir Thomas Spring, was a crucial component of that survival as it did a great deal to normalise the Gages' relationship with the Protestant gentry. By being prepared to use the expedient of Acts of Parliament, Sir William maximised his ability to raise funds at a time of great financial hardship for Catholics, although the sale of Chevington and Lackford in 1716 and 1717 is an indicator that he was not entirely successful. However, Hengrave does not seem to have been the centre of any missionary activity at a time when Coldham Hall hosted both a Benedictine and a Jesuit mission, the Tyldesleys perhaps produced a Franciscan priest and the Daniels of Acton gave a home to Sir William's brother, the Rector of the College of the Holy Apostles. This may have had something to do with the presence at Hengrave of Merelina Jermyn and her Protestant daughters. On the other hand, as a pre-Reformation house, Hengrave was unsuited to secret missionary activity. If it is possible to draw this conclusion from the limited evidence available, the incomer families such as the Burtons, Staffords and Tyldesleys, together with the Shorts, were a more vibrant force in Bury's Catholic community in the early eighteenth century than the Gages. To the extent that the Catholic convert Delariviere D'Ewes was the driving force behind the establishment of the Benedictine mission after Sir William's death, the influence of newcomers (whether to the locality or to the faith) was set to continue into the 1730s.

4

HENGRAVE AND THE BENEDICTINE MISSION, 1727–41

The period that followed the death of Sir William Gage, 2nd Baronet, in 1727, saw the establishment of what was effectively a single Benedictine mission with two foci: Hengrave Hall and the Bonds' house in Bury. The mission's principal patrons were Delariviere D'Ewes, mother of Sir Thomas Gage, 3rd Baronet, and Henry Jermyn Bond. In contrast to the preceding period, the 1730s onwards are well documented. A mission register from 1734–51 survives (Appendix 4), in addition to a personal diary kept by one of the monks, Alexius Jones, from 1731–43. Although correspondence from this period is scarce in the Hengrave manuscripts, the register and diary together constitute an invaluable documentary record of the Catholic community. The Benedictines laid the foundations of the mission that the Jesuit John Gage the Younger would take forwards in the 1750s, and the returns of Catholics refusing the Oath of Allegiance at the 1745 quarter sessions demonstrate that a small but well-established population comprising all social classes existed at the time.

The surviving evidence for the second quarter of the eighteenth century portrays a community and a mission emerging from gentry control and establishing a firm identity within a relatively tolerant wider community. The realities of ministry to a growing urban Catholic community required the Benedictines to deviate from a stereotyped model of gentry chaplaincy. For instance, in 1741 Francis Howard was hurled into the position of 'town' missioner, whether he liked it or not, and Alexius Jones seems to have had a fluid role that involved almost as much ministry at Hengrave at times as it did in the Bond family's household in Bury. The surviving personal documents of both men (the *Hengrave Register* and the *Diary*) serve not only to give a human face to the individual missionary priests; they also portray a mission that was prepared to assume an identity distinct from that of its immediate patrons.

Gages, Bonds and Rookwood Gages

In February 1727 Sir William Gage, 2nd Baronet, who was then aged about seventy-seven, was thrown from his horse against the wrought-iron gates of Hengrave Park, 'by which he received so much Injury that he survived only a few days'.[1] He died on 8 February, and the *Suffolk Mercury* of 13 February had fulsome praise for Sir William that testifies to the respect he commanded from his fellow gentry: 'All the years he lived, he lived not only loved but admired by all degrees of men, in proportion to the just notions they had of loving and admiring true charity, hospitality, generosity, honour, and politeness, all the virtues which he so eminently possessed, few can reach, very few can equal.'[2] Sir Thomas Gage, 7th Baronet reported that Sir William had a very strong constitution, and would have lived for as long as his father had his accident not occurred.[3] By his concise will of 2 May 1715, proved on 23 June 1727, Sir William left his whole estate to his wife Merelina.[4] She did not long outlive her husband and died on 29 August 1727,[5] leaving the estate to her step-grandson, Thomas Gage.

Thomas Gage had been heir to his grandfather since the death of his own father, Thomas, Sir William's eldest son by Mary Charlotte Bond, on 1 March 1716. When he succeeded to the baronetcy he was only fourteen years old, and in the absence of a father it was his mother, Delariviere D'Ewes, who dominated the family. Delariviere was one of four sisters from the once staunchly Protestant D'Ewes family to convert to Catholicism; her younger sister Mary was married to Francis Tasburgh of Bodney (d.1747),[6] while her elder sister Merelina married Richard Elwes and then Richard Holmes, who was involved in England's trade with Portugal.[7] A fourth sister, Henrietta, was married to Thomas Havers of Thelveton, whose family kept Catholicism alive in the Waveney Valley.[8] Delariviere's mother, Delariviere Jermyn, was the

---

[1] CUL Hengrave MS 1/4, fol. 338.

[2] Gage, *Hengrave*, p. 245.

[3] CUL Hengrave MS 1/4, fol. 338.

[4] PROB 11/615; Payne (1889), p. 64.

[5] Gage, *Hengrave*, p. 246.

[6] F. Blomefield, *An Essay towards a Topographical History of the County of Norfolk* (London, 1805–10), vol. 6, pp. 15–19. Francis Tasburgh was the son of John Beaumont Tasburgh and Elizabeth Blount and a cousin of the Flixton Tasburghs.

[7] Diary of Dom Alexius Jones, 1732–43 (CUL Hengrave MS 69) (hereafter *Diary*) 1 October 1731.

[8] Thomas Havers married Henrietta D'Ewes in 1726; in their marriage settlement it was stipulated that Delariviere would pay Thomas Havers £1,000, which may indicate the financial inability of her brother, Sir Germane D'Ewes, to provide her with a dowry

sister of Sir William Gage's second wife Merelina, meaning that Delariviere D'Ewes was Merelina's niece as well as her daughter-in-law.

The fact that Sir William made his wife executrix, combined with her subsequent death so soon after his own, rendered the Baronet practically intestate. This left Delariviere, the mother of the new Baronet (who was still a minor) to contest the estate with Sir William's other children. 'The affair with the younger children of S[i]r Will[iam] Gage' was still Delariviere's major concern at the end of 1729. Delariviere's agent, Ralph Pigot, prepared an agreement dividing the revenue of part of Sir William's estate between Sir William's other children.[9] However, matters were complicated by the fact that the younger children demanded that Edmund Howard, who had been Sir William's agent, should be 'receaver' of the rents on their estate;[10] the fact that Catholics could not legally inherit land made the appointment of such an individual necessary. However, Howard apparently behaved in an obstructive manner towards Delariviere, who claimed that Howard 'refuses to yeild up my sons court rolls notwithstanding his Patent ceased with S[i]r Will[iam] Gage and spurns at My power and athoritty'. Howard had once been entrusted with documents by Elizabeth Rookwood and Sir William Spring, who now no longer trusted him.

Delariviere reported that Howard 'applyes himself reliably to get the better of me, with the assistence of Mrs Gages and Mr Lamb'.[11] The 'Mrs Gages' were probably the two unmarried daughters of Sir William Gage living in Bury in 1745,[12] Ann and Henrietta (older unmarried women were usually referred to as 'Mrs'), while 'Mr Lamb' was either Fitznun Lambe of Troston, the husband of Sir William's daughter Charlotte, or their son John Lambe of Frimley. Howard's intransigence in his dealings with Delariviere, the widow of Thomas Gage, may have been a legacy of the financial disputes between Sir William and his eldest son shortly before Thomas Gage's death. However, Pigot believed that Howard's behaviour had more to do with his unwillingness to serve in the role that Sir William had assigned him:

> Mr Howard has often told me He did not want the authority and that the younger Children haveing the Equitable Estate Their authority was suffi-

---

(SRO(B) HA 528/42). The Havers paid a visit to the Bonds on 31 December 1736 (see *Diary* for that date).

9 Delariviere D'Ewes to unnamed recipient, 28 October 1729, CUL Hengrave MS 88/4/28.

10 Ralph Pigot to Delariviere D'Ewes, 6 November 1729, CUL Hengrave MS 88/4/30.

11 Delariviere D'Ewes to unnamed recipient, 7 November 1729, CUL Hengrave MS 88/4/29.

12 SRO(B) D8/1/3 bundle 2.

cient, he keeps all the Court Rolls refuses to deliver them & will keep Courts & have a Salary.[13]

Pigot noted that an attorney could be found who, for less than Howard was being paid, would look after the necessary documents on behalf of the family. Howard, then, was holding on to the documents in order to justify the salary he was receiving, yet at the same time he was unwilling to do his job. The case of Edmund Howard demonstrates the potential dangers that a Catholic family could encounter through the necessity of appointing Protestant intermediaries to conduct the affairs that it was legally problematic for them to transact directly. Many such interme- diaries, such as the Covells, were evidently trustworthy to the highest degree, but some could become greedy or obstructive. In the case of Edmund Howard, his actions seem to have divided the Gage family, although Delariviere seems to have been united in a common grievance against Howard with Elizabeth Rookwood, the widow of John Gage. Delariviere remained friendly with the Rookwood Gages, which was fortunate given the fact that they eventually succeeded to the baronetcy.

Delariviere and her sons were close, and Sir Thomas Gage, 7th Baronet recorded that a painting once at Hengrave depicted Delariviere 'reclining under a Tree, with a Chaplet of Flowers in her Hand – her eldest son Sir Thomas Gage was standing near her – The other two sons had hold of a favorite Deer by the Horns and Neck.'[14] The evidence suggests that Delariviere was a very protective mother; again and again, she insisted in her letters that she did not act in her own interests but on his behalf, and it seems that little changed when Sir Thomas came of age. Since he never married, Delariviere remained mistress of Hengrave, and she frequently appeared in public with her son.[15] In 1735 Delari- viere, together with her sister Mary, made unsuccessful efforts to secure a marriage for Sir Thomas. In a letter to Delariviere, Mary referred to 'utmost indeavours to gain [Sir Thomas's] fair Vallintine for life' and seemed to allude to other young marriages among the Catholic gentry: 'I have often heard of Lord Arrundles Son ... and that somer Mr Arrundle was but seventeen years old.'[16] Little evidence remains of Delariviere's estate management, although in December 1730 she sold '6 loads of bricks' from the kiln at Hengrave to Lord Cornwallis at Culford.[17] Sir

[13] Ralph Pigot to Delariviere D'Ewes, 6 November 1729, CUL Hengrave MS 88/4/30.

[14] CUL Hengrave MS 1/4, fol. 343.

[15] Sir Thomas visited the Bonds forty-five times between December 1736 and his death, and was accompanied by his mother on nineteen occasions.

[16] Mary D'Ewes to Delariviere D'Ewes, 23 February c.1730, CUL Hengrave MS 88/3/90.

[17] Receipt for 54s, 12 November 1712, CUL Hengrave MS 92.

Thomas came of age in September 1733 and, by an indenture of 18 January 1734, the limitation of the Gage family estates to the use of Delariviere, as the widow of Thomas Gage, was terminated in favour of new uses for the benefit of Sir Thomas.[18] However, Delariviere retained Flempton Hall Farm for her own use.

The extent of the estate described in the indenture of 1734 illustrates the diminution of the Gages' possessions since 1675. In addition to the manors of Chevington, Lackford and Little Whelnetham, by 1734 the Gages' lands in Whepstead, Cavenham, Great and Little Horringer, Great and Little Saxham, Chelsworth, Culford, Great and Little Livermere, Great Barton, Timworth and Denham had also disappeared, presumably sold. The remaining manors were Hengrave, Risby, Fornham All Saints, Flempton, Fornham St Genevieve, Harleston and Charmans in Risby. Harleston, which had originally been bequeathed to Sir Edward's brother Henry, reverted to the descendents of Sir Edward on the failure of Henry's line, and was thus the only significant gain since 1675. The Gages continued to own the advowsons of Flempton-cum-Hengrave, Westley and Harleston. They had lost Grange Farm in Bury by the 1730s, but retained Toll Gate Farm and 'Water Corn Mill' in Bury, 'the Woods in Barrows called Will meer Wood', Bayfield Hill and 'the old Grove'. In addition, the Gages owned lands in the parishes of Coddenham (a new addition), 'Barker' (Barrow?), Darnesden, Lackford and West Stow. Given the determined execution of the penal laws in the early eighteenth century to prevent the inheritance and ownership of property by Catholics, the depredations of the Gage estates were comparatively modest.

Delariviere and her sister Mary shared a common interest in the supernatural, and Mary shared a ghost story in which 'a parfect Busto of a man, with Head, neck and Breast, bruis'd' appeared on a mahogany slider that had been given to her husband's cousin George Tasburgh of Flixton (d.1736) by a certain Humphrey Burgoine, who evidently died in some sort of fall, perhaps from a horse. The appearance of the letter 'B' convinced George Tasburgh and his guest, Henry Bedingfield of Coulsey Wood, that Burgoine's ghost had left the message – and George Tasburgh had a copy made by a local painter on vellum, intending 'by the first opportunity to send the originall to be ingrav'd on a Copper Plate at London'.[19] The interest in ghosts shown by the Bedingfields, Tasburghs and Gages is unlikely to have been idle; in an age when spiritual phenomena were increasingly denied by members of the Estab-

---

18 CUL Hengrave 1/4, fol. 342.
19 Mary D'Ewes to Delariviere D'Ewes, 23 February c.1730, CUL Hengrave MS 88/3/90.

lished Church, belief in spirits was both a distinctive feature of Catholics and a demonstration of the truth of the doctrine of Purgatory.[20]

During this period the Gages acquired more Catholic literature as it became more easily obtainable in England.[21] Two works by Richard Challoner, *Catholic Authority: The Unerring Authority of the Catholic Church in Matters of Faith* (1732) and *Memoirs of Missionary Priests* (1741–42) made it into their library. On a similarly hagiographical theme was Cornelius Morphy's account of the deaths of the martyrs Edmund Arrowsmith and Richard Herst in 1628, *A True and Exact Relation of the Death of Two Catholicks* (London, 1737). The compilation *A Select Collection of Sermons Preach'd before Their Majesties King James II, Mary Queen-Consort, Catherine Queen-Dowager, etc.* (1741) harked back to an earlier era but demonstrated that Catholics remained fascinated with the House of Stuart. Sir Thomas Gage was also musical, and a set of manuscript music books surviving from the first half of the eighteenth century, with notes on tuning a harpsichord, may have been his.[22]

After Merelina Jermyn's death her two youngest daughters by her first marriage to Sir Thomas Spring, Delariviere and Harriet, remained at Hengrave. Merelina's eldest daughters, Merelina and Mary, were already married to Thomas Discipline and John Symonds respectively. In addition to these two step-cousins (who were in their late twenties in the 1730s), Sir Thomas shared Hengrave with his two maiden aunts, Henrietta and Anne, as well as his unmarried great-aunt Basilia, the only child of Sir Edward Gage still living there. Sir Thomas's brother (and heir) William and his youngest brother Edward completed the household. On 18 June 1735 the Rector of Flempton-cum-Hengrave, William Wilson, noted twenty-one 'Popish Recusants' in the parish over sixteen years of age out of an adult population of 113.[23] It is likely that all twenty-one were either members of the Gage family or their Catholic servants.

Sir Thomas's uncle, John Gage, lived at Coldham Hall with his wife Elizabeth Rookwood and their two sons: Thomas, destined to inherit the baronetcy in 1767 and John, the future Jesuit. Elizabeth's father,

---

[20] On the importance of ghosts and hauntings for the Catholic mission see O. Davies, *The Haunted: A Social History of Ghosts* (Basingstoke: Palgrave MacMillan, 2007), pp. 106, 166–67; P. Marshall, *Beliefs and the Dead in Early Modern England* (Oxford: Oxford University Press, 2002), pp. 236–64; F. Young, *English Catholics and the Supernatural, 1553–1829* (Farnham: Ashgate, 2013), pp. 103–9.

[21] CUL Hengrave MS 52.

[22] SRO(B) 449/5/10.

[23] SRO(B) 806/1/61. The note was appended to the assessment of parish income for 1735.

Thomas Rookwood, died on 21 August 1726, and John Gage adopted the surname Rookwood Gage as a condition of his wife's settlement.[24] Besides the Rookwood Gages, the Gages remained close to the Bonds in Bury St Edmunds. Henry Jermyn Bond, the second son of Thomas Bond and Henrietta Maria Jermyn, was related to the Gages twice over by marriage. His aunt Mary Charlotte had been the first wife of Sir William Gage, 2nd Baronet, and his uncle William Bond had married Sir William's sister Mary. Henry Jermyn Bond was married to Jane Godfrey, by whom he had two daughters (Charlotte and Judith) and three sons: James (b.1724), Henry[25] and Charles Jermyn Bond (b.1737).[26] The Gages seem to have visited the Bonds more than any other family in the area, and Hengrave was a home from home for the Bonds; the two families' social circles were virtually one and the same. The Bonds visited Hengrave twenty-seven times between 1732 and 1741 and members of the Gage family visited the Bonds sixty-seven times during the same period.

From the 1730s onwards Hengrave was a childless house, since Sir Thomas's brother William's marriage in 1741 produced no heir, and his youngest brother Edward died in battle in the service of Austria. Some evidence suggests that the Gages became a somewhat inward-looking family in this period. In 1735 Ann Pooley, the widow of John Lambe and a granddaughter of Sir William Gage, 2nd Baronet, set out to investigate whether the Gages had rightfully inherited the lands of John Gage of Harleston, including a place called Pipp's Farm. John Gage was the son of Henry Gage of Harleston, the brother of John Gage of Stoneham, who inherited the lands when John died without issue. When John Gage of Harleston died in 1723 'at a very great Age' and without an heir, Sir William Gage inherited his lands, which included a house in Arlington Street, London, which Sir Thomas Gage, 3rd Baronet later sold to Mary, Duchess of Norfolk.[27] It is possible that Pipp's Farm and the Arlington Street house constituted the estate that was disputed between Sir William Gage's younger children and Delariviere D'Ewes in 1729, in which Ann Pooley's husband, John Lambe, had been involved.

Ann Pooley was the niece of Judith Pooley, the wife of Henry Jermyn, Lord Dover.[28] Ann Pooley's brother enlisted the help of the Gages' friend and fellow Catholic, Thomas Short, to examine documents in the Evidence Room at Hengrave, in particular the will of Penelope Darcy

24 Payne, *Records of the English Catholics of 1715*, p. 16; Gage, *Thingoe*, p. 211.
25 Payne, *Records of the English Catholics of 1715*, p. 65.
26 *Diary*, 24 September 1737.
27 CUL Hengrave MS 1/4, fol. 343.
28 CUL Hengrave MS 1/4, fol. 333.

and her provisions for her son John Gage of Stoneham.[29] A few weeks later Ann Pooley visited Hengrave for herself and was unimpressed:

> I was at first received with great Coldness, I told him I had heard from the Council before whom the writings were paid, That the Title [to Pipp's Farm] was by no Means satisfactory, I was assured that the Title was as good as They could make it, That if I did approve of it, I might let alone.

Ann Pooley persuaded Sir Thomas to show her Penelope Darcy's will, but she complained that: 'As to the Writings They know Nothing; exact Pedigrees they have none, nor can They tell whether S[i]r. Will[iam] was Heir at law to Mr. John Gage or not ... In a word, They are the most trifling or the most ignorant People in their own Affairs.'[30] Ann assured her brother that 'I will leave no stone unturn'd since they have behaved so scandalously to disappoint them [the Gages]', and determined to examine a pedigree in the possession of Sir William Spring. There is no indication in the Hengrave papers of the outcome of the Pooleys' land claim, but it illustrates the importance of the Evidence Room and the validity of titles in a society where genteel status depended almost entirely upon land ownership and inheritance. Individuals at the fringes of the landed gentry, such as the Lambes and Pooleys, worked hard to establish land claims, even when they had laid dormant for generations. The Gages' apparent unawareness of their own history is, perhaps, a mark of their complacency in a period of relative security from hostile claims and sequestrations. The earliest known Gage family pedigree was drawn up by Dom Francis Howard, perhaps in reaction to the Pooleys' complaint. Although this original pedigree does not survive, a family tree begun in 1737 and added to by subsequent generations bears the legend 'copied from a ped[igree] on paper drawn out by Mr Francis Howard of the Ord[er] of St Benedict in possess[ion] of Mr Gage of Hengrave'.[31]

The Rector of Flempton-cum-Hengrave, William Wilson, found the Gages' administration of the Kytson almshouses in Hengrave village to be secretive, and he had little idea of how the 'hospital' was run, noting in 1735:

> There is also an Hospital in this Parish founded by the Lady Kitson about the year 1630 for Four Poor or Infirm Persons, with a yearly allowance of £7 10s Each & the mannour of Lackford tied for the Payment, but who are

---

29 Thomas Short to Mr Pooley, 15 October 1735, CUL Hengrave MS 93/1.

30 Ann Pooley to Mr Pooley, 27 November 1735, CUL Hengrave MS 93/1. CUL Hengrave MS 88/4/26 appears to be an earlier draft of Ann's letter.

31 CUL Hengrave MS 1/1, interleaved between fols 88 and 89.

Feoffees in Trust or how the money is disposed of We cannot tell, S[i]r Tho[ma]s Gage solely ordering & managing the same.[32]

The foundation of almshouses was often one of the few ways in which Catholics could influence the community in the absence of political power and, indeed, compete with parish charity – one famous Suffolk instance being the large almshouses constructed directly in front of Long Melford church by the Catholic Martin family. It is not surprising that the Gages had no desire for Wilson to get involved.[33] The inmates of the almshouses were family servants and so some, at least, were probably Catholics.

In 1735 Edward 'Teddy' Gage, Sir Thomas's youngest brother, took advantage of one of the few legitimate opportunities for military service open to Catholics, and volunteered to fight in Italy with the army of the Austrian Emperor in the War of the Polish Succession.[34] As a Catholic, Edward was unable to obtain a commission in the British Army, as it involved taking the Oath of Allegiance. This was not the first time Teddy had been to the Continent; on 24 August 1732 Jones recorded that he was leaving for Leghorn. Glickman has drawn attention to the encouragement given by the British government to Catholics to enter the Austrian service, given Austria's friendly relations with Britain compared to France.[35] Teddy Gage's decision to fight for Austria may have had more to do with the ease of obtaining a commission rather than consciously pro-Hanoverian sentiments, but it could also be an indication of the Gages' continuing political loyalism. In April 1741 Teddy Gage received a wound in an engagement with Prussian forces near Vienna. As the soldiers were carrying him from the battle lines to a field hospital, a cannon ball blew off his head.[36] Teddy was buried at an English convent in the Austrian Netherlands, possibly Bruges. Sir Thomas Rookwood Gage, 5th Baronet remembered of Delariviere D'Ewes that 'the early loss of her Husband and two favourite sons gave her a Melancholy Air, but interesting appearance'.[37]

William Gage travelled on less hazardous business, leaving for Portugal on 13 October 1737. William traded in a dark red wine – a Portuguese wine that is now known from its region of origin, Bairrada, but then was called 'annadia wine' after the vineyards at Anadia where the grapes were grown. Annadia wine was shipped from Coimbra and

32 Notes appended to the assessment of parish income, 18 June 1735, SRO(B) 806/1/61.
33 On the 'hospital' or almshouses see Gage, *Hengrave*, pp. 5–6.
34 *Diary*, 31 December 1735.
35 Glickman, *The English Catholic Community 1688–1745*, pp. 149–50.
36 Gage, *Hengrave*, p. 246; *Diary*, 27 April 1741; CUL Hengrave MS 1/4, fols 343–344.
37 CUL Hengrave MS 1/4, fol. 345.

the trade was in direct competition with the 'Port chaps' who shipped their wine from Oporto.[38] Both trades were largely controlled by the English. When William married Frances Harland in June 1741 a London newspaper described him as 'an eminent Portugal Merchant'.[39] As an ally of Britain and a friendly Catholic power, Portugal was an ideal location for a Catholic gentleman to pursue his mercantile interests; indeed, in Portugal it was a positive advantage to be both English and Catholic, which may explain why the Bishop of Coimbra personally rebaptised Delariviere's nephew Richard Holmes when he converted to Catholicism in March 1743.[40]

William was not the only member of the family engaged in foreign commerce; from time to time Hengrave played host to Sir Thomas's cousin Devereux Gage, the only son of Francis Gage of Packington in Staffordshire,[41] who in turn was the only son of Sir Edward Gage, 1st Baronet and his second wife Frances Aston. Devereux owned a plantation on the island of Montserrat. He stayed with the Bonds when he visited from 21 May to 3 June 1737, but dined at Hengrave. He returned from 19 September to 9 October. When he visited for a third time in July 1739 he was staying at Hengrave.[42]

In May 1739 Delariviere Gage bought a new house belonging to Sir John James.[43] Except in the summer months she did not live at Hengrave,[44] and until she bought a house of her own she may have occupied the Gages' townhouse in Northgate Street.[45] Alexius Jones visited Delariviere at her new house on 8 September 1741. However, on 13 August 1741, four days after he had last dined at the Bonds, Sir Thomas was taken ill. Two days later Jones rode out to Hengrave and Sir Thomas was taken to the doctor, probably Henry Short. Jones visited Hengrave on 17 August and again on 20 August; to make matters worse, 'Charly', the Bonds' youngest son, who had returned to them not long before,[46] came down with a fever on 26 August. On 31 August 1741, Sir Thomas drafted a will and bequeathed his entire personal estate to

---

[38]   Richard Holmes to Delariviere D'Ewes, 3 August 1743, CUL Hengrave MS 88/4/54; Thomas Bray to Sir William Gage, 23 October 1741, CUL Hengrave MS 88/4/41.

[39]   *London Evening Post* 2121 (13–16 June 1741).

[40]   Richard Holmes to Delariviere D'Ewes, 4 March 1743, CUL Hengrave MS 88/4/53.

[41]   Francis inherited Packington from his mother (Gage, *Hengrave*, p. 243).

[42]   *Diary*, 20 July 1739.

[43]   *Diary*, 19 May 1740.

[44]   *Diary*, 9 May 1741, 'Mrs Gage etc, to Hengrave for Summer'.

[45]   Jones made numerous references to short visits 'to Mrs Gage' before May 1740, implying that she was living in Bury, e.g. 4 January 1738, 'Our folks to Mrs Gage's'.

[46]   *Diary*, 23 June 1740, 'Master Charles home'. Presumably he had been staying with relatives.

his mother as well as the manor of Harleston and lands in the parish of Haughley. He nominated Delariviere as his sole executrix.[47] The will was witnessed by Thomas Short and Dr Henry Short, who was probably present as Sir Thomas's doctor. Charly Bond survived his fever but Sir Thomas, in spite of hopes of his recovery, died at Hengrave on 1 September 1741, with Jones in attendance, presumably to administer the last rites. His memorial inscription in Hengrave church described him as 'avid in religion, supremely tenacious (*tenax*) in the worship of God'.[48] *Tenax* in this case was probably a euphemism for Catholicism; he had successfully held on to the old faith.

The Benedictine mission

Benedictine missions of the eighteenth century cannot be understood in terms of a simple division between sedentary domestic chaplaincies to the gentry and independent urban missions. Geoffrey Scott has drawn attention to cases of town chaplaincies supplying priests to rural centres and rural chaplains spending time in their patrons' townhouses.[49] In the case of Bury both situations occurred; Dom Francis Howard, originally chaplain to the Gages at Hengrave, effectively became the 'town' missioner from 1741, and may have spent much of his time at the Gages' townhouse in Northgate Street. Furthermore, Alexius Jones, who was originally chaplain to the Bonds in Bury itself, spent periods serving the Gages at Hengrave outside the town. However, unlike Alban Dawney's East Anglian 'riding circuit' mission, patronised and funded by the Bedingfields and Southcotts,[50] the Hengrave and Bury mission was largely stable and located in two fixed places (Hengrave and Bury).

Francis Howard's background is elusive, but he may have belonged to the Howard family of Corby Castle in Cumberland, who provided a number of monks to the English Benedictine Congregation in the first half of the eighteenth century.[51] Alternatively, he may have been a

---

47 PROB 11/715.

48 Gage, *Thingoe*, p. 232.

49 G. Scott, *Gothic Rage Undone: English Monks in the Age of Enlightenment* (Bath: Downside Abbey, 1992), p. 83.

50 Glickman, *The English Catholic Community 1688–1745*, p. 55.

51 These included Dom Augustine Howard (1644–1718), see Birt, *Obit Book of the English Benedictines, 1600–1912*, p. 78; Dom Joseph Howard (d.1733), see Birt, *Obit Book of the English Benedictines, 1600–1912*, p. 88; Philip Howard, who was educated at St Gregory's Douai and was the only lay member of the 'Society of St. Edmund', the monks' Enlightenment 'college', see G. Scott, *Gothic Rage Undone: English Monks in the Age of Enlightenment* (Bath: Downside Abbey, 1992); his son Henry Howard who became a monk, see Scott, *Gothic Rage Undone*, pp. 185–86; and Dom Placid Howard, President of the Congregation 1753–66, see Birt, *Obit Book of*

descendent of Sir Charles Howard of Croglin by Dorothy Widdrington; Sir Charles was the sixth son of Lord William Howard, the second son of Thomas Howard, 2nd Duke of Norfolk, and had a number of sons.[52] Francis Howard was a novice at St Laurence's, Dieulouard in 1707 and he was professed in 1708. On the occasion of a visitation of the monastery on 13 March 1716 he was acting as Cellarer, apparently an important role at Dieulouard,[53] but this appointment came to an end when St Laurence's burnt down in 1717. On 23 April the South Province accounts record that he was given money to make the journey from Bath, where the Benedictines had a headquarters at 'the Bell-tree house',[54] to 'Whallam Hall in Suffolk'. There is no such place, and Allanson concluded that Whallam must have been a mistake for Coldham Hall. Howard was certainly in Bury in 1720, as he testified that Bishop Stonor had confirmed the three sons of Delariviere D'Ewes in that year.[55] In 1725 Howard was elected Secretary to the Provincial Chapter of Canterbury (the South Province) and he was Provost of Cambridge in 1733. Howard was appointed a General Preacher in 1741.[56] In 1749 he was appointed a Definitor,[57] and in the same year he was created titular Cathedral Prior of Norwich.[58]

Francis Howard laboured in relative obscurity at a particularly challenging time for the English Benedictine mission. Between 1720 and 1740 the number of monks in England declined as a result of the policies of Thomas Southcott, the virulently Jacobite President of the English Benedictine Congregation.[59] Southcott's hostility to the vicars apostolic, who were generally more sympathetic to the expedient of establishing friendly relations with the Hanoverian regime, made life

---

the English Benedictines, 1600–1912, p. 105, and Scott, Gothic Rage Undone, pp. 44, 197.

[52] 'The Junior Branches of the Howards', The Gentleman's Magazine 103 (1833), pp. 404–6.

[53] In the 1780s, and presumably earlier, the brewing-house was one of Dieulouard's main sources of income; see Aveling, The Handle and the Axe, p. 312.

[54] On the Bell-tree house see Scott, Gothic Rage Undone, p. 47.

[55] Hengrave Register, 10 June 1720.

[56] Allanson, Biography of the English Benedictines, p. 190.

[57] South Province Book R, p. 87. The General Chapter of the English Benedictine Congregation elected five Definitors to assist the President; these ran the Congregation, together with the two Provincials; see Lunn, The English Benedictines 1540–1688, p. 106.

[58] Birt, Obit Book of the English Benedictines, 1600–1912, p. 101; Bellenger, p. 73. The idea that the English Benedictines had inherited the ordinary jurisdiction of the sees of the Benedictine cathedral-minsters of pre-Reformation England was confirmed by Pope Urban VIII in the Bull Plantata, although in practice the Cathedral priors did not control the Benedictine mission unless they held other posts such as Definitor.

[59] Scott, Gothic Rage Undone, p. 84.

difficult for monks in England.[60] Given the strong taint of Jacobitism on the English Benedictines it is, perhaps, surprising that the Gages welcomed a Benedictine mission in this very period, in the light of Sir William Gage's record of support for the political status quo. The only hints of Jacobitism in Alexius Jones's diary are occasional references to political events such as the Porteous Riots, which became a focus of anti-Hanoverian feeling in Scotland,[61] and a remark on 28 December 1736: 'K: George like to be cast away'. It was rumoured in Rome that riots in London that year were in favour of King James,[62] although the anti-Irish Rag Fair Riots could scarcely be described as pro-Jacobite, and Jones was evidently out of touch with events in the capital. However, unsurprisingly Jones expressed no overt preference for a Hanoverian or Jacobite king in his diary.

During the 1720s and 1730s Benedictines endeavoured to separate themselves from complete dependence on gentry patrons in order to have the freedom to minister to poor Catholics. Howard's mission was centrally funded to a certain extent; on 27 November 1752 the South Province bought 150 'East India Bonds' to fund his work.[63] Bonds and stock investments were an important source of missionary income, although both the religious orders and the seculars suffered financially from the collapse of the 'South Sea Bubble' in 1720.[64] The extent to which the mission was funded by Delariviere and Sir Thomas Gage is hard to know with certainty, but if they did give money it was to Howard personally; the South Province accounts contain no donations from the Gages. However, Delariviere was the custodian of two treasures for the South Province in 1730, and it seems likely that the special relationship between the chaplain and the lady of the house pertained at Hengrave as it did in other Benedictine missions.[65] The South Province Book R, of contracts and rents, contains the following entry, evidently written after 1741:

> Item the same Mr Banister mentions an old valuable vestment supposed to be given by St Edward the Confessor, w[i]th a silver guilt Chalice in the hands of Mrs Gage Mother to late S[i]r Thomas. Mr Fran[cis] Howard says mr Banister took the said Vestment & carried to Bath An: Dom: 1730.[66]

---

60   Ibid. pp. 60–61.

61   *Diary*, 7 April 1737: 'Great bustle about Capt[ain] Porteus's affair'.

62   A. Shield and A. Lang, *The King over the Water* (London: Longmans, Green and Co., 1907), p. 403.

63   Allanson, *Biography of the English Benedictines*, p. 190.

64   Aveling, *The Handle and the Axe*, pp. 311–12.

65   Scott, *Gothic Rage Undone*, p. 93.

66   South Province Book R, p. 71.

The vestment's destination in Bath was the Benedictine headquarters at the Bell-tree house, where Banister had also stowed 'two large Reliquaries of Silver, a Crucifix, [and] two Silver Bread Boxes' given by Mrs Banks. In 1725 the Conquest family of Houghton Conquest in Bedfordshire gave the South Province a golden pyx and a silver-gilt chalice; Mrs Conquest in turn looked after relics belonging to the Province on its behalf.[67] Under the circumstances of the time it is not surprising that the laity were entrusted with items belonging to the monks, but it is unclear in the case of Delariviere D'Ewes whether the vestment and chalice mentioned were heirlooms of the Gages given to the South Province and retained by Delariviere for safe-keeping or whether they had been entrusted to Delariviere and had no particular connection with Hengrave. It is very unlikely that the vestment was as old as Edward the Confessor, but there was evidently a story and a tradition attached to it. The preservation of mediaeval vestments was part of that 'squirearchical culture of public virtue, grounded in principles of lineage and patriotism', harking back to the Middle Ages that characterised some early eighteenth-century gentry families.[68] Furthermore, it should not be forgotten that devotion to St Edward the Confessor was an important symbolic element of the Jacobite mythos, especially among Benedictine writers.[69]

The appearance of mission registers in the 1730s was a sign of a growing need to serve the whole Catholic community in a locality, and register-keeping was a key feature of what Marshall and Scott have called the 'Catholic gentry congregationalism' of the eighteenth century.[70] Mission registers were not so much legal or even ecclesiastical records, but 'personal documents' belonging to a particular monk and testifying to his pastoral care for the local Catholic community. The *Hengrave Register*, which is the third oldest Benedictine example to survive after Everingham (1719) and Brindle (1722), and the oldest from the South Province, belongs to this category.[71] The keeping of registers was a requirement of the Provincial Chapter, which insisted

---

67   South Province Book R, p. 70: 'Memorandum Mar: the 26. 1742. There belongs to the South Province several valuable Relicks in the Widow C[on]quest's Hands. Item a Gold Pix in the present Provincials Hands. Item one silver guilt in Mr Greenwoods hands. These were given by Mrs Conquest for the Use of the South Provincial. Item there belongs to the South Province, w[hi]ch are now at the Bell tree House in Bath given by my Lady Banks two large Reliquaries of Silver, a Crucifix, two Silver Bread Boxes. Witnessed by Mr Banester. July the 16. 1725.'

68   Glickman, *The English Catholic Community 1688–1745*, p. 68.

69   Ibid. pp. 97, 211–12.

70   Marshall and Scott, *Catholic Gentry in English Society*, p. 19.

71   Scott, *Gothic Rage Undone*, p. 86.

in 1733 that they be kept in order to resolve difficulties,[72] presumably concerning baptisms and weddings. Catholic priests did not conduct funerals, since by law these took place in the parish church, and Francis Howard recorded only baptisms and confirmations (his successor John Gage also recorded deaths and marriages). The survival of the *Hengrave Register* is probably an accident, and there were doubtless other early Benedictine registers that have not survived. The blank quarto notebook in which the register was written was later reused for the Cash and Account Book of the North Province from 1806–9, which may explain its survival.

The personal character of Howard's register is reinforced by the fact that he noted his favourite maxims, commonplaces and books in Latin at the beginning of the document: 'If you know Christ, it matters not that you know nothing else; if you do not know Christ, it matters not whatever else you know.' Howard quoted from St Bernard: 'From where may a man be proud whose conception is blame, to be born is punishment, life, necessity, and to die?' He also included some maxims with a rather Benedictine flavour: 'Say without end prayers, lead a life empty of crime, do your work wisely and bear your burden patiently'; 'To pray before the time is providence, after the time, negligence, at the time, obedience.' Howard copied a section from a book on the fall of Constantinople; perhaps the plight of the Greeks might have struck a chord with the situation of Catholics in England: 'Now the Greeks are under the tyranny of the Turks, so much so that while their Bishops elect the Patriarchs, they have to be confirmed by the Turk, and they must pay each year a very heavy tribute.' Perhaps Howard was thinking of the burden of recusancy fines and proposals by some, such as Thomas Strickland, that the Hanoverian King should approve the appointments of vicars apostolic.

All of the baptisms in the register were conducted by Howard and there is no mention of Jones at all. Between 1734 and 1751 Howard performed thirty-five baptisms, an average of just over two per year. However, the register makes plain that Howard's role changed considerably from 1742, when he baptised Laurence Crask, son of William Crask 'a Shoomaker in Bury'; up to that point, he had baptised only children born in Hengrave village or with an association with the Gage family, indicating that he was only the chaplain at Hengrave at this time. Between 1734 and 1740 he baptised three children of Richard Gardener, who lived in Hengrave, and two children of Thomas Morley. It is unclear whether Morley lived in Hengrave village or not, but the godmother of his daughter Anne was 'Mrs Dowager Gage of Hengrave', Delari-

---

72 Ibid. p. 87.

viere D'Ewes. It is highly likely that these baptisms were performed at Hengrave; John Stockings, 'Gardener at Hengrave Hall' and Mary Monker, 'housemaid at Hengrave', became the godparents of Richard Gardener on 9 December 1734, while Francis Humbarston 'Steward at Hengrave' and Mary Nice, the Hengrave housekeeper, were godparents to John Gardener on 30 May 1740.

The reason for Howard's change of role from domestic to urban chaplain was the death of the secular priest Hugh Owen in October 1741. After 1742 Howard, as priest to the urban Catholic community, baptised more children and did so more frequently. Of the godparents of these children, seventeen are specifically stated as 'both of Bury' and several more were probably inhabitants of the town as well. From 1742 the only individuals who appear in the register who were not from Bury are Edward Sulyard and 'Mrs Dunne' (who travelled up from London), Francis Sulyard of Buxhall (later of Haughley) and George Simpson of Coldham. There seems little doubt that Howard did not move from Bury and people came to him.

Appearances of the gentry in Howard's register are fairly infrequent, although they occasionally acted as godparents. Delariviere D'Ewes and Henry Jermyn Bond were godparents to Anne Morley on 31 May 1737, and Sir William Gage and his aunt Laelia Huddleston were godparents to William Morley on 22 May 1743; the Morleys were evidently favoured with the Gages' special attention, perhaps because they were senior servants at Hengrave. The only gentry children to be baptised during this period were Edward Sulyard on 9 August 1744 and Elizabeth Sulyard on 19 June 1746, both children of Francis Sulyard, younger brother of Edward Sulyard, the head of the family, who lived in London at this time. Francis was living at Buxhall in 1744 but by 1746 he was at the family seat, Haughley Park.

Francis Howard took care to record, in most cases, the date of birth of the child as well as the date of baptism; this was information that John Gage did not provide in the 1750s and 1760s. Furthermore, it went beyond the information usually recorded in parish registers. The average time that elapsed between birth and baptism for the seventeen children whose dates of birth were recorded was nine days; many children were baptised the day after their birth.[73] In an age when parents were anxious to have their children baptised as soon as possible, this indicates that the priest was readily available and that Catholic baptisms were less than furtive; indeed, the fact that Howard wrote his register

---

[73] I have excluded children who were considerably older when they were baptised such as Elizabeth Sulyard, whom Howard thought to be about six months old (*Hengrave Register* 19 June 1746), and James Betts who was six or seven months old (*Hengrave Register* 7 August 1746).

in plain English indicates that he had little fear of anti-Catholic feeling around him. However, the Catholic community in Bury seems to have been fairly insular at this period; only one child with a Protestant father (James Betts) was baptised by Howard, and it is interesting that this child, at six or seven months old, was the oldest child to receive the sacrament. Either Betts had already been baptised in the parish church and Howard's was a conditional rebaptism, or it had taken the child's mother six months to persuade the father that he should be baptised a Catholic.[74]

There is evidence in the register to suggest that Howard never fully embraced his role as an urban missionary and did not know his congregation particularly well; he baptised no less than five children of a certain Mr Horseman (probably the 'James Horsman, labourer' of the 1745 list of Catholic nonjurors)[75] but on every occasion left the man's Christian name blank. It is surprising that Howard had not come to know the man's name when he baptised so many of his children, even if he was a mere labourer. Likewise, Howard was able to name the mothers of only twelve of the thirty-five children he baptised.

Although the Benedictine mission was to a greater or lesser extent wholly dependent on the patronage of the Gages and Bonds, the keeping of a mission register was an important symbol of a mission's independent existence beyond a mere chaplaincy to a particular family. It is very likely that Alexius Jones ministered in and from the domestic chapel in the Bonds' house in Eastgate Street, later mentioned in John Gage the Younger's mission register,[76] while in the 1730s Francis Howard may have ministered at Hengrave in the same chapel that existed there in the 1670s, and of which no trace survives. Although Jones and Howard both strongly identified with their patrons' families (Jones referred to the Bonds as 'our folks'),[77] they were a great deal more than gentry chaplains.

If the *Hengrave Register* was all that survived of the Benedictine mission we would have a limited idea of how it operated. However, in the early nineteenth century John Gage the antiquary came into possession of an anonymous diary kept between 1731–43, which was given to him by Lady Bedingfield.[78] John Gage attempted to deduce the identity of the diarist, who never identifies himself directly, by assembling all the personal information he could find in the diary, but he was unsuccessful.

[74] *Hengrave Register*, 7 August 1746.
[75] SRO(B) D8/1/3 bundle 2.
[76] *Bury Register*, 21 May 1759.
[77] *Diary*, 10 September 1737; 4 January 1738.
[78] CUL Hengrave MS 69. The diary runs from 1 September 1731 to 15 July 1742.

However, it is obvious from the nature of the author's life that he was a missionary priest; he was without financial means and completely dependent on the patronage of the gentry he served. His regular visits to London and his role in accompanying his patrons to the Continent from 3–31 July 1735 are also suggestive. The priest was scrupulous to avoid any mention of his sacred functions, which were then theoretically still punishable by death, and like many missionary priests he seems to have masqueraded (or actually acted) as a private tutor; John Gage deduced this from the references to James Bond as 'Master Bond',[79] or simply 'Master'.[80]

Rather than referring to the sacraments and missionary activity by euphemisms the Bury diarist, like William Mawhood, a Catholic diarist of a slightly later period,[81] confined his daily record to a few formulaic and often unilluminating sentences, giving the time at which he woke up, a description of the weather in the morning, the location where he spent the day and night, a description of the evening weather and the time he went to bed. The only overt signs that the diarist was a Catholic, in fact, are his annual noting of the feast of Corpus Christi, a solitary reference to a Plenary Indulgence,[82] and the notes he made of those who 'died P[rotestant]'.[83] Of course, to anyone in the know it would have been obvious from his social circle that he was a Catholic. Although he never referred to conversations or activities, he did record who he met, and this is an invaluable record of the nature of the Catholic social network in the Bury area.

The surviving records of the Bury mission provide circumstantial evidence that demonstrate beyond reasonable doubt that the diarist was Dom John Alexius Jones, who served the mission at Hengrave and Bury from 1732 until his death. Jones was born in Middlesex in 1679 or 1680 and professed a monk at St Gregory's, Douai on 15 August 1699. He was ordained a priest in 1705 before he embarked on the English mission three years later; the South Province accounts noted money 'given to Mr J at his coming to town' on 6 October 1708.[84] Jones began his missionary work in the north of England (in the 1730s he paid visits to York, Pocklington and Wyton). According to Allanson, Jones sided

[79] *Diary*, 7 January 1733.

[80] *Diary*, 3 July 1735.

[81] The London woollen draper William Mawhood kept a diary 1764–90 and used terms such as 'Prayers' for the Mass and 'the necessary' for confession; see E. E. Reynolds (ed.), *The Mawhood Diary* (London: CRS, 1956).

[82] *Diary*, 4 May 1741.

[83] *Diary*, 8 June 1736; 19 December 1737; 6 March 1738; 14 June 1738; 13 August 1738; 3 October 1738; 25 May 1740.

[84] Allanson, *Biography of the English Benedictines*, p. 189.

with President Laurence Fenwick in the unsettled period after Fenwick's election in 1717, when the finances of the English Benedictine Congregation were left in a parlous state by the British government's response to the 1715 Jacobite rising. Fenwick, unlike his opponent Thomas Southcott, was not a strident Jacobite, and he was supported mainly by younger monks who had not experienced the revival under James II. Fenwick was seen by his opponents as an ally of the vicars apostolic and a loyalist.[85]

By 1731 Jones was based in London, from where he came to Bury in 1732.[86] The *Obit Book of the English Benedictines* records that in 1737 Jones became the chaplain at Hengrave, where he remained until his death on 10 August 1755.[87] Such a change of role seems to be indicated by Jones's remark of 17 October 1738, 'I began at Hengrave for the 1st time'. This does not seem to have meant a change of role for Francis Howard, although Anselm Cranmer, the editor of Gregory Allanson's *Biography of the English Benedictines*, thought that Howard 'changed places' with Jones.[88] Howard's role certainly changed in 1741 with the death of Owen, and Jones rather than Howard seems to have served the Gages at Hengrave after this point.

Francis Howard and 'Mr Owen' make regular appearances in the diary, but Jones himself is never mentioned, an argument in favour of the author being Jones himself. The diarist arrived in Bury in the same year as Jones (1732), he had apparent links with Douai (Jones was a monk of St Gregory's) and he paid a visit to Wyton in the East Riding of Yorkshire; this was a Benedictine mission recently established by Dom Henry Augustine Brigham (d.1738).[89] The diary notes Brigham's death on 5 January 1738. Unless the diarist was a monk, there would have been little reason for him to visit Wyton. The diarist was clearly a Benedictine, and Jones was the only priest in Bury at the time who fitted this description.

Jones began his diary in London on 1 October 1731. He made frequent references to Lincoln's Inn Fields, the Portuguese Embassy and Warwick Street, all of which were the locations of Catholic chapels. Among Jones's London friends was 'Mrs Holmes';[90] John Gage the antiquary informs us in an annotation that Mrs Holmes was born Mere-

85 Scott, *Gothic Rage Undone*, p. 54. On Fenwick and the discord in the Congregation see ibid. pp. 51–63.

86 Allanson, *Biography of the English Benedictines*, p. 189, quoting South Province Accounts: 'Paid to Mr J his expenses going to Bury 1732'.

87 Birt, *Obit Book of the English Benedictines, 1600–1912*, p. 101; Bellenger, 77.

88 Allanson, *Biography of the English Benedictines*, p. 190.

89 Birt, *Obit Book of the English Benedictines, 1600–1912*, 91.

90 *Diary*, 1 October 1731; 10 October 1731; 6 October 1732.

lina D'Ewes and was Delariviere's eldest sister.[91] Jones gives no indication of the circumstances of his being invited or sent to Bury, but he went 'to Mr Bond's' on 18 July 1732.

In the absence of correspondence from this period, we can only guess at the possible reasons for the establishment of the Benedictine mission at Hengrave. The Gage family's connections with the Benedictines go back to the 1660s, when Sir Edward Gage paid them an annuity for the privilege of holding former monastic lands, but there is no evidence of a specific Benedictine link after 1679, when Jerome Hesketh was linked to Sir Edward's house in Bloomsbury Market. In the short term, the marriage of John Gage to Elizabeth Rookwood may have prepared the ground for the monks; after all, Francis Howard was chaplain to the Rookwoods at Coldham before he arrived at Hengrave. Two of Delariviere D'Ewes's sisters were associated with the Benedictines. Mary D'Ewes was married to Francis Tasburgh of Bodney, cousin of George Tasburgh of Flixton who was the patron of one of the oldest Benedictine missions in East Anglia, established at Flixton in 1657. As we have seen, another of her sisters, Merelina, was an acquaintance of Dom Alexius Jones in London before his departure for Bury. For the present, the precise impetus for an expanded Benedictine mission in West Suffolk remains obscure.

Jones paid his first visit to Hengrave, 'a noble house', on 29 July 1732. Thereafter he paid regular visits,[92] albeit not as many as his patron Henry Bond. Jones rarely used the form 'we to Hengrave', as he did on his first visit, implying a trip by the Bond family, preferring 'I to Hengrave'. Jones's solitary visits could mean that he went there to celebrate the sacraments; he noted explicitly when he went to Hengrave for dinner (as on 25 May 1736), suggesting that his other visits were not mere social calls. Jones designed his diary to conceal his pastoral duties as the social round of the gentry, and only the pattern of visits can suggest their true nature. Whatever their character, the visits

---

[91] Merelina married first Richard Elwes and her son by her first marriage, Richard, was in Portugal when Delariviere wrote her will in December 1744 (Payne, *Records of the English Catholics of 1715*, p. 65).

[92] For Jones's visits to Hengrave up to the death of Sir Thomas, *Diary* 7 September 1732; 17 February 1733; 30 October 1733; 20 September 1734; 9 October 1734; 28 November 1734; 10 January 1735; 29 May 1735; 11 October 1735; 16 March 1736; 1 April 1736; 25 May 1736; 16 November 1736; 29 March 1737; 30 March 1737; 13 April 1737; 27 May 1737; 9 June 1737; 13 June 1737; 16 June 1737; 27 February 1738; 1 March 1738; 18 April 1738; 18 May 1738; 23 May 1738; 22 August 1738; 30 January 1739; 1 March 1739; 23 April 1739; 18 June 1739; 7 June 1739; 16 October 1739; 26 October 1739; 26 November 1739; 11 April 1740; 16 May 1740; 20 May 1740; 21 May 1740; 12 June 1740; 24 June 1740; 23 October 1740; 18 May 1741; 14 June 1741; 12 July 1741; 2 August 1741.

to Hengrave were reciprocated by the Gages, who frequently dined with the Bonds in Bury. 'The 2 Mrs Gages', meaning Delariviere D'Ewes and Elizabeth Rookwood, were guests, as well as Sir Thomas Gage himself and his brothers.

The *Obit Book of the English Benedictines* (as well as Allanson's accounts of Howard and Jones) assumed a structure for the Bury/Hengrave mission based on gentry chaplaincy, and attached Howard and Jones to Hengrave as if both were entirely dependent on the Gages. Alexius Jones's diary reveals that the reality was considerably more complex. If there was ever a resident priest at Hengrave, it is likely that he was Francis Howard, who often appears in the diary in the company of the Gages. The diary provides no evidence of Howard's 'cover story', but he may well have posed as tutor to Sir Thomas's youngest brother Edward in the 1730s. There are several references to Jones visiting 'Mr Howard at the Angel', a large coaching inn (and now a hotel) on Angel Hill, facing the Abbey gateway.[93] It is possible that Howard based himself at a large inn, but on the other hand this is an isolated reference, and it may have suited Howard's purposes at the time to be in Bury rather than at Hengrave. The priests seem to have used the Angel and another inn, the Greyhound, to meet up.[94] Another favourite haunt was 'Hannibal's' or 'Bal's', probably a coffee house.[95] Among these meeting places the Greyhound, which was on the east side of the Buttermarket and later became the Suffolk Hotel, was particularly significant since its landlord, William Adams, was a Catholic.[96] It is possible that the Greyhound was one of the locations in the town where Owen conducted his ministry and said Mass.

Jones visited Hengrave an average of every four months between July 1732 and November 1736, although there were periods when he visited as often as every month (September–November 1733 and March–May 1736). From March 1737 until Sir Thomas Gage's death in September 1741, Jones was at Hengrave much more frequently (around twice a month), and he did not spend any time outside the Bury area during this period. Unless he was dining with the Gages, Jones never specified the purpose of his visit. If Howard was the resident priest, then it is likely

---

93 The Angel was one of Bury's largest inns, on Angel Hill facing the gateway of the Abbey, *Diary* 17 June 1736; 3 March 1737; 20 July 1737; 19 August 1737; 21 September 1737; 21 December 1737; 16 July 1742.

94 G. Nixon, *Old Inns and Beerhouses of Bury St. Edmunds* (Brandon, 1996), p. 20. For the Greyhound, *Diary*, 12 September 1737; 21 June 1738; 21 September 1738.

95 For Hannibal's, *Diary*, 8 August 1737; 21 September 1738.

96 *Hengrave Register*, 11 May 1740: 'Mr Will[ia]m Adams Master of the Greyhound Tavern in Bury' was godfather to Frances Morley. The site of the Greyhound is now occupied by Waterstone's bookshop and the Edinburgh Woollen Mill.

that he would have said Mass for the family. One possible reason for Jones's occasional visits would have been to hear Howard's own confession, another could be that he was covering for Howard's absences on the Continent or elsewhere. This was certainly the case from October 1738 to June 1739, when Howard was at Dieulouard.[97]

Jones's conventional and formulaic record could not disguise the magnitude of the crisis that enveloped the town in September 1732. Jones noted 'Smallpox at Bury' on 1 September. Bury Fair opened as normal on 21 September, but the gentry reacted to the outbreak much as they had to bubonic plague in the previous century, by leaving town. Just over a hundred years earlier, in 1631, Bury had experienced a serious outbreak of plague, and in many ways smallpox was the plague's eighteenth-century successor. Howard accompanied Sir Thomas to London and then Bath on 25 September, Sir Thomas's birthday; perhaps Delariviere was fearful that her son would contract the disease, and sent him away. On 30 September Jones remarked, 'Never was known such a scarcity of water', and the suffering of the poor in Bury is hinted at by the fact that the Jesuit College of the Holy Apostles sent 'to the poor at Bury distressed by the smallpox, at Mr Owen's request, £1:3:0' in January 1733.[98] In November 1732 Jones paid a brief visit to London; in January 1733 James Bond, his tutee, contracted the smallpox but survived.[99]

Hengrave did not fare so well, and Jones recorded the death of Henrietta Spring (Harriet in the *Diary*), Sir Thomas's cousin, on 24 January, at the age of thirty. Only four days later her sister Delariviere, the 'little Dilly sly and sleek' of Richardson Pack's poem, suffered the same fate at the age of twenty-seven.[100] Both are buried in Pakenham church, where their memorial slab is still visible in front of the high altar. It seems highly likely that Harriet and Delariviere were victims of smallpox. Sir Thomas's aunt Catherine, the wife of Dr Henry Sorrel, who died on 5 April, may also have been killed by the outbreak,[101] and her tomb remains in the south aisle of St Mary's Church in Bury. Since the disease showed no sign of abating, on 18 June 1733 Jones left for Thetford with Mr Bond as well as Sir Thomas, Francis Howard and Dr

---

97   On 17 October 1738 Jones wrote 'I began at Hengrave for the 1st time', on 25 October he recorded 'a letter from Mr. Fr. Howard, Dieulouard Church robb'd some time ago' and on 15 June 1739 he wrote 'Mr Howard home to Hengrave'.

98   Foley, vol. 5, p. 538.

99   *Diary*, 7 January 1733.

100   CUL Hengrave MS 1/4, fol. 335.

101   Tymms, *An Architectural and Historical Account of the Church of St. Mary, Bury St. Edmunds*, p. 201.

Short.[102] The gentlemen amused themselves as best they could in the small Norfolk town, Mr Bond attending 'a Raffle'[103] while Jones went fishing in the River Thet.[104] Sir Thomas's brother William paid them a visit on 28 June.

On 14 July the party returned to Bury, and on 22 July the 'Corporation attested Bury free from the Smallpox'. The Thetford holiday was uncharacteristic, and it is likely that it was taken, like Sir Thomas's and Howard's trip to Bath, in an attempt to avoid the disease or at least to keep away from Bury, which in light of the water shortage could not have been a pleasant place to be. The blandness of the diary disguises what must have been a tragic event for the town, and Jones may have been largely insulated from the suffering that the secular priest Hugh Owen was left to address. It was not the last time that Bury was to be visited by an epidemic; on 4 May 1737 Jones noted 'Measles rage in town, many die'.

On 3 July 1735 Jones left Bury with Mr and Mrs Bond, their son James and the housekeeper Mary Wilson,[105] and set sail for Calais, arriving at Douai on 20 August. Jones stayed there until the 22nd when he set out for Cambrai to the south, leaving on 24 August. He returned to Douai on the 25th and was in Béthune on 27 August on his way to St Omer, where he stayed for only one day. From 28–31 August Jones stayed at Calais before sailing for Dover. He remained in London until 13 September when he set out for Yorkshire, dividing his time between York, Pocklington and Wyton. On 14 October he returned to London, and he did not resume his duties in Bury until 22 October. The record of Jones's travels is very brief and, for obvious reasons, contains no detail, but the entry on 24 October, 'They [i.e. the Bonds] rec'd a letter about Mr. Jemmy', makes it almost certain that the purpose of the trip to France was to deliver Jones's tutee to the English College at Douai for his 'Humanities'.[106]

Visits to the Continent, as the diary of William Mawhood relates in rather more detail, were a feature of life for Catholic families, who would not allow their sons to be educated at Protestant schools, or who

---

102   There were two Dr Shorts alive at this time, Henry and Philip, the sons of Thomas Short and Ursula Daniel of Acton; see Young, 'The Shorts of Bury St Edmunds', pp. 193–94. However, since the diarist does not differentiate two Dr Shorts, presumably only one of them was living in Bury in the 1730s.

103   *Diary*, 3 July 1733.

104   *Diary*, 7 July 1733, 'Caught some fish'.

105   'Molly' in the *Diary*. Mary Wilson, 'housekeeper to hen: Jermyn Bond Esq.' was the godmother of Frances Morley (*Hengrave Register*, 11 May 1740).

106   At a later stage Henry was also sent to school and seems to have fared badly; Mr Bond received a 'dismal account' of his son on 27 November 1741.

wanted their daughters to become nuns. Very often it was the priest, under the family's patronage, who arranged for a boy to go 'beyond seas', and so it is likely that Jones was in charge of setting up the trip. The college was probably the English College, although the fact that there were several English educational institutions in the city makes it impossible to say with absolute certainty which one Jemmy was sent to, and Jones's involvement could suggest that he was being sent to St Gregory's. Jemmy was eleven years old in October 1735,[107] which was the usual age for a boy to begin his formal studies at what was effectively a junior seminary that trained the sons of gentry destined for the secular life alongside those who would choose the priesthood.

Although the Benedictine mission could not have functioned without the patronage of the Bonds and Gages, it is evident from Alexius Jones's diary that missionary activity extended well beyond the limits of the family providing patronage. The fact that the Gages owned a townhouse in Bury and that Delariviere D'Ewes acquired her own house in 1739 ensured that Francis Howard was never trapped at Hengrave. The closeness of the Gages and Bonds certainly helped the mission, as it made it natural for Jones to serve at Hengrave during Howard's absence at Dieulouard in 1738–39. Howard and Jones may have trained at different monasteries, but they must have felt a spiritual affinity that allowed them to work together very closely. However, the smallpox outbreak of 1732–33 demonstrated that there was still a role for the 'town mission', since both Jones and Howard were tied to the movements of their patrons, who left the town, leaving poor Catholics to be attended to by the secular priest Hugh Owen.

Hugh Owen (or Owens) was born in 1669 on the Isle of Man, the son of Robert Owens. He entered the Venerable English College in Rome in 1689 and was ordained in 1692.[108] Owen was at Douai for a time before leaving for the English mission.[109] He was certainly in Bury in 1718, when he officiated at the clandestine wedding of John Gage and Elizabeth Rookwood.[110] Jones mentioned Owen considerably less frequently than Francis Howard,[111] and the fact that he recorded his visits 'to Mr Owen' would seem to imply that Owen had lodgings of his own in Bury.[112] Owen died from a fall on 19 October 1741, and it is possible

---

[107]   Alexius Jones recorded Jemmy's ninth birthday in his *Diary*, 15 October 1773.

[108]   G. Anstruther, *The Secular Priests* (Ware: St Edmund's College, 1969–77), vol. 3, p. 156.

[109]   Bellenger, p. 93 thought that Owen was trained in Malta.

[110]   CUL Hengrave 76/1.

[111]   Less frequently than Mr Howard, *Diary*, 20 December 1733; 5 February 1735; 21 May 1735; 7 November 1735.

[112]   *Diary*, 21 May 1734; 7 November 1734.

that he was the 'Mr Henry Oweing' buried in St James's churchyard on 21 October.[113] The Benedictines were on friendly terms with Owen, and Jones certainly bought books from him.[114] In addition to Owen, the monks met with other priests from time to time. The 'Carteret' of the diary was probably the Jesuit Philip Carteret (1694–1756), Provincial of the English Jesuits from 1751–56.[115] On 16 July 1742 Jones met with Howard and a man called Rigby at the Angel coaching inn; on 15 July 1743 he noted 'Mr Rigby turn'd P[rotestant]'. Since the Angel was a meeting place for Jones, Howard and Owen, Mr Rigby may have been a fellow priest as well.[116]

The Gages' and Bonds' social circle

One aspect of Catholic life that Jones unfailingly recorded in his diary was the socialising of the gentry. The names of everyone who dined with the Bonds were noted meticulously, and thus the diary presents a comprehensive picture of the social universe of the Bonds, with whom the Gages were associated so closely that it is as much a record of their social contacts as well. The names of guests ranged from the familiar, local and Catholic to local Protestants, visiting Catholics and far-flung family members.

Outside their own family members,[117] the most well-established of the Bury Catholics to visit the Bonds were the Shorts. Thomas Short, 'Dr Short' and Charlotte Short were fairly regular visitors.[118] Thomas Short may have been the brother of the doctors Philip and Henry (and 'Dr Short' may have been either of these); Charlotte Short was their unmarried aunt, since Jones refers to her as 'Mrs Charlotte' (an honorary 'Mrs' was often bestowed on elderly unmarried ladies). Charlotte was still living in 1767 at the age of 101,[119] and finally died in 1775 at the astonishing age of 109 (if the Census of Papists is to be believed).[120] Dr Short acted as a physician to the Bonds on at least one occasion, and a

113   *St James Burials*, p. 263.
114   *Diary*, 21 May 1734.
115   *Diary*, 29 August 1738: 'I with Carteret to Hengrave'; G. Holt, *The English Jesuits in the Age of Reason* (Tunbridge Wells: Burns and Oates, 1993), p. 95; Bellenger, p. 46.
116   Rigby could have been the secular James Rigby (1705–51), the Jesuit John Rigby (1712–58) or the Benedictine John Placid Rigby (d.1764) (Bellenger, p. 102).
117   Family members included the Gages and Rookwood Gages.
118   One or more of the Shorts visited on 7 May 1735, 3 October 1732, 7 May 1734 and 1 December 1735.
119   Rowe, 'The 1767 Census of Papists in the Diocese of Norwich', p. 227.
120   *Bury Register*, 6 January 1775.

mark of the effectiveness of Georgian medicine was his misdiagnosis of Mrs Bond in May 1737 with a serious illness – she turned out to be pregnant.[121]

Other local Catholics who visited the Bonds included Dr Henry Sorrel who had married Sir Thomas's aunt, Catherine Gage,[122] and the Sulyards of Haughley.[123] From slightly further afield came 'Mr Mayer',[124] who was probably one of the Maires who later patronised missionary activity in High Suffolk, a relative of the Maires of County Durham, a Catholic banking dynasty. Mrs Mary Maire, a Bedingfield by birth, was the benefactress of the 'Bacton mission' and died in 1784.[125] Jones visited the Tyldesleys at Fornham St Genevieve on several occasions,[126] although they do not seem to have dined with the Bonds in Bury. The Bonds received several visits from two counts known in the diary as 'Count Senior' and 'Count Junior', who were either foreigners or English or Irish Catholics with foreign titles.[127] Sir Robert Martin of Melford Place,[128] who was a relative of the Rookwood Gages by marriage,[129] also visited.

Non-Catholic guests were not uncommon in the Bond household. The 'Mr and Mrs Simons' who visited on 7 January 1737 were probably John Symonds and Mary Spring. The Springs and the L'Estranges from Pakenham were occasional visitors,[130] and so were the Desbor-

[121] *Diary*, 4 May 1737.
[122] *Diary*, 27 August 1732; 25 June 1737; 19 July 1737.
[123] *Diary*, 6 February 1737; 7 August 1737.
[124] *Diary*, 16 January 1737; 17 January 1737; 2 August 1737.
[125] Rowe, '"The Lopped Tree": The Re-formation of the Suffolk Catholic Community', p. 188. G. Holt, 'Some Letters from Suffolk, 1763–80: Selection and Commentary', *Recusant History* 16 (1983), p. 309, identified the 'Mr Maire' mentioned in John Gage's letter to Edward Galloway of 23 August 1765 as John Maire of Lartington and Hardwick, Co. Durham, counsellor-at-law.
[126] *Diary*, 13 January 1736; 2 December 1736; 13 January 1737.
[127] *Diary*, 29 December 1736; 17 March 1737.
[128] *Diary*, 22 March 1737; 15 May 1737.
[129] Sir Robert Martin's aunt Tamworth Martin (1664–1712) was the mother of Elizabeth Rookwood; *East Anglian Notes and Queries* (hereafter *EANQ*), 1 (1885–86), p. 345.
[130] *Diary*, 30 November 1736 (Spring), 20 March 1735; 26 January 1737 (L'Estrange). Hamon L'Estrange (1674–1767) of Barton Mere, Pakenham or his son Nicholas (b.1681) could well have been acquainted with the Gages; Merelina Jermyn, second wife of Sir William Gage, 2nd Baronet was buried at Pakenham in 1727 (Gage, *Thingoe*, p. 205). Her first husband was Sir William Spring of Pakenham. For the L'Estranges see S. H. A. Hervey (ed.), *Biographical List of Boys educated at King Edward VI Free Grammar School, Bury St Edmunds from 1550 to 1900* (Bury St Edmunds: Paul and Mathew, 1908), pp. 233–34. On 26 January 1737 the Bonds paid the L'Estranges a return visit.

oughs from Huntingdonshire.[131] Even the Church of England clergyman 'Parson Bird' dined with the Bonds on at least two occasions.[132] At one point Sir Thomas Gage dined at Euston, presumably with the Duke of Grafton, who was the leading peer of the county and a crucial ally;[133] the Gages' friendly relations with the Duke would prove useful at the time of the Jacobite rising of 1745.

On 27 May 1736 Jones dined with 'Mr Stonor' and on 20 June 1737 with 'Ld. Stonor'. The Stonors did not make good their claim to the barony of Camoys until 1839, so there was no Lord Stonor in the 1730s other than John Talbot Stonor, Baron de Lard and Vicar Apostolic of the Midland District. Howard and Owen joined Jones for dinner with the Vicar Apostolic, who according to Howard's register had confirmed seven people at Hengrave Hall earlier in the day. These included the steward, John Stockings, his wife Susan and their son Thomas. The other four (John Southgate, Jane Crisp, Mary King and Mary Church) may also have been servants at Hengrave. It is likely, given the number of people John Gage would later record as having been confirmed in his register and the infrequency of the Vicar Apostolic's visits, that Bishop Stonor also confirmed people in Bury during this visit.

Conclusions

Whatever the origins of the Benedictine mission and the reasons for its establishment, it proved adaptable to changing circumstances, and what had begun as two separate chaplaincies to the Gages at Hengrave and the Bonds in Bury expanded to become a mission to the whole Catholic community in the Bury area. After the death of Hugh Owen, with whom the monks seem to have worked closely, Francis Howard succeeded the secular priest as town missioner. By starting a mission register Howard made an important statement about the mission's independence and the status of the Catholic community as an entity in its own right, as well as preserving the records of the mission for posterity.

Under the patronage of Delariviere D'Ewes, the 1730s were a period of modest growth for the Catholic community, which enjoyed an understated 'second spring' after the dissolution of the Jesuit mission in the 1690s and the uncertainty that followed. The Benedictines undoubtedly

---

[131] *Diary*, 31 May 1734. The Desboroughs of Holywell and Buckden in Huntingdonshire were descendents of the Major Desborough who secured Bury for Parliament in 1648; their continuing Suffolk connections are suggested by the fact that Farrer, *Portraits in Suffolk Houses (West)*, p. 231, recorded portraits of Desborough family members at Ixworth Hall.

[132] *Diary*, 23 March 1737; 15 October 1740

[133] *Diary*, 25 June 1738.

made it possible for John Gage to take over a more than viable mission in 1755–56. At the same time, however, the 1730s and 1740s must have been a period of tragedy and disappointment for the Gages; Delariviere's third son, Teddy Gage, was killed in battle and Sir Thomas died without having married and produced an heir. The family's dynastic hopes rested on Delariviere's second son William or, failing him, on the Rookwood Gages of Coldham, who would increasingly come to influence Bury's Catholic community and eventually supplant the Hengrave Gages.

5

GENTRY CHAPLAINCY TO PROTO-PARISH,
1741–67

Many changes took place in the Catholic community between the death of Sir Thomas Gage, 3rd Baronet in 1741 and his brother William's death in 1767. Sir William Gage, 4th Baronet, an experienced merchant with an illegitimate son, was a very different man from his brother. The Bonds, who had shared the patronage of the Benedictine mission with the Gages, declined in influence after the death of Henry Jermyn Bond in 1748. Sir William's failure to produce an heir,[1] combined with the death of Delariviere D'Ewes in 1746, tipped the balance of influence in favour of the heir presumptive to the baronetcy, Thomas Rookwood Gage and his mother Elizabeth Rookwood. In the 1750s church politics divided the Gage and Rookwood families, at least temporarily, with the Rookwoods championing the cause of the Jesuits against the vicars apostolic. On the extinction of the Benedictines in 1755, it was Thomas Rookwood Gage's brother John who re-established the Jesuits in Bury, after an absence of sixty years. However, John Gage the Younger ministered primarily to the ordinary Catholics of the town and a wide hinterland, and his independent income, combined with family donations, allowed him to build a privately owned mission house and chapel long before such an arrangement became legal under the second Catholic Relief Act of 1791.

John Gage's mission resembled a continuation of the Short family's 'town mission', or even a revival of the Jesuit mission of the 1680s, rather than the successor of a Benedictine mission that, however successful it may have been, remained dependent on the gentry for finance and premises for worship. John Gage may have been of the gentry, but he did not exist only to serve them, and on his death he bequeathed his successors a flourishing and independent mission. While the 'revolt of the plebeians' discerned by Aveling in the second half of the eighteenth

---

[1]   This was the fate of many Catholic families in the period. See Aveling, *The Handle and the Axe*, p. 260.

century did not occur in any dramatic sense in Bury, the eighteenth-century Jesuit mission was undoubtedly part of a national trend that saw the number of Catholics increase by around 60 per cent between 1674 and 1804.[2] In the 1680s, less than one-third of priests served urban missions maintained by trust funds or collections; by the 1780s, led by the likes of John Gage, three-quarters of missioners were independent of the gentry and 'public chapels' were becoming the norm.[3]

This chapter offers a glimpse of the beginnings of John Gage's mission and the declining years of the Hengrave Gages, to be succeeded by their cousins the Rookwood Gages of Coldham. Between 1742 and 1757 Hengrave Hall was rented to the Protestant Carteret Leathes and ceased to be a centre of local Catholic activity,[4] although it is possible that Mass continued to be said there occasionally for local Catholics. The centre of gravity of the Catholic community inevitably shifted south to Coldham Hall, where it was to remain until 1794 when the Rook-wood Gages discovered a use for Hengrave as a refuge for the English Augustinian canonesses of Bruges. That period, however, lies outside the scope of the present study.[5]

The diary of Dom Alexius Jones ended in 1743, and the principal source for the Bury mission during the period 1756–67 is the mission register kept by John Gage himself (Appendix 6). Gage made little or no effort to disguise the nature of his ministry in this document, perhaps because he wrote it entirely in Latin, or else because he had little to fear from informants in a friendly neighbourhood and a more tolerant era. In addition to the register, Gage's correspondence from 1763 with Edward Galloway, a fellow Jesuit in Norwich, adds valuable detail to our understanding of the operation of his mission and the nature of local gentry involvement. A few personal letters of the Gage family survive from this period, and a touch of historical colour is occasionally added by the personal anecdotes gleaned by Sir Thomas Gage, 7th Baronet in the early nineteenth century.

---

2   Ibid. p. 286.

3   Ibid. p. 287.

4   Carteret Leathes gave notice that he would give up his tenancy of Hengrave at Michaelmas 1757 (Carteret Leathes to Sir William Gage, 4 April 1757, CUL Hengrave 88/4/69).

5   On this phase of Hengrave's history see my article 'Mother Mary More and the Exile of the Augustinian Canonesses of Bruges in England: 1794–1802', *Recusant History* 27 (2004), pp. 86–102.

From Gages to Rookwood Gages

In the will of 31 August 1741 of Sir Thomas Gage, 3rd Baronet, drawn up on the day before his death, he left the manor of Harleston and the lands he owned in Haughley to his mother Delariviere, along with the entirety of his personal estate including silver plate, jewels and cattle. Delariviere was also the executor of his will.[6] Sir Thomas was succeeded as baronet by his brother, Sir William Gage, who had recently married (on 14 June 1741) Frances Harland (1705–63), sister of Admiral Sir Robert Harland, 1st Baronet of Sproughton, and widow of John Ellis of Cotton.[7] The *London Evening Post* described Mrs Ellis as 'a very agreeable Lady, with a Fortune of 15,000l'.[8] Following the example of her mother-in-law, Delariviere D'Ewes, Frances converted to Catholicism on her marriage.[9]

Sir Thomas's death elicited condolences even from fairly remote relatives, indicating the extent to which the Gages could still command a network of non-Catholic friends. Tilman Hinckell (one of Sir William's fellow merchants in the Portuguese wine trade) met Thomas, Viscount Gage at Richmond who 'took it a little amiss' that he had not been informed about the death before he heard it in the newspapers.[10] Sir William's second cousin by marriage, Cordell Spring of Pakenham, also wrote with his condolences while Thomas Bray, a fellow merchant of Sir William in Portugal and possibly his agent there, arranged for two hundred Masses to be said for the repose of Sir Thomas's soul and ensured that 'Dicky' (Sir William's cousin Richard Holmes, his apprentice) went into mourning. However, Bray also had other, more self-interested, anxieties on his mind; when he inherited the baronetcy Sir William had no more need of his mercantile activities, but Bray was keen to encourage him to continue them: 'pray Lett me intreat you now not to drop it but Steal time to persue the same, for I take Merchandizing rather a feather in great mens Caps, then a blur to their names'.[11]

Bray was still more anxious a week later when he had heard nothing from Sir William, and he endeavoured to persuade the Baronet not to 'bury himself' at Hengrave 'since yo[u] are known to be alive in the world'. Bray feared that his employer was turning into a different kind

---

6   PROB 11/715.

7   Aveling, *The Handle and the Axe*, p. 284; Gage, *Thingoe*, p. 210.

8   *London Evening Post* 2121 (13–16 June 1741).

9   CUL Hengrave MS 1/4, fol. 366.

10 Tilman Hinckell to Sir William Gage, 8 September 1741, CUL Hengrave MS 88/4/38; Thomas, Viscount Gage to Sir William Gage, 8 September 1741, CUL Hengrave MS 88/4/37.

11 Thomas Bray to Sir William Gage, 23 October 1741, CUL Hengrave MS 88/4/41.

of man, and begged him, 'pray dont lead the rest of y[ou]r life away w[i]th hearing of y[ou]r farmers Stories, nor Country Esq[ui]r[e]s tales of fox hunting'. He encouraged Sir William to write to his usual customers and acquaintances, encouraging them to renew their wine orders, probably anticipating the beneficial effect of Sir William's new status on his business.[12] Eventually, in March 1743, it was left to Richard Holmes to explain in a letter to his aunt Delariviere that Bray was very much 'provok'd', since he had not heard from Sir William since August 1742.[13]

On 19 September 1741 Alexius Jones noted that Delariviere D'Ewes 'quitted Hengrave'. She moved permanently into her house in Bury, as social protocol demanded, since Frances Harland had displaced her as mistress of Hengrave. In December Delariviere, accompanied by Francis Howard, paid a visit to London where she called on Mrs Rookwood Gage and Mrs Bond, among others. Delariviere attempted to persuade Sir William not to sell her horse, a sign that she did not exercise the same influence over 'Billy' as she had over Thomas.[14] On 13 November Jones described his ministry as 'at Bury al[l] nights, & days except Hengrave, & Noughton'. Presumably Jones's visits to Hengrave were to Sir William and Lady Gage; the reasons for his visits to 'Noughton' (either Nowton or Norton, both villages close to Bury) are harder to guess at. On 8 June Jones wrote that 'Mr. Howard returned to Merry', which may have been a reference to the Merry family, although it is unclear why Howard would have moved from his position as chaplain to Delariviere D'Ewes in order to live with the staymaker Richard Merry, and the meaning of this statement remains obscure. Howard was certainly with Delariviere in December 1741.

On 28 March 1742, Sir William and Lady Gage left Hengrave for London, where they may have spent a considerable amount of their time. When Sir William died in May 1767 it was at his house in Carrington Street, Mayfair.[15] However, so many letters were sent to Sir William in Bury during the course of the 1750s that he seems to have spent a good deal of time there as well. He certainly remained close to the local Catholic community and maintained relations with the Rookwood Gage, Sulyard and Farrell families. In 1752 Ralph Sulyard asked for Sir William's advice on the matter of whether he should send his son to 'a Roman Catholicke School in Lancashire where he will be well settled in his principles of Religion'.[16] However, Sir Thomas Gage, 7th Baronet

12 Thomas Bray to Sir William Gage, 30 October 1741, CUL Hengrave MS 88/4/42.
13 Richard Holmes to Delariviere D'Ewes, 4 March 1743, CUL Hengrave MS 88/4/53.
14 Delariviere D'Ewes to Sir William Gage, 29 December 1741, CUL Hengrave MS 88/4/43.
15 *London Evening Post* 6819 (16–19 May 1767).
16 Ralph Sulyard to Sir William Gage, 1 March 1752, CUL Hengrave 88/4/59.

(grandson of Sir William's heir, Thomas Rookwood Gage) was critical of Sir William, and doubtless his historical commentary reflected something of what his grandfather felt in 1767: 'The writer of these pages cannot refrain from observing, that he did not possess all the Cardinal virtues – for, by his want of prudence the Family Estates were greatly reduced – and the Wreck of his property descended to his Heir in a ruinous and encumbered state'.[17]

Whatever the condition in which Sir William left his fortune, when he first inherited Hengrave he would have been a wealthy man. On 7 November 1742 Sir William's brother-in-law Captain Robert Harland wrote to him from the *Princess* to inform him of the death of his cousin Devereux Gage, apparently in unpleasant circumstances ('the rest of the story was not pleasing to me').[18] As Devereux's closest living relative, Sir William had a claim to inherit his entire estate and consulted lawyers concerning the matter who informed him that, since Sir William and Devereux were descended from different wives of Sir Edward Gage (Mary Hervey and Frances Aston respectively), the Hengrave Gages 'were onely of half blood' and thus could not inherit.[19] However, Sir Thomas Day, with the help of John Martin of Long Melford, advised Sir William to claim Devereux Gage's estate, since he had 'Right & Title to it'.[20] Sir William was eventually successful and inherited 'Gage's Fee', a plantation on the island of Montserrat that Devereux had inherited from his mother. However, Sir William seems to have had little interest in running a plantation and he sold it soon afterwards to Thomas Meade.[21] Sir William was not the only member of the Gage family to have interests in Montserrat; in 1745, Thomas, 1st Viscount Gage of Castlebar (the head of the Firle branch of the family) mortgaged two hundred acres to Meade.[22] Until the volcanic eruption of 1997 that rendered most of the island uninhabitable, an area of Montserrat was still named after the Gages.

Sir William's questionable private virtue was suggested by the fact that he fathered an illegitimate son by a Portuguese mistress, William 'Olivarez' Gage, long before inheriting Hengrave. The annuity of £8 that Sir William bequeathed to 'Mrs Elizabeth Holder otherwise Howe' in his will is puzzling, and it is possible that Mrs Howe was another of

---

17 CUL Hengrave MS 1/4, fol. 367.
18 Robert Harland to Sir William Gage, 7 November 1742, CUL Hengrave MS 88/4/44.
19 Sir William Gage to Sir Thomas Day, undated [January 1743], CUL Hengrave MS 88/4/49.
20 Sir Thomas Day to Sir William Gage, 11 January 1743, CUL Hengrave MS 88/4/48.
21 CUL Hengrave MS 1/4, fols 313–14.
22 R. B. Sheridan, *Sugar and Slavery: An Economic History of the British West Indies, 1623–1775* (Baltimore, MD: Johns Hopkins University Press, 1974), p. 177.

his conquests. Nevertheless, Sir William was praised in verse by 'Dr. Winter of Bath' in 1746:

> To Hengrave turn, where lives my steadfast Friend,
> Attempt not what you can't enough commend.
> Here, shunning smoke, and noise, and Courtly Gold,
> He tills the Ground as Cincinnate of old.[23]

Sir William had no choice but to shun 'courtly gold', given the laws still in place against the participation of Catholics in public life. However, Sir William seems to have been neither an effective estate manager nor a natural leader of the Catholic community in Bury. He failed to produce an heir, although Frances Harland gave birth to a stillborn daughter in January 1743.[24] The death of Delariviere D'Ewes on 18 October 1746, 'as much a most excellent woman as a most beloved mother', deprived the Benedictine mission of its patron.[25] Delariviere seems to have had little or no money when she died; Sir William was obliged to pay some of her legacies out of his own pocket, to the surprise of Thomas Havers of Thelveton, who thought that Delariviere's house in Northgate Street would be sold for this purpose.[26] Sir William told his nephew Richard Holmes that 'my mother did not leave a shilling behind Her'.[27]

The Benedictine mission was soon to lose another patron. Henry Bond, Jones's patron, was buried in Hengrave church on 3 March 1748.[28] His widow, Jane Godfrey, remarried the Protestant Thomas, Viscount Gage,[29] thus maintaining the long-standing Gage–Bond connection, albeit with a different branch of the family. However, her connections with the Hengrave family were strong enough that when she died in London, her body was taken to Hengrave rather than Firle to be interred on 18 October 1757.[30] Henry Bond was succeeded as head of the Bond family by his eldest son, also Henry. On his twelfth birthday, on 18 August 1749, at Hengrave, Charles Jermyn Bond received as a gift from his aunt Judith Bond the manuscript 'Testament de l'âme chrestienne'

---

23 CUL Hengrave MS 1/4, fol. 367. Unfortunately, Sir Thomas Gage declined to transcribe the next few lines of Dr Winter's verse, which apparently made an obscene allusion to Sir Thomas Kytson and Anne Boleyn.

24 Ralph Sulyard to Sir William Gage, 20 January 1743, CUL Hengrave MS 88/4/51.

25 Gage, *Thingoe*, p. 237 incorrectly gives 1756 as the date of her death. She was buried at Hengrave church on 25 October 1746 (Gage, *Hengrave*, p. 77) and her will was proved on 7 November 1746 (Payne, *Records of the English Catholics of 1715*, p. 65). For her memorial inscription in Hengrave church see Gage, *Thingoe*, p. 237.

26 Thomas Havers to Sir William Gage, 25 February 1757, CUL Hengrave MS 88/4/63.

27 Sir William Gage to Richard Holmes, undated [1746], CUL Hengrave MS 88/4/34.

28 Gage, *Hengrave*, p. 77; Gage, *Thingoe*, p. 235.

29 Estcourt and Payne (eds), *The English Catholic Non-Jurors of 1715*, p. 256.

30 Gage, *Hengrave*, pp. 72 (memorial inscription), 77.

that his grandfather Thomas had written for the use of his mother, Marie Peliot, in 1683. Concerned to maintain family traditions, Judith wrote that she gave the book to Charles 'that he be oblidged to keep it in memory of his Grandfather; who writ it'.[31]

The lingering representatives of an earlier era finally slipped into history during this period. Henrietta, the fifth daughter of Sir William Gage, 2nd Baronet, died on 25 June 1757, followed by her sister Ann (the ninth daughter) who died on 29 March 1760. Frances Harland ailed throughout the summer of 1763 and eventually predeceased her husband Sir William Gage, 4th Baronet on 20 July of that year.[32] She may have died from the 'ague' from which Sir William suffered at the same time. With the death at a young age of Sir Thomas Gage, 3rd Baronet, the death of Teddy Gage in a far-off battle and the failure of Sir William Gage and Frances Harland to produce an heir, the senior branch of the Gages slipped into extinction to be supplanted by the more vigorous Rookwood Gages.

The matriarchal tradition of the Gage family did not end with the death of Delariviere D'Ewes, since Elizabeth Rookwood, the mother of Thomas Rookwood Gage and the Jesuit priest John Gage the Younger (who never used the Rookwood name), became the patroness of a new Jesuit mission in Bury to replace the Benedictines, who simply died out in 1755. Elizabeth died on 30 January 1759, aged seventy-six, having established her younger son as the spiritual pastor of the local Catholic community and her eldest son as its lay leader and financial pillar. At Coldham Hall, Thomas Rookwood Gage had a numerous family by Lucy Knight, the daughter of William Knight of Kingerby in Lincolnshire, whom he married in 1746. At Hengrave, the household consisted only of Sir William and Lady Gage. No records for the house survive from this time, but it is likely that the establishment that the Bonds and Alexius Jones had visited so frequently in the 1730s and 1740s was very much reduced. Hengrave was a house in decline, and it was soon to become a mere property rather than a family home. Maps of the Hengrave estate were made in 1742 and 1769; by 1769 the house was occupied by a tenant, William Otley, and the size of the park itself had shrunk from 291 acres in 1742 to 254 acres.[33] On Sir William's death in 1767 the Jesuits discussed the possibility of buying mortgages on the Hengrave estate with the proceeds of the sale of their property of

---

[31] CUL Hengrave MS 57 (inscription on flyleaf in the hand of Judith Bond).

[32] John Gage to Edward Galloway, 15 July 1763 (Holt, 'Some Letters from Suffolk, 1763–80', p. 304): 'How long poor Lady Gage may last God knows; this is the twentieth week she has been allmost confined to her Room, I might have said Bed, & I myself to the town.'

[33] SRO(B) 712/58 (1742 map); SRO(B) 712/60 (1769 map).

Newnham in Bedfordshire, and investing the proceeds in 'India Bonds' and turnpikes.[34]

The Catholic community in 1745

Between the official exposure of French plans to invade England and restore the Stuarts in February 1744 and the final defeat of Prince Charles Edward Stuart at Culloden in April 1746, Catholics in England came under a heightened scrutiny reminiscent of the seventeenth century. Measures were taken to confiscate their arms in the fear that they might participate in a rising in favour of the Pretender. Furthermore, magistrates and constables were empowered to confiscate from a Catholic any horse worth more than £5. There was a genuine fear that East Anglian Catholics would be incited to join the rebellion by their clergy – a priest was supposed to be doing this in Bungay and Wymondham.[35]

On 13 March 1744, Sir William's tenant at Hengrave, Carteret Leathes, went to Euston Hall in the hope of speaking with the Duke of Grafton, then Lord Lieutenant of the county, on Sir William's behalf.[36] The purpose of Leathes's visit was probably to persuade the Duke to meet publicly with loyalist Catholics. Such a gathering did take place at some point in 1744 or 1745. John Marchant, who gathered together a mass of material relating to the Jacobite rising and published it as *The History of the Present Rebellion* in 1746, recorded that: 'In Suffolk, Sir William Gage, and some other Roman Catholicks, waited on the Duke of Grafton at Euston-Hall, to assure his Grace of their peaceable Disposition, &c. at this Juncture.'[37] The Dukes of Grafton, direct descendents of Charles II and Lady Castlemaine, were the leaders of the Tory faction in Suffolk throughout the eighteenth century, and more inclined to be sympathetic to loyalist Catholics than the Whig aristocracy. Catholics were required to surrender their horses and firearms to local constables, but Leathes invited Sir William to leave them with him for safekeeping (which meant, ironically, that they would have been kept at Hengrave):

> I gave Orders to my Servants to receive y[ou]r Horses, as Mrs Gerrard will y[ou]r Fowling Pieces or any other things you think propper to send; and if it should be necessary you part with them absolutely, If you will present

---

34   James Dennett to Edward Galloway, 19 November 1767 (Holt, 'Some Letters from Suffolk, 1763–80', p. 311).

35   N. Rogers, 'Popular Jacobitism in a Provincial Context: 18th Century Bristol and Norwich' in E. Cruickshanks and J. Black (eds), *The Jacobite Challenge* (Edinburgh: J. Donald, 1988), p. 133.

36   Carteret Leathes to Sir William Gage, 13 March 1744, CUL Hengrave MS 88/4/56.

37   J. Marchant, *A History of the Present Rebellion* (London, 1746), p. 69.

them to me, I shall alwayes think myself under such obligations for it, as to deserve a gratefull return whenever opportunitys offer.

It seems likely that Sir William did give his larger guns and horses to Leathes. When he received a visit from the constables of the borough of St Edmundsbury on 7 October 1745, they seized 'a Brace of pistols & three swords' and declared '[we] have not taken or seen on such search any Horse of the value of five pounds in our Judgm[e]nt'.[38] The constables must have realised how unlikely it was that Sir William Gage would own no horse worth £5 or more, but they evidently did not ask many searching questions. Leathes noted that 'the Justices in most Counties, especially in the North, are very rigorous and strict in putting the Laws in execution', as if to imply that Suffolk was an exception. For Sir William, the principal drawback of the Jacobite rising of 1745 was that it 'interrupted' his favourite sport of shooting.

Sir William's visit to Euston (and the fact that he was the only Catholic gentleman named by Marchant) is an indication of the position he occupied as the 'leading man' among Suffolk Catholics in the 1740s, probably on account of the size of his estate. Sir William unswervingly maintained the tradition of Hanoverian loyalism established by his grandfather, the 2nd Baronet, in spite of his patronage of Benedictine monks (often characterised by their strongly held Jacobite views at this time). It seems likely that Sir William had little interest in politics at all, however. The dominant figure of Delariviere D'Ewes continued to provide a highly visible link between the Gages and a leading Protestant family of the locality, and Carteret Leathes was evidently a useful friend to have.

Marchant singled out Suffolk Catholics for special mention for their loyalty in 1745, albeit his account retained a trace of suspicion:

> The Catholicks in that Country are very numerous, who have behaved very quietly, which I won't be so uncharitable as to suppose was owing to their Fear of Frampton's Regiment which was quartered amongst them, but had rather impute it to their own Prudence, and the Consideration, that they could never be better used, if so well, under a Popish Government, as they were under the present.[39]

Marchant's preference for the term 'Roman Catholick' over 'papist' in his book is a sign of the growing tolerance towards loyal Catholics among the educated population, which was scarcely damaged in the south of England by the events of the Jacobite rising of 1745. After all,

---

[38] SRO(B) D8/1/3 bundle 2. The 'Brace of pistols' were perhaps the 'six Gunnes' that Ralph Sulyard bought for Sir William in January 1743 (Ralph Sulyard to Sir William Gage, 20 January 1743, CUL Hengrave MS 88/4/51).

[39] J. Marchant, *A History of the Present Rebellion* (London, 1746), pp. 69–70.

East Anglia's most active Jacobite, Sir John Hynde Cotton of Madingley Hall just outside Cambridge,[40] was a Protestant, and there was no immediate historical reason to single out East Anglian Catholics for suspicion; the active Jacobitism of the Rookwoods was long past. However, anti-Catholicism remained a living force among ordinary people in Suffolk, who considered the popish threat sufficiently real to repeat the actions of their ancestors a hundred years earlier:

> The People were very jealous of some under-hand Practices among them, as appears by the following Instance. One Day, as a Cart-load of Goods was coming to the House of a Roman Catholick, the Country People stopt it, and search'd to see if there were any Arms conceal'd among them; but not finding any, they suffer'd the Cart to pass on.[41]

At the quarter sessions on 30 September 1745 those who refused to take the Oath of Allegiance to George II were presented, 'being Papists or reputed or suspected to be so'. In preparation for these presentments, the same constables who had confiscated Sir William's pistols drew up provisional lists of Catholics in Bury by wards, on the basis that no Catholic would take the Oath, which still contained an explicit repudiation of transubstantiation. These rough lists survive, along with the names of those actually presented. Many of those who appear as Catholics in the lists do not appear in the presentments, and there may be a number of reasons for this. First, it could be that they were never tendered the Oath. Second, it may not have been established with certainty that they really were Catholics (several individuals were marked on the lists as 'reputed papists'). Third, it is possible that the constables and magistrates were selective in their desire to incriminate local Catholics, and decided to remove some names from the list.

Six members of the Gage family appeared in the constables' original lists, but none appeared in the presentments. Only those members of the family living in Bury itself were included; if a list was made for Hengrave as well it has not survived. The daughters of Sir William Gage, 2nd Baronet were living in Bury at this time: 'Ann Gage, spinster'; Mary, the widow of Dr Henry Huddlestone and her daughter Lelia Huddlestone; and Charlotte, the widow of Fitznun Lambe of Troston.[42] In addition, Delariviere D'Ewes, who may have been living in the

---

[40] The Cottons of Madingley acted as trustees for the Rookwood family on numerous occasions, demonstrating that links existed between Catholic and non-Catholic Jacobites in East Anglia.

[41] Marchant, *A History of the Present Rebellion*, p. 70.

[42] Fitznun Lambe was buried in Hengrave church on 4 June 1733 (Gage, *Hengrave*, p. 77).

Gages' townhouse in Northgate Street, was also recorded.[43] The presence of members of the Huddlestone family in Bury may have had an additional significance to the Jesuit mission, since John Champion, who was Superior of the English Jesuits from 1741–58, was the resident chaplain at Sawston Hall in Cambridgeshire;[44] Champion visited Bury in 1763.[45]

Ordinary Catholics far outnumbered gentry in the constables' lists. The total number of Catholics counted was 119, or 84 not including children. Unlike in 1715, when only Catholics who owned property were counted, the constables of 1745 attempted to count even labourers, and this list is consequently a valuable record of the total make-up of the mid-century Catholic community (Appendix 5). Only 40 of the 84 adults listed were presented at the quarter sessions as nonjurors. Few of the women in the 1745 lists were Catholics married to non-Catholics, with the exceptions of Sarah, the wife of Robert Stowe, and Elizabeth, the wife of William Hawkins, watchmaker. William Hawkins (1703–75) was one of the longest-established watch and clockmakers in Bury, and a leader in what had become one of the town's most profitable industries; he was the grandson of Mark Hawkins the Elder (1674–1750) and the son of Mark Hawkins the Younger (1707–67), who made and sold their clocks at the Crown and Dial on Cook Row (present-day Abbeygate Street), between the corners of Whiting Street and Hatter Street.[46] The fact that one of Bury's most respected tradesmen in the prestigious clockmaking trade was prepared to marry a Catholic is surely an indication of the level of tolerance in the town.

From Benedictine to Jesuit mission

The mid-eighteenth century saw a concerted effort by the vicars apostolic to gain control of the English mission. This was more effective in some parts of the country than others, and East Anglia presented a particular problem. The counties of Norfolk, Suffolk, Cambridgeshire and the Isle of Ely had been part of the Midland District since 1687, but since the vicars apostolic were based in Staffordshire and Warwickshire, East Anglia was extremely remote from the centre of authority. This situation allowed the regulars, and the Jesuits in particular, to flout

---

[43] SRO(B) D8/1/3 bundle 2.

[44] G. Holt, *The English Jesuits in the Age of Reason* (Tunbridge Wells: Burns and Oates, 1993), pp. 94–95.

[45] John Gage to Edward Galloway, 15 July 1763 (Holt, 'Some Letters from Suffolk, 1763–80', p. 304).

[46] A. L. Haggar and L. F. Miller, *Suffolk Clocks and Clockmakers* (Ramsgate: Antiquarian Horological Society, 1974), pp. 93–95.

the authority that the vicars apostolic claimed over all clergy. On 10 September 1642 John Talbot Stonor, Bishop of Thespiae and Vicar Apostolic of the Midland District, appointed James Brown as Vicar Forane in East Anglia, describing his role in ideal rather than realistic terms: 'that he should have keen eyes not only for the laity who dwell in any of the said counties, but even for the priests, whether seculars or regulars: may his ministry faithfully cherish those filled with grace, direct the doubting, confirm the wavering'.[47]

However, Stonor also acknowledged the reality of the pastoral situation when he conceded that a new fund to support the work of Brown could only be raised from 'churches … whose use and administration pertain to the secular clergy' (*eccl[essi]arum … quorum usus & administration ad Clerum secularem pertinent*). In the event, four funds were created: the 'Common Fund of Norfolk', the 'Itinerant Fund' and funds for Bury St Edmunds and King's Lynn.[48] The Bury fund, which was worth £50, was presumably the continuation of support given by Stonor to Hugh Owen; Francis Howard, even though he was a Benedictine, had taken over the town's secular mission on Owen's death.

On 30 May 1753, Pope Benedict XIV published a papal brief that was intended to combat some of the corruptions on the English mission and, in particular, ensure that the regular clergy led a life distinct from that of the seculars. It was a perennial paradox of the English mission that the regular clergy were crucial to its survival and yet, by spending long periods of time living as chaplains, they dispensed with aspects of what made them distinctive as regulars, such as community life and the renunciation of personal property. Among other things, the brief required that 'any regular missionary, in order to cast off worldly dust and renew his spirit, should return to his own religious community every six months; he should put on the habit and remain there for three months together'.[49] This was potentially a very disruptive measure to the English mission, since many Mass centres and chapels were served by a single regular priest who, according to the brief, would be absent on the Continent for at least three months of the year.

---

[47] John Talbot Stonor to James Brown, 10 September 1742 (Birmingham Archdiocesan Archives A14): … *ut non in Laicos modo sed etiam in Sacerdotes seu Seculares seu Regulares qui in aliquot dictorum Comitatum degunt … attentos habeat oculos; ministerium suum fideliter adimplentes foveat, dubitantes dirigat, vacillantes confirmet.*

[48] Note in the hand of Bishop Stonor (Birmingham Archdiocesan Archives A38).

[49] Pastoral Letter of the vicars apostolic promulgating Pope Benedict XIV's Brief of 30 May 1753 (Archives of the Archbishop of Westminster, A 40/96), p. 7: *Cuilibet missionario Regulari, ut ad mundanum pulverem excutiendum, & spiritum suum renovandum, post singula sexennia ad suam propriam familiam Regularem regrediatur, habitum induat, ibique per tres integres menses commoretur.*

It fell to the vicars apostolic to promulgate this brief, which was very unpopular indeed with patrons of regular clergy and, indeed, with the regulars themselves, especially the Jesuits. Whereas monks and friars were intended to return to their 'mother house' from time to time, the Society of Jesus was a missionary order by its very nature, organised in local 'colleges', and there was no requirement in the Jesuit rule for Jesuits to return to a mother house or live together in community. Lay patrons and regular clergy were unwilling to obey the vicars apostolic at the best of times, let alone when they were the bringers of such unwelcome news from Rome. Bishop John Joseph Hornyold, Coadjutor to Bishop Stonor, tasked the secular priest Alban Butler (1709–73), famous for his *Lives of the Saints*, with enforcing the brief in East Anglia. Butler had recently been appointed chaplain to Edward Howard, 9th Duke of Norfolk at his palace in Norwich. As chaplain to East Anglia's (and indeed England's) leading Catholic layman, he seems to have enjoyed some sort of informal pre-eminence amongst the secular clergy in the region. Butler arrived in Bury at the end of 1753, but met only with Sir William Gage, with whom he left copies of the instructions from the vicars apostolic, which were to be signed by Francis Howard and two Jesuits then in Bury, James Dennett and John Gage (this is the first mention of John Gage the Younger in Bury). Dennett and Gage initially refused to sign the document, but were subsequently ordered by their superior to do so. Butler sent a second copy to Sir William, but the Jesuits objected to the fact that the document had been sent to the Baronet, and still refused to sign. Butler noted that they 'are angry with Sir Will[ia]m for taking them from me for them'.

Sir William then received an angry letter from Thomas Rookwood Gage, John Gage's brother, calling into question the motives of the vicars apostolic and their supporters:

What else can mean their partial scheme of procuring r[e]g[u]l[a]rs to be sent abroad for 3 months every 5 years, but to engross their places after tiring them out with large expences & the family with the want of due assistance during the time of their banishment. Do seculars who are bound by fewer vows from worldly vanities, stand in less need of renewing their spirit? Or does their not being obliged to the rule of poverty, cause them to squander so much on secular affairs as not to be able to pay their residence at a college for 3 months as well as a regular? But to excuse all absurdities, I am willing to suppose these gentlemen design to put themselves upon the same footing as those R[e]g[u]l[a]rs who have no houses to go to, and so leave the mission and all pastoral functions to those who have been at pains and expence of travelling abroad to shake off the worldly dust, w[hi]ch having already much weakened, must in time quite put out the eyes of those who have not the opportunity of doing the same.

Thomas was accusing the vicars apostolic of imposing the burden of travel to the Continent on regular chaplains, and the burden of replacing them on their patrons, in order to discourage people from having regulars in the first place, thus making way for secular chaplains. He was not alone in seeing the new rules as a conspiracy of the secular against the regular clergy; Alban Butler noted that 'Sir H. Benefield is the hottest'. Not all regulars, however, seem to have responded like the Jesuits and their supporters. Butler reported that 'the monks are very civil and ready', and that Francis Howard 'writ to me that he received respectfully and would conform in all things to Mr Stonor's mandate'. Furthermore, Sir William Gage behaved 'very genteely', even after he received his cousin's 'bitter' letter.

What seems to have annoyed Butler most was Thomas Rookwood Gage's proprietory attitude to the clergy: 'He says he shall take it unkind for one to send them (the late mandate & the Regulae before) to any person belonging to me' (underlined in the original letter).[50] Thomas's response to the brief was probably driven as much by family loyalty to his brother John as it was by his interest as a patron, yet the letter that Butler sent to Bishop Hornyold explaining the situation in Bury is the clearest evidence we have that the perennial conflict of the seculars and regulars divided the Gage family in the eighteenth century, with the Rookwood Gages championing the Jesuits, and the Hengrave Gages content with the authority of the vicars apostolic. The letter also demonstrates that John Gage was probably at Coldham Hall in 1753. The pairing of his name with that of James Dennett, who was certainly chaplain there, and the fact that Thomas complained so bitterly that the new regulations would leave him personally out of pocket, suggests that Thomas was thinking of the effect on the mission at Coldham; the Rookwood Gages were not, as yet, involved directly in the Bury mission.

John Gage the Younger (so-called in order to distinguish him from his Jesuit uncle of the same name) was born in 1720, the second son of John Gage and Elizabeth Rookwood, and educated at St Omer. He was ordained at Watten in 1740, and studied philosophy at Liege before his departure for England.[51] Foley claimed that Gage was not professed as a Jesuit until 2 February 1756,[52] but this must be an error; if Gage had been a secular priest up to 1756 it is unlikely that Butler would have referred to him as a Jesuit. A letter of 15 November 1793 from Sir Thomas Gage, 6th Baronet to Gage's successor, Charles Thompson,

[50] Alban Butler to Bishop John Hornyold, 23 December 1753 (Westminster Diocesan Archives, A 40/97).

[51] Foley, vol. 7:1, p. 283.

[52] Ibid. vol. 5, p. 539.

stated that Gage 'knew Father Howard, the last Benedictine there',[53] and it may be that an agreement was reached that Gage should succeed Howard. However, in 1753 the Benedictine mission was still very much active, and in that year Howard and Jones were even joined by another young monk, Dom Maurus Heatly (1722–1802).

Jones died on 10 August 1755, and Howard followed him a few months later on 12 December.[54] Heatly returned 'Mr Jones's spolia who died at Hengrave' to the South Province of the English Benedictine Congregation[55] ('spolia' were the personal property of a monk, which reverted to the province after his death). Jones's spolia evidently did not include his diary, as it would otherwise have found its way to Downside Abbey along with the rest of the material from the South Province. Heatly was a young monk at the time he was sent to Bury; he was born at Salmesbury in Lancashire and professed at Lambspring in 1740, although he spent the next years at St Gregory's, Douai. In 1755 he was sent to Cheam in Surrey. He would go on to hold one of the highest offices in the Congregation, as the rather despotic Abbot of Lambspring, where he had the opportunity to rule a small German principality.[56]

The South Province accounts recorded money 'Received back of Mrs Webb for Gloves given at Mr Jone's Funeral to the servants of Lady Gage'.[57] Sir William arranged with the Benedictine Henry Wybarne, then a missionary in Norwich, for a memorial tablet to be erected to Howard's memory, although where this was located is unclear.[58] One of Francis Howard's legacies seems to have been the interest shown in joining the Benedictines by Sir William Gage's illegitimate son, Olivarez. In August 1755 Olivarez was at St Gregory's, Douai, where he intended to make a trial of the monastic life. John Placid Howard, President of the English Benedictine Congregation, gave Sir William a positive account of Olivarez:

> W[he]n I was at Douay, August last … I left him very well & hearty, & am persuaded greatly pleased with the calling he was to enter on a trial of about 6 weeks after. w[he]n I wrote my sentiments about it to poor Mr Howard whose loss I sincerely lament, I told him th[a]t I thought th[a]t sort of life

53 Ibid. vol. 5, p. 538.

54 Downside Abbey, South Province Book R, 1717–1826, p. 82.

55 Allanson, *Biography of the English Benedictines*, p. 256.

56 On Heatly's abbacy at Lambspring see Scott, *Gothic Rage Undone: English Monks in the Age of Enlightenment,* pp. 27–35.

57 Allanson, *Biography of the English Benedictines*, p. 190.

58 Henry Wybarne to Sir William Gage, 10 July 1756, CUL Hengrave MS 88/4/65. Wybarne was a prominent East Anglian Catholic in his own right, as heir-general of the Tasburghs of Flixton through his mother Lettice.

suited the youths turn, being of a meek & [*illeg.*] temper, & really believe he will be happy in it.[59]

Placid Howard cautioned that he would let Sir William know at once if he thought there were any grounds for regarding Olivarez as unsuitable: 'I am of opinion th[a]t unless such as settle to th[a]t calling, prefer it to all others on proper motives; it is an equal misfortune to those who under take it as to those, with Whom they settle.' There is a note of caution in Howard's letter that may indicate he was suspicious of Olivarez's motives; as the illegitimate son of a baronet he had few prospects, especially if Sir William produced a legitimate heir, and the religious life offered him security. For whatever reason, Olivarez never attained his ambition, as he was not professed as a Benedictine monk. He later married and took charge of an alum works.[60]

Even after the demise of Bury's Benedictine mission, the Jesuit John Gage was not the only priest in the town. In the mid-eighteenth century the Short family patronised a mission that may have been the successor of Hugh Owen's 'town mission', continued by Francis Howard after Owen's death in 1741. The Dominican missioner happened to be a member of the Gage family as well, James Ambrose Gage (1721–96), who was present in Bury 1758–61. Ambrose was born in Suffolk in 1723; according to John Gage the antiquary he was a son of one of the five youngest sons of Sir Edward Gage and Elizabeth Feilding. He had a brother, Thomas Gage, who lived in Bury (according to Sir Thomas Gage, 7th Baronet),[61] as well as a sister, Augustinian Canoness Catherine Mary Xaveria Gage.[62] It is possible that the Jane Gage who had a house in Bury in the 1750s was his sister or sister-in-law.[63] James Ambrose was professed as a Dominican friar at Bornhem on 1 February 1745. He was ordained in 1747 and appointed Prefect of the Dominican College at Bornhem on 9 November 1748, in which post he remained for ten years, before leaving for the mission at Bury on 15 March 1758. According to his obituary: 'He was stationed at St Edmundsbury as Chaplain

---

59 John Placid Howard to Sir William Gage, 23 November 1756, CUL Hengrave MS 88/4/66.
60 William Olivarez Gage to Sir Thomas Rookwood Gage, 27 June 1767, CUL Hengrave MS 88/4/72.
61 CUL Hengrave MS 1/3, fol. 317.
62 Gage, *Thingoe*, p. 209. A letter from Canoness Catherine Gage is preserved in the Hengrave MSS (Catherine Mary Xaveria Gage to Frances Harland, 8 June 1743, CUL Hengrave MS 88/4/55).
63 Jane Gage to Sir William Gage, 8 July 1756, CUL Hengrave MS 88/4/64; Jane Gage to Sir William Gage, 13 June 1757, CUL Hengrave MS 88/4/70.

to the Short family, which had many Dominican connections.'[64] The 'Dominican connections' of the Shorts consisted of two members of the family who had joined the order: John Jordan Short (1685–1754) was a younger son of Dr Thomas Short, personal physician to Charles II, and his wife Ursula Daniel. Professed in 1719 and ordained in 1721, Jordan Short never went on the mission but spent his life teaching at the University of Louvain.[65] An individual with a closer connection with Ambrose Gage was William Benedict Short (1723–1800), the son of Dr Thomas Short's brother Francis and his wife Jane Harrison. Benedict Short was elected Provincial of the English Dominicans in 1766.[66]

At the Dominican Provincial Chapter of 1758 Ambrose Gage held the honorary title of Prior of Sudbury and, supported by Benedict Short amongst others, a petition was presented for Gage, 'who now labours strenuously in England', to be elected Preacher General, but it was denied on procedural grounds.[67] In 1762 Ambrose Gage was elected a Definitor of the Province and succeeded in being appointed Preacher General,[68] and he continued to be elected Definitor at subsequent Provincial Chapters. In 1766 he was elected Master of Theology, following the death of Anthony Thompson. The Chapter records described Ambrose thus:

> endowed with doctrine and religious morals, professed for twenty-two years, forty-five years old, for ten he took upon himself faithfully and knowingly to imbue the young with studies as much as with humane letters and religious morals, and for nine years with fertile fruit he laboured strenuously in the Apostolic Mission.

Ambrose Gage was promoted numerous times and was titular Prior of Norwich in 1762,[69] Oxford in 1770,[70] Cambridge in 1774,[71] London in 1782[72] and York in 1786.[73] He died on 5 March 1796.[74] From 1770–73 Gage served as Prior of Bornhem before returning to the mission at Stourton Lodge in Yorkshire, where he built a chapel.[75]

---

64 W. Gumbley, *Obituary Notices of the English Dominicans from 1555 to 1952* (London: Blackfriars Publications, 1955), p. 78.
65 Ibid. pp. 66–67.
66 Ibid. pp. 79–80.
67 C. F. R. Palmer, *Acta Capitulorum Provincialium Provinciae Angliae Ord. Praed. 1730–1916* (London: Westminster Press, 1918), pp. 35–36, 39.
68 Ibid. p. 56.
69 Ibid. p. 46.
70 Ibid. p. 59.
71 Ibid. p. 63.
72 Ibid. p. 74.
73 Ibid. p. 76.
74 Ibid. p. 299.
75 *Dominicana* (London: CRS, 1925), n. p. 120, 134.

Ambrose Gage's obituary provides the only evidence we have that the Short family patronised their own chaplain. It is possible, although Alexius Jones's diary unfortunately provides no proof of this, that Hugh Owen was also patronised by the Shorts. The Benedictines were primarily gentry chaplains, and the Shorts may have wanted a separate pastoral identity for the 'town' Catholics. The idea that the Shorts sustained a clerical presence in Bury between the dissolution of the Jesuit mission in 1688 and the departure of Ambrose Gage is appealing and, given the Shorts' antipathy to the Jesuits, their original intention may have been to forestall a need for the Jesuits to return. Unfortunately, there is no direct evidence for the Shorts' involvement in the pastoral life of the town until the appearance of Ambrose Gage in 1758.[76] However, judging from his refusal to co-operate with the vicars apostolic in 1753 and his intolerance of the presence of secular clergy in Bury in 1789,[77] John Gage may well have resented a Dominican rival as well.

Ambrose Gage remained in Bury for three years until 1761,[78] when he became the chaplain at Coulsey Wood, a house in the village of Stoke Ash between Needham Market and Scole.[79] Coulsey Wood had been served from 1715–59 by the Benedictine Dom Maurus Rigmaiden (alias Smith),[80] who succeeded Francis Howard as Provost of Cambridge in 1749.[81] Coulsey Wood was the Suffolk home of a branch of the Bedingfield family from 1693,[82] but by the mid-eighteenth century the house was rented by James and Laelia Farrill, until they sold their furniture and moved to Bury in 1768.[83] The departure of Ambrose Gage in 1761, leaving Coulsey Wood without a priest, created enormous problems for John Gage and the Bury mission, with Gage expected to come up with a solution to fill the pastoral vacuum. In April 1765 John Gage wrote to

---

[76]   Rowe, *The Story of Catholic Bury St. Edmunds, Coldham and Surrounding District*, p. 11.

[77]   John Gage to Edward Beaumont, 23 January 1789 (Birmingham Archdiocesan Archives, C935f). Gage was angry that Beaumont and his congregation used his chapel without permission.

[78]   C. F. R. Palmer, *Obituary Notices of the Friar-preachers, or Dominicans, of the English Province* (London: Burns and Oates, 1884), p. 20.

[79]   Holt, *The English Jesuits in the Age of Reason*, p. 306.

[80]   Allanson, *Biography of the English Benedictines*, p. 191.

[81]   Downside Abbey, South Province Book R, p. 87.

[82]   In 1715 Henry Bedingfield of Stoke Ash owned the manor of Denham, valued at £508 14s 9d (Estcourt and Payne (eds), *The English Catholic Non-Jurors of 1715*, p. 254). Henry married Mary, daughter of William Havers of Winfarthing (whose son Thomas Havers of Thelveton married Delariviere's sister Henrietta D'Ewes) so he was Delariviere's brother-in-law. He died in 1738 (Foley, vol. 5, p. 568).

[83]   Rowe, '"The Lopped Tree": The Re-formation of the Suffolk Catholic Community', p. 188.

Galloway about the lack of a priest to serve the house. A number of the Coulsey Wood congregation lived in the neighbourhood of Haughley. Francis Sulyard, in the presence of John Reilly and James Farrill, asked John Gage to officiate there. John Reilly insisted that Gage should officiate every Sunday, but Gage explained that this would be impossible as he was already serving Sudbury. He suggested the Jesuit chaplain at Coldham, Richard Laurenson (alias 'Mr Billinge'), for the task.[84]

By the summer of 1765 the situation had still not been resolved, although Laelia Farrill seems to have proposed that a young priest named Charles Billing (1735–1805, not to be confused with Richard Laurenson alias Richard Billinge), who was then serving the Tasburgh family at Bodney, should move to Coulsey Wood.[85] John Gage objected on the grounds that 'he w[ou]ld be judg'd too young for so solitary a place'.[86] In the event, the younger Billing was transferred to Staffordshire, and Dennett instructed John Gage to host a new Jesuit chaplain, Henry Molyneux (1693–1771) on his way to Bodney,[87] having procured him 'a suit of cloths & a Doeskin pair of Breeches'.[88] Haughley remained without a priest.

The Coulsey Wood problem illustrates the challenges created by the vast geographical extent of John Gage's missionary oversight, which reached from the Waveney to the Stour. It also illustrates the logistical problems raised by the desire of the gentry to have Mass said in their local area. Gage remarked that 'were [Laurenson] to go to either place he must certainly go over night'. For an elderly priest, who was going deaf, this was no small matter. Later on, Mass seems to have been said at Haughley itself, rather than Coulsey Wood. On 20 October 1773 John Gage wrote to Bishop Hornyold, the Vicar Apostolic, that he was 'in the habit of serving once in six weeks at Mr Sulyard's of Haughley Park'.[89]

Joy Rowe has estimated that, in addition to John Gage's congregation at Bury, he was serving a congregation of around thirty at Stoke-by-Nayland, and about the same number in High Suffolk or the Waveney

---

84   John Gage to Edward Galloway, 4 April 1765 (Holt (1983), p. 306). See also Holt (1984), p. 143.

85   Holt, 'Some Letters from Suffolk, 1763–80', p. 307. On Charles Billing see Bellenger, p. 39.

86   John Gage to Edward Galloway, 16 July 1765 (Holt, 'Some Letters from Suffolk, 1763–80', p. 308).

87   Molyneux had been serving the Hedgecourt Chapel near East Grinstead under the patronage of the Gages of Firle since 1724 (Foley, vol. 7:1, pp. 513–14; Bellenger, p. 88; *Miscellanea VIII* (London: CRS, 1913), p. 185).

88   John Gage to Edward Galloway, 13 August 1765 (Holt, 'Some Letters from Suffolk, 1763–80', p. 308).

89   Foley, vol. 5, p. 539.

Valley at Haughley, Coulsey Wood or Thelveton.[90] Lay leadership in the
scattered community of High Suffolk was crucial, as was indicated by
the fact that John Reilly, not John Gage, called the shots on where the
priest ministered on a Sunday. For Rowe: 'The chaplaincies had indeed
done much to keep Catholicism alive but it was the tenacity of the laity
to hold on, even in extremes of isolation, that provided the congregations for these new public chapels.'[91] Not for nothing was Sir Thomas
Gage, 3rd Baronet described as *tenax* on his monument in Hengrave
church, and the epithet might have been justly applied to any of the
gentry (or indeed non-gentry) Catholic families in Suffolk. The social
diversity in the congregations of small missions such as Coulsey Wood
must have been striking, but Catholics remained united by a common
loyalty to one another and to the Mass.

In contrast to the small but durable community of High Suffolk,
Catholicism in the Stour Valley seems to have gone into decline in the
second half of the eighteenth century. In 1786, John Baptist Newton,
the chaplain at Coldham, reported that while there had once been a
chapel at Long Melford, now 'nothing is to be met with but ignorance,
stupidity and sometimes a total neglect of religion'.[92] The only Stour
Valley Catholics who emerge from John Gage's register in the period
1756–67 are the Hales and Lotts of Bulmer Tye; the Normans and
MacGowans of Great Cornard; the Codlins, Griggs, Goldsmiths and
Hermans of Sudbury; and the Wellums of Long Melford. Of the twelve
baptisms performed by John Gage outside of Bury, seven were at Long
Melford, Sudbury or Bulmer Tye.

John Gage began a mission register on 1 January 1756 entitled 'Status
Miss: S: P: B:'. 'Miss: S. P. B.' may stand for *Missionis Sanctorum
Patrum Benedictinorum*, i.e. 'Mission of the Holy Benedictine Fathers';
alternatively it may be the name of the mission, *Missio Sancti Patris
Benedicti*, 'The Mission of our Holy Father St Benedict'. If the initials
do refer to St Benedict or the Benedictines this would be an indication
that John Gage simply took over the Benedictine mission to begin with
and continued to maintain the monks' practice of keeping a register. In
the register, Gage recorded baptisms, deaths and marriages. Of these,
the baptisms were the most important record, since Catholics were not
obliged by law to baptise their children in the parish church in the same
way that they were obliged to bury their dead and marry in the parish,

---

[90] Outside of the Liberty of St Edmund, High Suffolk had the largest Catholic population
in the county, see Rowe, '"The Lopped Tree": The Re-formation of the Suffolk
Catholic Community', pp. 169–70.

[91] Ibid. p. 187.

[92] Rowe, 'The 1767 Census of Papists in the Diocese of Norwich', pp. 195–96. See also
Foley, vol. 5, p. 544.

at least after Lord Hardwicke's Marriage Act of 1753. Gage's record of *defuncti* should not be taken as a record of funerals since, by law, these took place in the parish church. However, requiem masses may have been said for all or some of those whose dates of death were recorded.

The marriages recorded in the register were Catholic marriages with no legal standing, which might take place before or after the parish wedding, obligatory since Hardwicke's Marriage Act in 1753. The vicars apostolic encouraged Catholics to 'exchange consents' before a missionary priest before going to the parson. However, far from being the 'furtive affairs in private houses' suggested by Aveling, Catholic marriages in Bury after 1753 were openly recorded in the register.[93] However, since many Catholics married non-Catholics, it could not be guaranteed that the non-Catholic party would agree to a Catholic ceremony as well, and consequently John Gage's list is unlikely to represent an exhaustive list of every wedding involving a Catholic in the Bury area.

In the annotations he added to the register, John Gage acknowledged the debt he owed to his mother when she died in 1759:

> In this year on 30th January died Elizabeth Gage Rookwood, signal benefactress, patroness and almost foundress (*paene fundatrix*) of this mission. It seems altogether proper and just that her anniversary should be celebrated, if possible, on the aforesaid day every year, and that each day thereafter whenever Mass is said the *De Profundis* should be added after the Liturgy of the Blessed Virgin Mary for her soul and the souls of the other benefactors in the chapel of this Mission.[94]

Elizabeth Rookwood had given Gage the financial independence that was crucial to his ability to expand and improve the Bury mission. In his collection of documents on the history of the Rookwood family, Sir Thomas Gage, 7th Baronet noted the existence of a memorandum in John Gage's hand, endorsed by his mother, written at Blandecque on 6 July 1741, 'being a private Agreement between his Mother and himself relative to the disposition of his Fortune in contemplation of a religious life'.[95] Since Gage was about to enter the Society of Jesus at this point, it is probable that the document put his inheritance in his mother's hands to administer on his behalf. In 1735 Elizabeth bought for him the manor of Fresels in the parish of Westley. By his will of 7 August 1788 (proved on 6 November 1790) Gage passed this manor to his successor in the

93 Aveling, *The Handle and the Axe*, p. 310.
94 *Bury Register*, fol. 101.
95 CUL Hengrave MS 76/1.

mission.[96] In this way it remained attached to the Bury mission as a financial guarantee of its independence of gentry control.

In addition to John Gage's ownership of a manor, he may well have benefitted directly or indirectly from the fact that his brother Thomas Rookwood Gage was charged with the administration of the manor of Newnham in Bedfordshire as principal trustee, which was used to fund Jesuit missionary activities in East Anglia.[97] In June 1765, Thomas gave his brother £132 6s 6d, 'repairs falling very heavy', an indication that John Gage's financial independence was not always entire. Gage himself did not always appreciate the fact that the Bury mission had no formal endowment: 'I have served this place above these seventeen years, entirely gratis, as there is not one penny foundation I know of', he wrote to Bishop Hornyold in 1773.[98]

When Gage began to minister in Bury he had access to a private chapel in Southgate Street that was able to accommodate a congregation of fifty, 'in which divine service was performed in secret, and which was afterwards tenanted by a Mrs White who was a friend of the Gages though a Protestant and from whom the lane which there branches off from the street is still called Madam White's Lane'.[99] A separate external staircase from Madam White's Lane led directly to the chapel, and permitted discreet access for local Catholics. Since this chapel seems already to have been in existence when Gage began his mission, it is possible that the substantial townhouse to which it was attached was the property that Delariviere D'Ewes bought from Sir John James in 1740.[100] Alternatively, as Joy Rowe suggests, it may have been a house belonging to John Gage's mother, Elizabeth Rookwood. The Rookwoods had owned a townhouse in Bury since at least 1674, and it probably played host to the family chaplain as well as the family itself.[101]

Between 1 January 1756 and 21 November 1767 John Gage baptised eighty infants and one 15-year-old girl named Mary Magdalene, who was given no surname and described as *N: Americana*, which probably stood for *Negrissa Americana* ('American negress').[102] Given the Gages' connections with Montserrat, it is possible that Mary Magdalene was a slave from 'Gage's Fee'. Her godparents were James and Laelia

[96]   Gage, *Thingoe*, p. 93.
[97]   Holt, 'Some Letters from Suffolk, 1763–80', p. 307–8.
[98]   John Gage to Bishop Hornyold, 20 October 1773 (Foley, vol. 5, p. 539).
[99]   Rowe, '"The Lopped Tree": The Re-formation of the Suffolk Catholic Community', p. 186.
[100] *Diary*, 19 May 1740.
[101] Hervey (ed.), *Suffolk in 1674*, p. 52.
[102] *Bury Register*, 9 May 1759.

Farrill, who may have employed her as a servant. Of the eighty infants baptised, the vast majority were the sons and daughters of Bury Catholics and were presumably baptised at John Gage's own chapel. On occasion, John Gage evidently travelled beyond Bury and baptised babies in private at home, such as the daughter of Richard Gardiner at Hengrave, Mary;[103] three sons of Nicholas Herman at Sudbury;[104] Susanna, the daughter of Elizabeth Tilson at Fornham All Saints;[105] John, the son of Elizabeth Girt at Great Finborough;[106] William, the son of William Caruthers at Hargrave;[107] the son and daughter of Joseph Lott of Bulmer Tye;[108] Mary, the daughter of James Vincent at Coldham;[109] Thomas, the son of Thomas Goldsmith at Sudbury;[110] and Anne, the daughter of Joseph Wellum at Long Melford.[111]

The vast majority of those baptised in Bury were native Bury Catholics, with the exceptions of Elizabeth, 'the daughter of an Irish traveller', who was the first child baptised by John Gage (on 1 January 1756), and John Atvers, 'a foreigner', on 25 January of the same year. However, even in Bury not all baptisms were performed in John Gage's own chapel in Southgate Street. The baptism of John Horseman on 21 May 1759 took place 'in Mr Bond's chapel'. Of the five baptisms performed 'at home', two were the children of John and Mary Reilly. Reilly was given the title *Dominus* in the register as a mark of his gentility. Thomas Reilly (b.1760), the son of John Reilly, may have been the Thomas Reilly who married Charlotte Steele of Mustow House.[112]

Apart from the Reillys, other gentry mentioned in the register included the Farrills and William Olivarez Gage, Sir William's illegitimate son. The Laelia Farrill who acted as godmother on four occasions was born Mary Laelia Huddlestone, the only child of Dr Henry Huddlestone and Mary Gage, daughter of Sir William Gage, 2nd Baronet. Her husband, James Farrill, died at the age of seventy-five on 19 October 1767.[113] Although Mary Laelia had no children, she gave her name to her goddaughter Mary Laelia Scarf, who was baptised on 10 February

---

103   *Bury Register*, 5 December 1759.
104   *Bury Register*, 21 January 1760 (John Herman); 16 October 1761 (Ambrose Herman); 10 April 1763 (Michael Herman).
105   *Bury Register*, 26 April 1761.
106   *Bury Register*, 22 June 1761.
107   *Bury Register*, 10 May 1762.
108   *Bury Register*, 9 January 1763 (Mary Lott); 28 July 1764 (John Lott).
109   *Bury Register*, 8 September 1763.
110   *Bury Register*, 10 February 1764.
111   *Bury Register*, 20 July 1764.
112   Farrer (1908), p. 66. Farrer associated the Reillys with Westhorpe.
113   Gage, *Thingoe*, n. p. 209 erroneously gave the name Dominick to James Farrill.

1760. In spite of the fact that they lived at Coulsey Wood until 1768, the Farrills were frequently in attendance at baptisms as godparents in Bury.[114] Olivarez Gage also acted as godfather on two occasions. He had a mortgage of £2,500 on the Hengrave estate during his father's lifetime (Frances Harland's sister had a mortgage on the estate for the same sum).[115] In Sir William's will, written on the day of his death, the Baronet bequeathed his house in Bury (presumably the Northgate Street property) to Olivarez, his 'natural son', who was described in the will as William Gage of Leith, near Whitby in Yorkshire.[116]

The name of a non-Catholic parent was usually omitted from baptism records, although it was occasionally included (as in the case of Elizabeth Stuart, the mother of William Stuart, baptised on 2 January 1762). Of the sixteen marriages performed by John Gage between 1757 and 1767, ten involved a non-Catholic party; four men married non-Catholic wives and five women took non-Catholic husbands. In one case (the marriage of the non-Catholic Robert Tillson to Elizabeth Birch on 7 July 1760), Gage noted that the marriage was performed with no witnesses 'that it might be done prudently', perhaps an allusion to family opposition to the match. One famous member of Bury's eighteenth-century Catholic community, the playwright and novelist Elizabeth Inchbald (née Simpson), was the daughter of the Catholic yeoman farmer John Simpson, and a Protestant mother, Mary Rushbrook of Flempton.[117] John Gage married the Frenchman François Le Comte to Anne Morley on 3 May 1761, but the couple moved to London soon afterwards and there is no evidence that any foreign Catholics were based in Bury at this period. William Last and Mary Gibben required a dispensation from the vicar apostolic for their marriage on 4 December 1767, probably on grounds of consanguinity; canon law, unlike English law, did not permit the marriage of first cousins.

Bury may have been a tolerant town, but John Gage's ministry was not altogether unhampered by clergy of the Established Church. On 31 October 1764 the 100-year-old Joan Parfery died 'in the hospital' without having received Holy Communion. Gage noted in the register

---

114 Holt, 'Some Letters from Suffolk, 1763–80', p. 306.
115 James Dennett to Edward Galloway, 14 November 1767; James Dennett to Edward Galloway, 19 November 1767 (Holt, 'Some Letters from Suffolk, 1763–80', pp. 310–12).
116 A daughter of William Olivarez Gage married George Anne of Burghwallis in Yorkshire, whose son Michael married the heiress of the Tasburghs of Bodney and changed his surname to Tasburgh-Anne (CUL Hengrave MS 1/4, fol. 367).
117 I have established Inchbald's mixed parentage in my article 'Elizabeth Inchbald's "Catholic Novel" and its Local Background', *Recusant History* 31 (2013), pp. 573–92.

that Joan's 'noise was so great that she was deprived of the Sacrament out of the envy (*invidia*) of non-Catholics, and especially of the minister Crask'.[118] The reference was to Walter Craske, Reader of St Mary's Church, who was elected by the parishioners on 14 November 1757 and held the position until his death in May 1790, along with the rectories of Bradfield Combust and Stowlangtoft.[119] However, Crasks appear in the *Hengrave Register*, and the fact that the family was divided along confessional lines may have contributed to Walter Craske's *invidia*.[120] The hospital in question was probably Clopton's Hospital, erected in St Mary's Churchyard in 1730, which admitted three poor men and three poor women from each of the two parishes of Bury St Edmunds.[121] This was the only hospital in Bury at the time and, since it lay in the precincts of St Mary's Church, it is likely that Craske had spiritual oversight of the inmates. Another Catholic, Robert Oxer, was also an inmate alongside Joan Parfery.[122] John Gage recorded the deaths of local Catholics even when they were not in the locality at the time, such as the five-year-old Elizabeth Reilly 'at Tours in France' on 5 November 1765, and the death of Sir William Gage, 4th Baronet in London on 17 May 1767.[123]

On 11 May 1759 Vicar Apostolic John Joseph Hornyold paid a rare visit to Bury to confirm 40 Catholics,[124] and in the same year 119 people took advantage of the Indulgence promulgated by Pope Clement XIII between Palm Sunday and Easter Day.[125] This was the largest number ever to receive Easter communion in Bury before 1770. Easter communions ranged from between 87 communicants in 1757, to 113 in 1762, the year in which the new mission chapel was consecrated. Christmas communions were always lower than at Easter, ranging from a high of 90 in 1758–59 to 63 in 1766–67. John Gage received a total of fourteen converts into the Catholic Church during the period 1756–67, the highest number being four in 1766. On the whole, the mission underwent modest growth in the years up to 1762 and experienced modest decline thereafter; however, numbers remained stable and there seem to

---

[118] *Bury Register*, 31 October 1764 (fol. 65).

[119] Tymms, *An Architectural and Historical Account of the Church of St. Mary, Bury St. Edmunds*, pp. 106–7.

[120] For the Catholic Crasks see *Hengrave Register*, 12 October 1742; 11 February 1750.

[121] E. Gillingwater, *An Historical and Descriptive Account of St. Edmund's Bury, in the County of Suffolk* (Bury St Edmunds, 1804), pp. 231–32.

[122] *Bury Register*, 7 October 1764.

[123] His body was brought back to be interred at Hengrave on 24 May 1767 (Gage, *Hengrave*, p. 77).

[124] The next confirmations did not take place until 17 July 1768 (*Bury Register*, fol. 103).

[125] *Bury Register*, fol. 101.

have been no dramatic demographic changes in the Catholic community in these years.

A new home for the mission

In July 1763 Gage wrote to Galloway to inform him of the arrival of James Dennett, Superior of the English Jesuits, at Coldham. Dennett was still at Coldham in 1767, which was, therefore, the nerve centre of the entire English Jesuit mission in England when the Superior was in residence there.[126] Dennett was, with Sir William Gage and John Gage's brother Thomas, the patron of the new chapel at Bury begun in 1761, as noted in the register:

> In this year was built from the foundations the Mission House to God Best and Greatest; [this was done] on account of Sir William Gage (*G. G. Eq.*) and Thomas Rookwood Gage (*T. R. G.*) putting forward the money, with James Dennett (*J. D.*) helping.[127]

Dennett's patronage, although it was probably financially insignificant, was symbolically important. It ensured that the new mission house was a project of the Society of Jesus, patronised by its Superior in England, as well as an endeavour of local gentry and family members. In this way John Gage's mission was quickly able to assume the identity of a mature proto-parish with its own identity. However, in spite of the financial help, the building of the new mission house and its chapel in Westgate Street was a protracted and troubled affair. In 1762 Gage recorded the consecration of the chapel:

> In this year on 20th December the Chapel of this Mission was consecrated to God under the dedication of the Immaculate Conception of the Blessed Virgin Mary, with the signal benefactors being Sir William Gage and Thomas Rookwood Gage. Mrs Tindesley[128] [gave] a silver hanging cross and two silver vases with six flowers.

However, John Gage was still receiving bills for work on the mission house in February 1764 (for the staircase and 'sash pulleys') from the

---

126   Dennett was chaplain at Coldham 1751–52, Provincial 1762–66 and again chaplain 1766–87 (Holt (ed.), *The English Jesuits 1650–1829*, p. 78).

127   *Bury Register*, fol. 102.

128   'Mrs Tindesley' may have been one of the Tyldesleys who settled at Fornham St Genevieve, although there is no evidence that Tindesley was a variant spelling of the Lancashire surname. She was probably the Joan Tindesley who died at the age of seventy-seven on 14 October 1766. It is possible that she was the widow of the Mr Tildesley who died in 1734 (*Diary*, 18 February 1734).

builder, Mr Dobson, and the less-than-competent plasterer Wilkins.[129] In July 1765 he reported that 'Part of one of Wilkins's ceilings is fallen and another is crumbling down',[130] and his brother Thomas Rookwood Gage, who had contracted Wilkins for plasterwork at Coldham Hall, was so exasperated with the plasterer that he wanted to speak to him before witnesses: 'I want my rooms & am a great sufferer by delays', he complained.[131]

The new mission house and chapel cost a total of £2,000 to build and furnish.[132] The chapel remained in use until the construction of the parish church of St Edmund, King and Martyr in 1836, when it became the presbytery's drawing room. The wall separating the chapel from the adjoining church was knocked through in 1979, and it has been the Blessed Sacrament Chapel ever since.[133] Although none of the original furnishings remain, some of Wilkins's plasterwork survives in the 'mock-gothic' coving around the edge of the ceiling.

Continuity and change in the Catholic community

While the list of Suffolk nonjurors in 1715 was somewhat meagre, the Benedictine and Jesuit registers, taken together with the constables' lists of 1745 and the November 1767 'Returns of Papists' to the Bishop of Norwich, give a fairly comprehensive picture of the Catholic community in Bury between 1734 and 1767. The 1767 list was drawn up in response to a vigorous campaign in the press for a census of Catholics. As a result, the most accurate record of the Catholic community yet undertaken was made by local clergy of the Established Church for each diocese in England.[134] These incumbents, having a greater degree of local knowledge than the constables who sought out papists and reputed papists for the 1745 quarter sessions, generally produced more accurate and complete lists. The questions posed to incumbents in 1767 did not require them to declare the names of papists, and the intention of the census was demographic and statistical rather than punitive; the

---

129   John Gage to Edward Galloway, 25 February 1764 (Holt, 'Some Letters from Suffolk, 1763–80', pp. 305–6).

130   John Gage to Edward Galloway, 16 July 1765 (Holt, 'Some Letters from Suffolk, 1763–80', p. 308).

131   Thomas Rookwood Gage to Edward Galloway, 23 August 1765 (Holt, 'Some Letters from Suffolk, 1763–80', p. 308).

132   Rowe, '"The Lopped Tree": The Re-formation of the Suffolk Catholic Community', p. 186.

133   M. Statham, *The Book of Bury St. Edmunds* (Whittlebury: Baron Birch, 1996), p. 47.

134   E. S. Worrall (ed.), *Returns of Papists Volume 2: Dioceses of England and Wales, except Chester* (London: CRS, 1989), p. x.

anonymous returns were edited by E. S. Worrall for the Catholic Record Society in 1989. However, for the Diocese of Norwich a counterpart list, which actually named Catholics, also survived. This was edited by Joy Rowe and published in 1996 as an appendix to her article on the censuses of 1676 and 1767.[135]

The 'Return of Papists' makes for an interesting comparison with John Gage's mission register. The census recorded ninety-seven adult Catholics in the parishes of St Mary and St James (139 including children), and we know from the register that ninety-one Catholics received Easter communion that year. This suggests that the census was largely accurate. However, beyond Bury the census illuminates the extent to which the Catholic population had changed. In the parish of Flempton-cum-Hengrave, the rector recorded only a French hairdresser, Anthony de Moin, and the labourer Richard Gardiner, who also appears in the mission register. The absence of a significant Catholic population in the village is strong evidence in favour of the virtual abandonment of Hengrave, where servants were no longer needed. By contrast, there were twenty-seven Catholics living in the parish of Stanningfield, in addition to Sir Thomas Gage, 5th Baronet and his family. This was the largest concentration of Catholics anywhere in Suffolk after Bury itself. By 1767 the gentry Catholics in the parish of Fornham All Saints (incorporating Fornham St Genevieve) had disappeared, leaving behind only the publican Thomas Ramplee (Ramplin?), probably the landlord of the Three Kings public house, his daughter and the poor woman Elizabeth Tilson and her daughter.

With the exception of Stanningfield, by 1767 Suffolk Catholicism was very much an urban phenomenon, and the population of gentry Catholics in particular was concentrated overwhelmingly in Bury. Ipswich returned just twelve Catholics. Rowe has estimated that Catholics represented 2.5 per cent of the town's population in 1767, compared with 0.97 per cent of the national population (around seventy thousand Catholics in 1750, according to John Bossy),[136] and 0.4 per cent of the population of Norfolk.[137] Rowe has argued that the availability of the Mass was a crucial factor in the survival of a Catholic population in those areas where one persisted.[138] The establishment of the public chapel at Bury drew in more communicants, as evidenced by the record number (113) receiving Easter and Christmas communion in the new

---

[135] Rowe, 'The 1767 Census of Papists in the Diocese of Norwich', pp. 202–34.

[136] Bossy, *The English Catholic Community 1570–1850*, p. 422.

[137] Rowe, *The Story of Catholic Bury St. Edmunds, Coldham and Surrounding District*, p. 13.

[138] Rowe, '"The Lopped Tree": The Re-formation of the Suffolk Catholic Community', p. 188.

chapel at Easter 1762. However, in the scattered communities of High Suffolk the faith survived, in spite of the absence of a sizeable Catholic community and a public chapel, simply because priests were prepared to minister there at the instigation of local gentry.

Comparison of the four main sources for Bury Catholics reveals a socially diverse community consisting of gentry, tradesmen, craftsmen, labourers and servants, as well as a significant number of widows at any one time (see Appendix 7). Overall, 138 separate family names can be found across all of the sources, and several families, such as the Hunts and Larretts, had multiple branches.

Table 5.1. The social composition of the Catholic community
in Bury St Edmunds, 1734–67

Gentry	Tradesmen	Craftsmen	Servants	Labourers	Unknown
9.3%	7.3%	22%	9.3%	8%	44%
(14/150)	(11/150)	(33/150)	(14/150)	(12/150)	(66/150)

Table 5.1 shows that almost 10 per cent of the Bury community consisted of gentry. Of these families, only the Gages, Rookwoods, Shorts and Sulyards were of long standing, although the Bonds and Burtons arrived in the late seventeenth century and were scarcely newcomers in 1734. However, families such as Dillon, Fergus and Reilly were newcomers of Irish origin, a trend remarked by Aveling in the rolls of the English colleges on the Continent as well as in mission registers.[139] Some of the new gentry families, such as the Farrells, married into older families like the Gages. Other names are familiar local Catholic or non-Catholic gentry with whom the Gages had contracted marriage alliances, such as Huddlestone and Lamb. The otherwise unknown Catholic physician Dr Nile, present in Bury in 1745, may have been attracted by the success of the Shorts.

For the purposes of this analysis I have classified as tradesmen those who derived their income from selling the produce of others rather than through craft and manufacturing; these include innkeepers, butchers, watchmakers, stewards, barbers and drapers. By 1767 Bury had two Catholic innkeepers, in addition to Thomas Ramplin of the Three Kings at Fornham All Saints, while the butcher Nicholas Brundle was

---

[139] Aveling, *The Handle and the Axe*, pp. 262, 292. Dr John Bergin drew attention to the increasing prevalence of Irish Catholics among the English gentry in a paper delivered to the Catholic Record Society conference on 26 July 2011, 'An Irish Catholic Elite in England, 1670–1800'.

a leading member of the community who frequently acted as godfather at baptisms. Lower down the social scale, the largest single identifiable social group within the community consisted of craftsmen such as carpenters, glovers, joiners, mantua makers, shoemakers, staymakers, tailors and woolcombers. Seven families were engaged in the shoe-making business, while eight were tailors. A little under 10 per cent of Catholics were in domestic service, and it is these names, unsurprisingly, that pass in and out of the registers fairly quickly; people were more likely to leave their local area in order to enter domestic service, and they did not necessarily stay long. Apart from the relatively small number of heads of household listed as labourers, we have no record of the social status of 44 per cent of the families recorded between 1734 and 1767, and many of these may have been labourers or piece-workers.

A limited degree of social mobility and self-improvement is evident over the course of thirty-three years. For instance, the prolific Horseman family, mere labourers in 1745, had produced a shoemaker by 1767. Likewise the Larretts, who were gardeners in 1745, had advanced to shoemakers by 1767, and Agnes Larrett was the mistress of a Catholic dame school, implying a certain degree of education. However, the Catholic community was a dynamic and changing one. Only seven families in addition to the Gages (Birch, Cranmer, Horseman, Hunt, Larrett, Lowdall and Merry) appear in four of the five lists, and only the Gages themselves feature in all five. Twenty families appear in three of the lists.[140] Overall, 29 families (21 per cent) feature in three or more of the lists, leaving the other 109 (79 per cent) appearing in two lists or fewer. However, this is not necessarily an accurate measure of the degree of change in the Catholic community; the registers did not record the names of every Catholic, only those of Catholics who produced children, married, died or acted as godparents during the years covered by the register. Families such as the Shorts, whom we know from other sources to have been in Bury at the time, are absent from the *Hengrave Register*, for instance.

A comparison of family names that occur in 1715, 1734–51 and 1746 with family names occurring ten years later in the Jesuit register and the returns of 1767 yields somewhat more informative results. Just over 20 per cent of the names that occur in the *Bury Register* and the 1767 returns can be found in the *Hengrave Register* or the 1715 and 1745 lists (28/138).[141] Whatever analysis is made, it is evident that in the

---

140   These are: Adams, Annis, Balls, Bennett, Betts, Bond, Browning, Brundle, Frost, Gardiner, Gillett/ Jellett, Huddlestone, Kenyon, Mann, Morley, Rhodes, Sulyard, Tyldesley, Twite and Wordwell.

141   These are: Adams, Balls, Bedingfeld, Betts, Birch, Bond, Browning, Brundle, Cranmer, Crisp, Frost, Gage, Gardiner, Gillett, Horseman, Huddlestone, Hunt, King,

period in question only around 20 per cent of the Catholic community remained in one place for more than a decade. Fortunately, the incumbents who compiled the 1767 returns noted how long individuals had lived in Bury; 49 of the 139 Catholics recorded in that year had been in Bury for ten years or longer, while 42 had been in the town for twenty years or longer. Only 34 of the 97 Catholic adults (thirteen years old or older) had been born in Bury, and therefore listed as 'natives'.[142]

Some Bury families who had been Catholic in earlier years seem to have conformed to the Established Church during the course of the eighteenth century. Although the Prettyman family numbered a Catholic nonjuror in 1715, the Bury wool merchant George Prettyman (1722–1810)[143] was not a Catholic, and his son George (1750–1827) went on to become Bishop of Winchester. It is possible that the younger George Prettyman's opposition to Catholic emancipation as a Lord Spiritual may have owed something to his embarrassment concerning his family's own Catholic roots.[144] The Crask family, who were Catholics in the 1740s, were still in Bury in the late eighteenth century, but had presumably conformed. Other families, such as the Betts and Birches, seem to have had both Catholic and non-Catholic members, and this may not have been uncommon.

The stable core of around thirty native Catholic families in Bury may well have been a crucial reason behind the arrival of other Catholics interested in launching themselves in the same trades, and the 'native' and incomer Catholics should not be seen as distinct groups. In the last years of the eighteenth century, French aristocrats would be added to the roll of incomers, but up to 1767 they were probably Catholics who either had family connections with Bury, came to work for the small group of Catholic gentry who were settling in the town, or who were attracted by a town that must surely have had an enviable reputation for its tolerance towards Catholics. The Catholic community was, in Joy Rowe's words, 'established as a recognised entity'[145] even if it was not, as yet, a legal one.

Larrett, Lowdall, Merry, Morley, Rhodes, Short, Simpson, Sulyard, Tyldesley and Wordwell.

[142] Rowe, 'The 1767 Census of Papists in the Diocese of Norwich', pp. 225–28.

[143] The usual spelling of this name was Prettyman; however, the *ODNB* lists this name as 'Pretyman'.

[144] G. M. Ditchfield, 'Tomline, Sir George Pretyman' in *ODNB*, vol. 54, pp. 934–37.

[145] Rowe, 'The 1767 Census of Papists in the Diocese of Norwich', p. 188.

EPILOGUE

In the second half of the eighteenth century, Bury's Catholic community continued to expand, and John Gage's chapel may have been the first in England to be licensed under the Act of 1791.[1] François de Rochefoucauld, who visited Bury with his brother Alexandre in 1784, viewed the position of the Catholics in England through the prism of what he witnessed in Bury, reporting that in spite of anti-Catholic legislation, 'the Justice of the Peace always evades the rigour of the law: never is it put into force'. As a consequence, 'Catholics feel completely at ease: despite the severity of the laws against them, they practise their religion without concealment, and everyone knows without demurring.' De Rochefoucauld remarked that: 'The chapel at Bury belongs to the priest himself and all the Catholics attend on Sundays and Feast Days without the least trouble.'[2] Nevertheless, the young Frenchman considered Catholics to be 'absolutely separated from the body politic of the English'.

De Rochefoucauld compared the fervour of English Catholics favourably with French religion:

> I find the Catholics much more zealous in England than in France: they are more scrupulous in their religious observance: it is because they are discriminated against. It is the disposition of all men in all countries to like doing what is forbidden.[3]

De Rochefoucauld's evocative descriptions of the Catholic community in Bury are far exceeded, however, by the portrayal of Catholic gentry society in Elizabeth Inchbald's novel *A Simple Story* (1791), the first novel by an English Catholic to feature Catholic characters, which drew on Inchbald's upbringing in the shadow of the Rookwood Gages of Coldham Hall.

Sir Thomas Rookwood Gage, 5th Baronet became 'one of the most intimate acquaintances' of the de Rochefoucauld brothers and they paid frequent visits to Coldham. According to de Rochefoucauld, Sir Thomas's eldest son (the future 6th Baronet) was at this time living 'on the other side of Bury' (Norman Scarfe assumed that his house

---

[1]   Rowe, *The Story of Catholic Bury St. Edmunds, Coldham and Surrounding District*, p. 12.

[2]   F. De Rochefoucauld (ed. N. Scarfe), *A Frenchman's Year in Suffolk* (Woodbridge: Suffolk Records Society, 1988), p. 67.

[3]   Ibid. p. 68.

was Hengrave, although this is not certain). Most importantly, we know from the Frenchman's account that the alterations to Hengrave begun in 1775 were still continuing in some form nine years later: '[The Gages] have been restoring an old-fashioned house, which is costing them a great deal and obliges them to economise.' Nevertheless, de Rochefoucauld described the Gages as 'rich, for their family is a very old one'.[4]

The 'restoration' was carried out by the Catholic landscape gardener Richard Woods. In the 1770s Sir Thomas significantly altered the Hall by pulling down the tower and east wing and filling in the moat;[5] he also levelled the bay on the east side of the south front corresponding to the chapel bay, rendering the Tudor house asymmetrical. Whatever improvements Sir Thomas intended for the Hall stopped there, and Woods's plans for the park came to nothing; the funds were not available for a recusant landlord to landscape on the scale being attempted by his Protestant neighbours.[6] Thereafter, Hengrave seems to have been abandoned and the Gages considered selling it; in 1790 James Cornwallis, Bishop of Lichfield and Coventry and the brother of the Marquis Cornwallis of neighbouring Culford, contemplated purchasing the estate.[7] Hengrave found a new purpose between 1794 and 1802 when it became the home of the exiled English Augustinian canonesses of Bruges and their school.[8] However, as late as 1809 Sir William Gage, 7th Baronet was discussing pulling down the Hall and selling the materials.[9]

It was probably changing tastes, and the intervention of John Gage the antiquary, that saved Hengrave from demolition, and the house was certainly lived in again by the 1820s. The Rookwood Gages (or 'Gage Rokewodes', as they styled themselves from 1843) finally became extinct on the death of Sir Edward Gage-Rokewode, 9th Baronet (1812–72) on 3 January 1872, although he was survived by his widow, Henrietta-Mary Beauclerk, second daughter of the Earl of St Albans, who died in 1887. By Royal Sign Manual of 9 May 1872, and in accordance with Sir Edward's will, Robert Darell of Calehill in Kent, the grandson of Elizabeth Rookwood Gage, daughter of Sir Thomas Gage, 7th Baronet (and

4   Ibid. p. 27.
5   Gage, *Hengrave*, p. 17.
6   F. Cowell, *Richard Woods (1715–1793): Master of the Pleasure Garden* (Woodbridge: Boydell Press, 2009), pp. 207–10.
7   C. Paine (ed), *The Culford Estate 1780–1935* (Ingham: Ingham Local History Group, 1993), p. 1.
8   F. Young, 'Mother Mary More and the Exile of the Augustinian Canonesses of Bruges in England: 1794–1802', *Recusant History*, 27 (2004), pp. 86–102.
9   Elizabeth Jerningham recorded in her diary for 4 June 1809: 'Sir Thomas [Gage] put me out of patience by talking of pulling down Hengrave Hall to sell the materials. Neither his Wife or Brother [John Gage the antiquary] seemed to like it' (E. Castle, *The Jerningham Letters* (London: Richard Bentley and Son, 1896), vol. 1, p. 341).

therefore the senior female-line descendent of the Rookwood Gages) took the surname Rokewode-Darell and added the Rokewode arms to his own.[10]

However, Hengrave passed to the Earl of Kenmare in 1887 on the death of Lady Henrietta; Mary Anne Browne, daughter of the Earl of Kenmare, had been the mother of both the 8th and 9th Baronets.[11] The Earl of Kenmare leased Hengrave to the Australian steel magnate John Lysaght (it is unlikely that he sold it, as there is no sale catalogue for the period and the contents of the house remained intact). The house was sold to Sir John Wood in 1897, who restored the interior to some semblance of its Tudor appearance and even rebuilt the east wing (albeit without the original tower). Sir John restored the chapel and the Great Hall to their original dimensions and made the church of St John Lateran a chapel of ease in the parish of Flempton-cum-Hengrave; the church had been the Kytson and Gage mausoleum since its amalgamation with the parish of Flempton in 1589.[12] Through the sales of 1897 and 1952, the contents of the Hall were irretrievably dispersed, with the notable exception of the Hengrave manuscripts, and in 1952 Hengrave became a convent school under the care of the Sisters of the Assumption. In 1974 the Sisters established an ecumenical religious community and conference centre at Hengrave, which was dissolved in 2005. Hengrave Hall is now in private hands.

John Gage, the former Jesuit, died in 1790 but the chapel he had built remained in the hands of the ex-Jesuits. In 1837, in response to growing congregations after Catholic emancipation and the expansion of the town, a large mission church (later the parish church of St Edmund King & Martyr) was built on the east side of John Gage's chapel of 1762. The Jesuits continued to serve the church in Bury until it was transferred to the secular clergy of the Diocese of Northampton in 1929.

Conclusion

The period from 1741–67 did not so much see the decline of the Gages and the rise to influence of their Rookwood Gage cousins as a more profound realignment of the Catholic community in Bury, as a fully fledged mission congregation. The death of Delariviere D'Ewes and the extinction of the Benedictine monks spelled the end of a mission based around domestic chapels in the households of the Bonds and

---

[10] *London Gazette*, 23858 (17 May 1872), p. 2361. The Darells of Calehill became extinct with the death of Ethel Mary Margaret Darell-Blount in 1953.

[11] Gage, *Thingoe*, p. 205.

[12] For a copy of the Deed of Consolidation (*unio realis*) see SRO(B) 449/3/12.

Gages. Although, paradoxically, a Gage himself, John Gage's financial independence and his decision to build his own chapel (albeit with the financial support of the Gages and Rookwood Gages) freed the Catholic community in Bury from gentry patronage. It is hard to imagine John Gage following his brother or his cousin into the countryside during a smallpox outbreak, as Francis Howard and Alexius Jones were obliged to do in the 1730s. John Gage combined his family connections with the leading families of the area with a strong sense of independent missionary purpose, and was thereby able to establish the Jesuit mission in Bury on the firm foundations that would allow it to pass without difficulty to other Jesuit priests; unlike the Benedictine mission, it did not end with his death.

While the numbers of Catholics in Bury had not swelled significantly between 1745 and 1767, the composition of the population was shifting, in the form of a modest influx of minor gentry (at least some of them of Irish extraction) along with their servants. Bury was a tolerant and, to some extent, a cosmopolitan provincial market town where Catholics had little to fear from popular violence and antipathy. The evidence suggests that Catholics of all ranks were thoroughly integrated into Bury society by the end of the 1760s, setting the stage for the sympathetic welcome that Bury (and other towns) offered refugees of the French Revolution twenty years later.

EDITORIAL METHODS APPLIED
TO THE APPENDICES

Appendices 1 and 2 are transcriptions of MS material, and in them I have observed the following editorial conventions.

Insertions in the original MS are shown between oblique lines thus \.../. Readable deleted sections are shown within angled brackets <...> while illegible words are marked [*illeg.*] and sections that cannot be read owing to damage are marked [*damaged*]. No attempt has been made to retain superscript in the text such as '8th' for '8th'.

Original spelling and capitalisation have been retained with the exception of the archaic letter thorn (y), which is expanded to 'th' in all cases. Light punctuation has been inserted in square brackets [thus] where necessary to aid understanding of the text. Abbreviations have likewise been extended in square brackets, except where obvious (e.g. 'Mr' and 'Dr'). The dates quoted in the original documents are unaltered, but in all references to those same documents, Julian dates are given with the year beginning on 1 January (so 1 January 1642 or 1 January 1642/3 becomes 1 January 1643). No attempt has been made to retain the original layout of documents.

Appendix 3 consists of extracts from a printed source. The spelling, capitalisation and footnotes of the original have been retained, but not the italicisation of numerous words that occurs in the original.

Appendices 4, 5 and 6 consist of transcriptions of registers. These are transcribed in a modern form dictated by the kinds of information contained in the text, whereas in the original MSS the authors changed their minds at various times about how much detail they wanted to include. All names are given in their original spelling. Notes on individuals are paraphrases or translations of Latin phrases (e.g. *obiit infans* becomes 'died in infancy', *subito* becomes 'suddenly' and *acatholicus* becomes 'non-Catholic'), unless they are in speech marks (in which case they are direct quotations from the English or translated from the Latin).

APPENDIX 1

SELECTED GAGE FAMILY LETTERS
AND PAPERS, 1640–1744

1. Penelope Darcy to Mary Kytson, 28 November 1640 [CUL Hengrave MS 88/2/147]

Deer Madame

yesternight came a noble personage to mee: who desiring my pardon tolde me I was to prepare for more ill newes. For my nephew Savage[1] & mr Gilbert were gone to Colchester to receive the guifte of your other manour in the westcountrie & that if it were possible, they desired to proclaime me no childe of yours.

Deerest Mother hold your hand & remember how often you have tolde mee that you could long since have enritched your selfe (when you were in necessitie) with the sale of those manours but you rather embraced suffering then to give way to it for the care you had of me and myne.

Remember how many yeares you withstood it & now at last were pleased out of your love to settle it on my beloved sonne Edward. I beseech you let not him bee the first on whom you repent your guift bestowed, who is the last and all that God hath left me of my nurselings. If your Ladyship see no desert in mee, & that my misfortune makes mee I can no way meritt from you, yet Remember you are my mother & for God and iustice sake destroy not with sorrow what you have made. let not my poor children suffer for my faulte, but as in the whole course of your life you have been ever holden charitable to strangers prove not otherwise to your cradle[.] Remember Madame for the passion of God what a deer childe I lost of late, and what a wound it hath given mee, doe not by unkindnesse upon unkindnesse bereave your childe of her senses send her to Bedlam & overthrow a whole posteritie that hath as it ought so yelded you all reverence and obedience. Consider I beseech you that if my L[ord] my father had survived halfe your fortunes had been my byrthright let not your surviving (which I alwaies begged of God) make my condition worse, when from you I expected to have my fathers want of affection repayred.

---

[1] Thomas Savage, 1st Viscount Savage (later 2nd Earl Rivers), husband of Penelope's sister Elizabeth Darcy.

Thinketh your Ladyship it was not enough for my father, out of your lands in so manie yeares to raise so great a fortune for my sister & her children (which out of his owne he could never have done) unless your selfe also seeing all this given so entirely for them should strive to heap more where is so great plenty alreadie[.] But God move your heart to compassionate your poore distressed childe, that submittes to your doome and humbly craves your blessing

s. Johns this 28. of November 1640

Pen[elope] Gage

At s[i]r John Jerrills coming over to us I submitted to live in Hengrave with my owne poor fortunes, rather then to molest your ladyship because you were unwilling to alter your wrightings. And would have lived in silence had it not now concerned my poore childe whose good I dearly tender

2. Penelope Darcy to Mary Kytson, 29 January 1643 [CUL Hengrave 88/2/150]

Deerest Madam,

On Tuesday last my physitian went for London, leaving me able, I thanck God, to walke about my chamber, which I have now kept these six weeks. On Munday heer came the High Sheriff, S[i]r William Castleton, my cozin Spring, and Mr. Maurice Barrow, with about thirty attendants to fetch away your Ladyship's armour, by appointment of the House of Commons. Had not S[i]r William Hervey by chance heard of it, and come in some quarter of an hour before to give me notice of theyr coming, I, being weak, had been much affrighted with so many coming sodoinly upon mee. I told them, the armes, house, or land, was none of myne, but I was only admitted heer awhile by your Ladyship's favour, and had I had health, I had not been heer at this present. Therefore I desired them to acquaint your L[adyshi]p with theyr authoritie, to whom it belonged, and I was content to submitt to any thing. They replyed that they had farr home, and must dispatch the business at that present. I told them, if theyr authoritie would reach so farr, I could not gainesay anything the Parliam[en]t commanded. Whereupon they presently went downe, and poor Peed, being very sick at his owne howse, was sent to for the key and inventorie, but could not redly tell where they were. They brake open the doore, and tooke up carts in the highe way, and tooke away all your armes. I desired the drumme might be left, being verie good for a stable, to inure horses not to be fear'd: they by no means would leave it, but tooke it into the coach with them. Some wished them, it being late, and the evening verie rainie, to seal up the doores and leave somebodie to attend it, which the sheriff thought fitt; but Mr. Barrow say'd he would stay till 12 o'clock, but he would dispatch it that night. They made great apologies to me at theyr coming inne, saying they hoped I would parden theyr unwilling employment, and that they wer forced to that they did. I told them the armes had been 100 yeares in caholike's hands, and never yet hurt a finger of any body, and I wished they never might. They are now all in the hands of the sheriff, and I wish your L[adyshi]p or my cozin Grimston had the keeping of them, but I submit myself in all things to your L[adyshi]ps pleasure, that am ever,

Madam, your most obedient, and affectionate daughter,
PEN[elope] GAGE.

Hengrave,
Jan[uary] 29, 1642

I have sent your L[adyshi]p here enclosed a letter of theyr's, with a copie of the order: – Madame, though I am thus disarmed, yet I am much comforted by hearing of the safe and happie deliverie of my daughter Petre. We are daily threatned by the common sort of people, and for our defence have nothing left us.

3. Henry Becket to Mary Kytson, 29 January 1643[2] [CUL Hengrave MS 88/2/151]

Madame
    Some thinck it will be an ill president for your L[adyshi]P being a Protestant to suffer your armes to be taken away & it is conceiued that if you make meanes to mr Grimston[3] & other your friends in the howse you may have them againe at your owne dispose ————— seeing they belong only to you & there is no statute lawe to take them from you & then you may place them wher you thinck fitt. I think s[i]r Thomas Jermyns howse[4] were a fitt place he being a Parlament man & not too farre off for carriage[.] I beseech your L[adyshi]Ps pardon presuming this farr to advise you that am

Madame your honours most humble servant
Henry Becket

Hengrave
Jan[uary] 29
1642

---

[2] On the outside of the letter: 'To the R[igh]t honorable the Countesse of Rivers at her house in Colchester present these'.

[3] Sir Harbottle Grimston.

[4] Rushbrooke Hall, home of Sir Thomas Jermyn (1573–1645), MP for Bury St Edmunds in the Long Parliament.

4. Penelope Darcy to Mary Kytson, 7 July 1643 [CUL Hengrave MS 88/2/156]

Dearest Madam

I am infinitlie trubled th[a]t I cannot for the season give yo[u]r La[dyshi]p soo full satisfaction as I desire upon the receyte of yo[u]r monies. I did for me what then was yo[u]r La[dyshi]ps pleasure, for the [*illeg.*] of it. God forbid you should not Command yo[u]r owne when you please, but I protest I know not how to come by it now w[i]th anie saftie, nor till my returne into the Countrie, w[hi]ch I intend a fortnight hence, I humbly beseech you be pleased not to thinke this anie excuse, for you shall foinde I will most willingly returne all or what you please soo soone as possible I can. it is true the concluding of the match[5] is at a stay in respect of these distractions, yett it would much trubble me if Nan should be hindred of the hopes of that preferment, howsoever you shall never foinde me to disobey yo[u]r La[dyshi]p in anie thinge whilst I have breath that am and ever will be Madam

yo[u]r. La[dyshi]ps Most affectionate and obedient daughter
Pen[elope] Hervey

London July the 7th
1643

5. Penelope Darcy to Mary Kytson, 11 July 1643 [CUL Hengrave MS 88/2/157]

Dearest Madam

This bearer and his wife, Lay in the Lodgings I tooke at my first coming to London, and soo I grow into theyre acquaintance, they have now layen at my house a fortnight or 3 weekes and I have had verie good Companie of them, I [*illeg.*] Maloncully [*illeg.*] they are now goinge to Yarmoth and passinge through Colchester[.] I have desired them to waite upon yo[u]r La[dyship]s and deliver you this letter, and had it not been for feare of bringing trubble upon yo[u]r La[dyshi]p I had waited upon you my selfe, haveing soo good an opportunitie as to return w[i]th theyre emptie Coatch and I should have been glad to have spoaken w[i]th yo[u]r La[dy]s[hip] concerninge the safe returne of what you writt for, and soo I would have done about other occasions, my husband hath used his best indevors to gett me a house at Buirry, but cannot light on anie fitt for a familie, I confess I would fayne have been in a Towne these dayngerous times, and I can find n[o] waye but

---

5 Probably the projected marriage of Penelope's daughter Ann to Sir Andrew Clifton.

to retire to the Towne at Hengrave w[i]th my familie for I am infinitely wearie of London, w[hi]ch I thought impossible, but how to leave my house and goods in s[ain]t Jonses, secure, taxes and payments beinge so greate, as I know not how to continue it. I heare my daughter Merry[6] whoe is now at Soffam,[7] is somwhat recovered, by Doct[o]r Shorte,[8] but poore wretch she cannot as yett heare of her husband though we have sent manie letters[.] thus humbly cravinge yo[u]r pardon and b[l] essinges for me and myne I take leave that am Madam

        yo[u]r La[dyshi]ps most affectionate and obedient daughter

                              Pen[elope] Hervey

London July the 11th
1643

6. Thomas Harrison to Penelope Darcy, undated (1640s) [CUL Hengrave 88/2/168]

Right Hon[ora]bl[e]

    It seemeth by Mr: wyndes relation that it pleased yo[u]r La[dyshi]p to vouchsafe the remembrance of yo[u]r poore old servant by [*illeg.*], w[hi]ch By some sinister meanes miscaryed, soe as it never came to my hands, thoe pressed in other two [*illeg.*] by yo[u]r Hon[our] to the La[dy] Gage to Bee informed of the extremity thereof. I should have thought my selfe unworthy of Longer Lyvinge if I had neglected that undergoinge of any of yo[u]r Hon[ou]rs command, the Bent of my Desire beinge always most steadily willinge to p[er]form serviceable respect to yo[u]r La[dyshi]p to whom I ever was and still am beyonde my expression obliged.

    Madam I shall fall of from ffyrl-house, for that I finde not such respect as deserved[.] I have beene no ill member to that house 33 yeares especially in these miserable last distractine tymes. I was hardly Dealt with by [*illeg.*] of my Noble M[aste]r in raysinge of my rent, w[hi] ch I founde pleeded for my dutifull affortinge yor Hon[ou]r and not submitting my selfe to them and theirs wanted not severall enemyes the coales, I patiently bore all, thinkinge that S[i]r Tho[mas] Gage[9] would in some sortes have considered my service w[hi]ch I p[er]formed in suppressing many noxious occurrences by my owne policy, or giveing notice to avoyde the dangers, the p[ar]ticulers wheirof I will not commit

---

6   Penelope Darcy's daughter Penelope Gage who married Henry Merry of Barton Blount in Derbyshire.

7   Probably Swaffham in Norfolk.

8   Probably Dr Richard Short (d.1668).

9   Penelope's eldest son, Sir Thomas Gage, 2nd Baronet of Firle.

to paper[.] I am very sorye that I have beene soe tedious. pardon the boldnes of him that will ever remaine

Yo[u]r Hon[ou]rs humble servant
Tho[mas] harrison

Mr wynde understandinge my intent to wryte to yor Hon[ou]r intreated me humbly to pray yor Hon[ou]rs direction to whom and wheire to play yo[u]r La[dyshi]ps [*illeg.*], and whether to the former appointed Krex-eyuor or not. this humble service to yo[u]r Hon[ou]r always promised. he told me that his honored M[aste]r S[i]r Thomas Gage hath beene much trouble[d] w[i]th his fitts since his returne into England so we he forced to Bee lett bloud, he hopes the worst is past. he told mee that he hath writt severall l[et]t[e]rs to yo[u]r Hon[our] but never were any answered. he further told mee that he intends soe soone as he hath [*damaged*] this half yeares rent to wayt upon yo[u]r Hon[ou]r and pass his accompts Boke for lady day & Michaelmas [*damaged*]

7. Edward Gage to Frances Aston,[10] **1 December [1659]**[11] [CUL Hengrave MS 88/3/61]

Decemb[er] 1

Deare Madame

it is now almost tenn of the clock att night and I am but just now released out of prison[.] I was this afternoone att a play and taken by the soldiers with all the men there and carried to St Jameses[.] I am a fraid the post will be gone and can only tell you that though the persons that render our busnes for y[ou]r father & my mother who mett this afternoon did not agree yet I feare not but my Indeavours will putt that conclusion to all which I am so ambitious of and that I shall be allowed for ever to beare the quality of [*illeg.*] [*illeg.*] Aston your most faithfull & most affection[ate] B[rothe]r   E[dward] Gage

---

10 Frances Aston was Edward's sister-in-law.
11 On the outside of the letter: 'for Mrs Frances Aston att Toxhall — present putt this in the Lichfield Stayge Staffordshire'.

8. Bridget Stanhope to Elizabeth Feilding, [December 1669][12] [CUL Hengrave MS 88/3/58]

My Deare Chilld I am very glad to heare you are all so well[.] I was desirous to have bin with you at London this winter but god has bin pleased to viset mee with such hevy afflictions as I am not able to give my selfe that trobell as to remove out of this settellment though it be not such as I would have it yett the venter of a chang will be worse to me now in this ill condision I am in so I resolve to sitt still till I heare what will become of your poure Brother who knows not what cours to take with his children which care I must now take upone mee though left with nothing to do it with all but a hope your Brother will give som helpe to itt and god will agane loocke upone us to helpe us[.] you could never have demanded any thing from mee in a worse time for I have many Detts and trobells upone mee and that Dett to mee which my sone Basel[13] thinkes so Desperate from the cappten pray desire your Brother not to trobell his thoughts with itt for I have pade use mony for that fiftypound ever sins he had it and I know a way to gett itt as well as he and shall paye it where tis now owing and not to discharge his suparssos Detts which will be the same agane[.] when so ever the[y] are payed he is like to paye them himselfe for I never will[.] I am very much trobled you can not obtane a [*illeg.*] of a place though he had wanted for it never so long it would have bin some comfort to him in thes afflictions which you know his temper is to be most passionate so with my blessing to my sone Gage and Kaete I am Deare Chilld

your most Affection[ate]
mother B[ridget] Desmon[d]

I have had most sad letters out of Fearland this last post
I was much trobled to heare of your sone will gages haveing the smallpox but I hope he is by this past all danger

9. Elizabeth Feilding to Sir Edward Gage, undated (1660s) [CUL Hengrave MS 88/3/63]

wensday night

My Dearest Dedre
    I was much troubled to know what was becume of my Dearest, but I

---

[12]   On the outside of the letter: 'this To the lady Elizabeth Gage my Deare Daughter at her house in Suthampton Buildings neere to Bloomsbery markett next the Bull London'.
[13]   Basil Feilding, eldest son of the Earl of Desmond.

had noe Cunsyearne for the wont of my Coch[.] I am glad with all my heart that you wentt throw with the Coch to nuportt but when I wred in your Letter that your over turned I was afrade you ade sume hurtt but time bee sides your Letter ded assure mee that you gott noe hurtt by your fale; only hee tould mee that you gott Could but I hope my Dearest you will gett it a way very quickly[.] [*damaged*]dy bee sure to Lie in A safe Loging and gett A good bed and see itt will eared for you have noe Care of your selfe but for my sake, My Dearest make much of your selfe and doe not dessorder your selfe, nor spend your mony my Dearest for god sake. thinke of mee and mind your bisnes that I may not bee Long absontt from my Dearest Dedre that I Love better then my one Life[.] I thinke of you night and day and I will bee as true to you; as you are to your selfe your Letter as giving mee great seattisfacktion and I hope I shall rest better this night then I have done sence you Left mee; for I Could not slepe for Thinking weare you ware and seeing the Coch not Cume home made me have many apprehensions for you; I thanke god for all his Blesings to mee and for your safty which I Countt one of the greatting I have in thes world; bee true to me my Dearest and Love mee and in this doing you will make hapy your Most obeadantt and most duttyfull wiffe to Cummand

E[lizabeth] Gage

10. Mary Gage[14] to Thomas Halsall, undated (1670s) [CUL Hengrave MS 88/2/174]

Mr Hallsal I receivd a letre from my brother last night and he sends me word that my box has bin kept all this time by the newmarket coach but whether it will come to bury or lyes at newmarket I doe not know[.] this I must desire you to give your self the truble to finde out and if it be at newmarket to some messenger to goe thether for it to morrow and to let me have it the next day[.] I should put you in mind of an other concern but I am confident you will not forget me[.] I hope to hear somthing of it when I see you upon Sunday[.] in mean time I give you thanks for the care you have already taken in my concern and shall alwais b[e] your friend

M[ary] Gage

---

[14] Mary Gage was the eldest daughter of Sir Edward Gage by his first wife Mary Hervey; she later married William Bond.

11. Mary Gage to Thomas Halsall, undated (1670s)[15] [CUL Hengrave MS 88/2/175]

I was extreamly disappointed mr Halsall when I came to town and found noe word of the mony[.] you may very well believe that I am in noe little want of it[.] I beg the continuance of your assistance in it[.] my brother has has promised his whensoever it shall be demanded[.] the getting of it done as sone as posible will ad very much to the obligation which I will always own to be a very high one[.] I well assure you if I reckond that I should want this very much though my father paid several things for me[.] I finde if I doe soe now more there being very little of myne paid I supose you have received my father['s] orders by my brother concerning the chapel[.] I tould my lady what you desired me and asked if I should say any thing to you but she toul[d] me she would write her self[.] pray mr hallsal let me hear from you for I have not mony to to buy me close till you helpe me to soone[.] I hope mr covell does not repent what he has proceeded which though you have a great deall of reason more to doe I doe not at all mistrust it and am only only ashamed I canot return you thanks proportionable to soe great a favor but if there be at any time any thing within my power to serv you you shall find me ready to perform the part of your obligd friend

M[ary] G[age]

pray my servis to your wif and to mrs pidg[eon]

12. Sir Edward Gage to Thomas Halsall, undated (1670s) [CUL Hengrave MS 88/2/178]

Tom Halsall I saw about a weeke since a doe killed here hard by the towne that was extraordinary fatt and I have longed ever since for some doe venison[.] I would have you therfor appoynt the keeper to kill me a good one if he can and send it up next weeke[.] I have more to say to you but I want time att the present for it,

E[dward] Gage

remember me to my Bro[ther][16] & will Gage, I beleeve my daughters & mr Sulyard[17] will be gone from Hengrave before you receave this & so I say nothing to them.

---

[15] On the outside of the letter: 'for Mr Halsall att Hengrave neere St Edmonds Bury'.
[16] Probably John Gage of Stonham.
[17] Sir Edward Sulyard of Haughley, husband of Sir Edward's eldest daughter Penelope.

13. Sir Edward Gage to Thomas Halsall, undated (1670s) [CUL Hengrave MS 88/2/179]

London
Maundy Thursday

I have considered of An allowance for my sonne will, & doe order you to pay him 200s per ann[um] which is more than ever I was allowed my selfe till I had a settlement made upon me upon marriage; butt my intention is to be att no other kind of Charge concerning him whatsoever; if he finds the country to chargeable for this proportion, he knows he has a home here, where he will be att no expence except of cloaths & pockett money.

14. Dr Francis Gage to Mr Enderby, 18 January 1668 [CUL Hengrave MS 88/3/109]

Paris Jan[uary] 18/28

Sir

The foule weather at sea this winter season is the cause that letters neither goe nor come so speedily as they should so that I know not whether you have recieved either of my two letters w[hi]ch some weekes agoe I writt unto you directed to the naggs head, one for y[ou]r selfe, and the other some dayes after for S[i]r Edward: In both w[hi]ch I gave you an accompt of the expences under w[hi]ch it was impossible for mr Gage to live in this College, since w[hi]ch I have received the bill of exchange you delivered to mr Platt, and have the mony: but by it I partly perceive S[i]r Edwards allowance will not extend to the necessary somme w[hi]ch I required: soe that sincerely I know not what to doe w[i]th the young gentleman when he comes. If I kepp any servant of my owne I could command him to doe all the busenesse for him, but I have none but one that putt by mr Draycotts mother to waite upon her sonne, for whom I pay both dyet and wages, so that it is not to be expected that I should command him to attend on any other. Really I think S[i]r Edward ought to spend one hundred at least upon his sonne; or if his occasions will not allow it, I conceive he would doe better to breed him in some place more out of the eye of the world. I shall doe him all the service I can, but I should be loth to see him in a meaner pension than I my selfe or any English are in. my most humble service to S[i]r Edward, his sonne is not yet come. I am S[i]r

y[ou]r most assured friend and servant
Gage

15. Dr Francis Gage to Mr Enderby, 15 February 1668[18] [CUL Hengrave MS 88/3/108]

Paris Feb[ruary] 15/25

Sir

I received y[ou]rs of the 4th instant, by w[hi]ch I perceive that S[i]r Edward intends to place his sonne in this college. The last letter I received from him gave me orders to finde out some convenient pension to put him into for a month or two: w[hi]ch I had donn. but the young gentleman had not been there above two days, but that he tooke such a dislike to the place, that no persuasion could prevaile w[i]th him to continue any longer in it: so that this resolution of his father comes very seasonable to the young mans inclination: who indeed is so nice and shiftlesse, that he can live no where, without a great helpe and assistance, and I fear, a greater than I shall be able to afford him; though I promise faithfully to doe him all the service I can, but desire it may not be knowne that I have any care of him, more than as a friend. I shall go about to furnish his chamber with all speede, and provide all necessaries for his coming into the College, whereupon I desire you to dispatch away the bill for the 90 pound you mention, for mony runnes away apace. his sute of clothes, with hatt, sword and belt, cost about <u>12</u> pistolls, besides w[hi]ch I was forced to lay out five pistolls in linnen for him, to witt 4 night shirts, 4 day shirts, 6 bands, 6 hand kerchers, 6 capps and six pairs of socks. his expence for dyet, lodging, fire and washing hath already been above 5 pistolls more. you neede not doubt but I shall manage his monies the best I can: the greatest difficulty will be to settle him at first, for afterwards things will goe on in a regular course. He is very well, begs his fathers blessing, and presents his best respects to his sisters and to y[ou]r selfe, as I render mine to S[i]r Edward and accompt me S[i]r

y[ou]r most faithfull servant
Gage.

---

[18] On the outside of the letter: 'To my much hon[oured] friend Mr Enderby at his lodgings at the naggs-head in Holbourn overagainst Giffords Buildings London'.

16. Dr Francis Gage to Sir Edward Gage, 4 March 1668[19] [CUL Hengrave MS 88/2/181]

Paris March 4/14 1668

Sir

According to y[ou]r order I have settled y[ou]r sonne in the College, in the same pension with mr Draycott and my selfe, and shall have as much care of him as possibly I can. All the furniture of his chamber I have bought new out of the shop, because old thinges are both dangerous for use, and of little profitt. He hath a couple of faire chambers of the [*illeg.*] in the pension, w[hi]ch I was forced to take, because all the [*illeg.*] are worth nothing: but he must pay for them ten pistolls a yeare, because they are in the first story. I send you here enclosed a particular accompt of what I have layed out for him, both for the furnishing of his chambers and other expences since his coming to town: his expence hereafter will be almost regular, to witt, for his and his mans pension 650tt for his chamber 100tt, for his mans wages 80, for his scooles 60. besides clothes and at other emergent occasions w[hi]ch cannot be easily computed. It will be necessary that besides his clothes w[hi]ch he weares dayly at home, he have our sute to appeare abroad in, especially when he goes to our English Court, w[hi]ch the queene doth expect of all the English that live in town, at least some times. As also that you be pleased to allow him something monthly for his private expences, as you shall thincke fitting. He goeth into the fourth schoole for this halfe yeare, where I am confident he will appeare among the first

I am y[ou]r most faithfull servant and affectionate kinsman

Gage.

17. Sir Edward Gage to Susan Hervey (Lady Hanmer); letter prefacing Sir Edward's translation of Nicolas Fouquet's *Essays* (London, 1694)

Dear Madam,

This comes to give you Notice of a Present I have sent you by your Carrier, which will yield an account how I have entertain'd myself since you made This a Solitary Place by your leaving it: The Present, it shocks my Modesty to term it so, is that little Volume put by me into English, which you liked when I lent it you in its Native Language, at the time

---

[19] On the outside of the letter: 'For the Hon[ora]ble S[i]r Edward Gage to be left with Mr Enderby at the naggs head in Holbourn overagainst Giffords buildings London.'

of your being in these parts. With the Alteration it receives by my Hand, I am sensible, Madam, I make you a very bad Compliment, to offer to entertain one of your Judgment with the Defects of Mine, and yet I am not able to forbear it. The Character you gave this Piece, when you told me you had attempted to take Notes out of it, but found you could not justly do it without writing out the whole Book, makes me bold to believe there is something in it that may shine quite through the Cloud of my Stile, and afford you a pleasing Beam. The Person, Madam, supposed to be the Author, was Monsieur Fouquet, who, besides his own vast Wealth, had the Management of the greatest Revenue that belongs to the Crown of France. Amongst a great many Accusations which happen'd to be brought against him, and which at last condemn'd him to a perpetual Imprisonment, one was, That he lived higher than the King himself, though he proved he had done it by the Ruine of his own Fortune. Now certainly this Person must needs be taken for a Witness of good credit, when he sets before our Eyes, as he does after Solomon, the little Value which the things of this World deserve to have with us: He writ this, and a former part of the same Work, in the solitude of his Confinement among the Mountains of Savoy, which, the Author says, did not a little contribute to the enlightning his Thoughts; and so it may be esteemed the fitter to be received by you, Madam, in your Retirement in Wales, whither you have withdrawn your self. If you find in places of this Volume, when you converse farther with it, a Spirit of Devotion, I hope you will take notice in what Perswasion it was written, and examine, whether you ever met with any thing truly of that kind, which has been written out of that Perswasion: And I wish, Madam, you may make such an advantageous Observation here as I could desire. If my Wishes do not suit with your Inclinations, at least, Madam, they agree to Perfection with the true Friendship and Respect I have for you, which would contribute, if they could, to your highest Felicity. I have much Pardon to beg of you, but chiefly for my Boldness in printing this Letter before my Translation, and in taking the liberty to place your Name before to weak a Work as my part of this comes to: But, Madam, allow me to give my Pen this Reputation, in consideration of the Honour I have of a Near Allyance to you, but more especially for that I am, beyond all the rest of the World,

Madam, Your most Affectionate, Faithful, and Obedient Servant,
E[dward] GAGE

18. Sir William Gage to John Hervey, 1st Earl of Bristol, 22 November 1725 [BL Add. MS 61457, fol. 182]

My Lord

My concerns with the Duke of Marlborough haveing been transacted by mr Gibson with much more friendlyness then expense[,] I cannot charge mr Guidott from mr Gibsons accounts or my owne rememberance[.] my lady Gives a much more lively one added, with any gratusly offer'd but y[our] L[ord]ship indeed and my L[or]d Godolphin were privy to a very unfaire push made att me by a countryman of ours mr Guidotts kinsman, which you and the L[or]d above named putt by with mr Guidott, but I alwaise lookd upon that matter as an effect of the gentlemans vanity and temper whome I forbeare to name, rather than as a memento that I was backword in my rewards.

Thus my Lord stands my knowledge of what you write to me upon, as does alwaise my greatest deferrence and respects to the Dutchess of Marlborough and as the observance that shall ever [be] payd to what you command

your obedient humble servant and near Kinsman

W Gage

Hengrave No[vember] the 22d 1725

19. List of documents in the Evidence Room at Hengrave in 1727[20] [SRO(B) HA 528/40]

An Exemplification att request of John Cogshall Gent,[21] It[e]m the paper Booke of the Mannor of Hengrave, One paper Book of Hengrave parish, Sir Tho[mas] Kitson's [*illeg.*] Burgundy [*illeg.*] to S[i]r Tho[mas] Kitson.

In a Form of Labelled Aumbry
Items
a parcell of Old writings belonging to the Hengrave Estate

---

20 On the outside of the paper: '15 Aprill 1727 Account of writings In the Evidence room in Hengrave House'. The folded paper was inserted into the Rentals Book of Lady Penelope Hervey, begun in 1656.

21 There were two armigerous branches of the Coggeshall family in Suffolk, at Benhall and Melton. The 1664–68 Visitation of Suffolk recorded a John Coggeshall as heir to the Coggeshalls of Benhall (see E. Bysshe (ed. W. H. Rylands), *A Visitation of the County of Suffolk* (Mitchell, Hughes and Clarke: London, 1910), pp. 46, 116). However, he would have been seventy-two years old in 1727 and the 'John Cogshall' mentioned here could have been his son or grandson. Why a Coggeshall would have taken such an interest in the documents at Hengrave is unclear.

On the high Shelfe
Our Deeds concerning the Hengrave Estate, Each one of some [*illeg.*]

In the Stout Cupboard
on the low Shelfe also
severall old Leases and papers relating to the Chevington Estate.

In the Third Cupboard
on low Shelfe
76 parcells of Antient Court Rolls belonging to the Mannors of Hengrave,
Flempton, Lackford, Charmans in Risby and other unnamed

On the Middle Shelfe
A parcell of Our planns and papers

On the high Shelfe
A parcell of our Court wills, Leases and old Deeds concerning the
Hengrave Estate.

In partitions over the Cupboards and Drawers on the right hand of the
room Also very many antient Court wills of Severall Mannors and
Copys of other Deeds.

In a Leather Case
Is the Exemplification of the Creation of S: Edward Gage a Baronett by
King Charles the Second, 15 July In the fourteenth of his reigne.

writings in 16 severall Drawers on the right hand of the room afore-
mentioned
The Severall little Drawers on the right hand of the room [*illeg.*] in
which there are any writings. Also Labelled, Showing the content of
aforesaid Drawers.

This last of all

The 27th of Aprill 1727
All the Goods, Chattells and Cattle mentioned in this inventory are now
[*illeg.*] and to Hengrave House and Parke pursuant to this Order above
so present[.] As witnesse our hands
Dorothy. —
John S[impson]
John Simpson Junior[22]

[22] Possibly John Simpson of Stanningfield, who was godfather to Thomas Hunt

These also testify to the Inventory of the Goods removed from Horningsheath to Hengrave.

20. Delariviere D'Ewes to unnamed recipient, 28 October 1729
[CUL Hengrave MS 88/4/28]

S[i]r

I beg leave to take this opertunity by Mrs Carter to tell you, that the reason why I did not send to you was waiting for Mr Folks sure Determination in the affair with the younger children of S[i]r Will[iam] Gage, I have heard from Mr Pigot since his coming to town to whom I sent the purpose of your letter, as also the proposals you were pleased to leave with me[.] he is intirly of the opinion, that I cant come into any other agreement but what he proposed to you and that though the sum is not set, yet its very fitt if we soe enter into articles that they oblige themselfs to keepe things in a manner fit for the purchaser, and mithinks since they say, without disput for their own sakes they will keep up the estate, it cannot be improper where such a Number is concern'd to have it fix'd. Mr Pigot does not think it convenient for me to joyn in it if they will please to come into those articles which I never thought there would have been the least demur then they are at Liberty to put in whom they please, and I shall be far from even saying any thing against their will and pleasure on that point[.] and as to any dispute can arise I cannot frazire my self any, at least am resolved to make none but what are very justifiable[.] you were pleased s[i]r to think at first there woud be no dificulty in my article, but the price set, and Mrs Gage of Coldem has both told me and writ from her self concerned that they did not think any thing unreasonable, but the price set so paid Mr Beble in town and had we not insisted on a price set I beleive things had there been concluded which withall my heart I wish had been, that I might not have had the morification of troubling you on a subject wherein I much aprehend you think me in the wrong, but beg youll do me the Justice to consider that as I act for my son and not for \my/self I cannot be too cautious and beleive me s[i]r did you know of the half quarter of what I have meet with since the Death of S[i]r Will[iam] Gage I question not but it woud rather cause compassion then blame[.] I will trouble you with a letter as soon as I hear from Mr Folks, and wish

---

(*Hengrave Register*, 15 January 1748) and the father of the actress, playwright and novelist Elizabeth Inchbald. Alternatively, he may have been the John Simpson who was mentioned in the parish register of Flempton-cum-Hengrave as the father of a son buried on 5 January 1743 (SRO(B) FL571/2).

most heartily in the mean time the younger children woud give in to
that little is ask by s[i]r

> Your most obedient serv[ant]
> D[elariviere] Gage

Hengrave oct[ober] the 28 1729

21. Delariviere D'Ewes to unnamed recipient, 7 November 1729
[CUL Hengrave MS 88/4/29]

> Hengrave: Nov[ember] the 7 1729

S[i]r since you are pleased not to alter the Article in your paper relating
to Mr Howard, give me leave to beg your patience, till I can acquaint
Mr Pigot therewith who knowing my inclinations to be intirly fixed on
making up this affair with the younger children in an amicable way,
perhaps may find out a Medium, that may be agreeable on all sid[e]s,
though I am asurd he is intirly against my Joyning in any thing relating
to Mr Howard and not without most substantial reasons since I may
safly say he has by him near a hundred lettis from me since the Death
of S[i]r Will[iam] Gage to acquaint him with all the circumstances, and
seldom one without mention of some hardships put upon me by the man
I am now desird to assist and who actually at this very time refuses to
yeild up my sons court rolls notwithstanding his Patent ceased with
S[i]r Will[iam] Gage and spurns at My power and athoritty, and passes
by all slights put upon him by S[i]r Will[iam] Spring and Mrs Gage
of Colddem who have disposed of their rolls from him though he was
one concerned in their affairs, and applyes himself reliably to get the
better of me, with the assistence of Mrs Gages and Mr Lamb. but if my
councel will asure me my son is safe I shall pass by all personal affronts
put upon me.

  its with the utmost regret all this trouble is given you from s[i]r

> your most humble ser[van]t
> D[elariviere] Gage

22. Delariviere D'Ewes to unnamed recipient, 14 November 1729
[CUL Hengrave MS 88/4/31]

S[i]r I take the Liberty of desiring your perrusal of the leter inclosed
from Mr Pigot, which sums up in short the hard useage I have had. I
woud do any thing for peace did I only act for my self, and had long
since given up all, as I did that part of my Joynture Claimd by the

younger children which though perhaps in the end I might have lost, yet I might have disputed it with them[.] they pretend peace and at the same time will doe nothing towards it and are resolved to fight Mr Howards cause to the end and afterwards to set him up against my son which is what sticks at my heart and causes all my uneasyness for I would not have my son to say afterwards I have confirmed his greatest enemy against him[.] I wish you had been pleased at first to have told me Mrs Gages woud insist on the warrent signd to Mr Howard then I could have spoke to Mr Folks about it and you s[i]r woud not have had so much trouble: so give you from me as little as possible. I must once more beg you to moderate that article makes me so uneasy and send me the paper to sign[.] please to take into consideration my son and then I leave it intirly to you to send me what I ought to set my hand too, and to put an end to all the trouble given you s[i]r

from your most humble ser[van]t
D[elariviere] Gage

Nov[ember] the 14 1729

23. Delariviere D'Ewes to unnamed recipient, 19 November 1729
[CUL Hengrave MS 88/4/32]

Sir Iv[e] been so very ill ever since Sunday that I could not acquaint you sooner that I consent that those words be put in as they stand in your leter, viz. of such agent as the younger children have apointed, or shall apoint, which I suppose will be sufficient satisfaction, from s[i]r your

humble serv[an]t
D[elariviere] Gage

Nov[ember] the 19 1729

24. Delariviere D'Ewes to unnamed recipient, 28 November 1729
[CUL Hengrave MS 88/4/33]

S[i]r I having been informed by severell of my friends that Mr Howard was gone to London in hopes of moving the court to order the sale of the term Estate, I did not expect an answer from you, till you could hear from him[.] Were I influenced by anger as you were pleased to accuse me of, or had the least tendency towards it in business, I have heard enough to raise passions of that nature but I asure you s[i]r the only use I have made of it, was in the first place to consider with my self what I had done to cause all these reports. on which consideration I found my self only to be guilty of not liking Mr Howard well enough to set

my hand to his preferment for I know not that ever I aimed at going of
from an amicable agreement, since the first time you favoured me with
menitioning it to me[.] as to the objection I made relating to Mr Folks, I
still am of the same opinion, and though I set my hand to the paper you
are pleased to send, yet shall justifie my self to him in all particulers,
he having all along in this affair showed his good will towards my son,
as well as the younger children, I hope s[i]r youll excuse all complaints
and troubles I have given you and depend that you will be pleased to
keep the paper I here sign, till my son is secure of the severill partys
hands to this agreement,

I am s[i]r your most obedient humble serv[an]t
D[elariviere] Gage

25. Mary D'Ewes (wife of Francis Tasburgh) to Delariviere D'Ewes, 23 February 1735 [CUL Hengrave MS 88/3/90]

Feb[ruary] the 23d

Dear Sister

   I recieved yours with much pleasure to hear you are better and
wonder not at your catching cold this bitter pinch of weather we have
had, I hope its now over, and that we shall all be able to get abroad
again, we have not once stir'd out since we came from Oxburgh. Poor
mr Tasburgh has had so violent a fitt of the Gravil he could not stand
right up – nor turn him in his Bed, without the utmost pain, and difficulty for near a fortnight, he is now thank God much better, but not yet
well. I have sympathised with him all the time with the same distemper,
but not quite so bad as he was. Our young ones are all well, we heard
this morning of Fanny, her eye houlds perfectly well. Molly desires her
Duty to you and ma[ny] thanks, she likes any Coulerd apron you please,
but if yo[u] are so good as to give her, her Choice she chuses a white
[o]ne. Our kind love attends S[i]r Thomas he will never want our good
wishes, and utmost indeavours to gain his fair Vallintine for life, master
Bedingfeld is only nine years old, I have often heard of Lord Arrundles
Son, Lady Arrundle his mother in law, tould me she never heard of it,
and that somer Mr Arrundle was but seventeen years old. I hope Mrs
Davers is [c]ome home well from Bath, I beg the favour of you soon
to desire her, if she has done with my Mitche Frame [*damaged*]ll send
it to me by Allens waggon, for as soon as the weather is warm Molly
will want it. Mis Dashwood is better now, with this grate-Belly then she
used to be, poor Mrs Chamberlain has been ill ever since she lost hers,
but is now somthing better. You desire an account of the wonderfull

appearance at Flixton, I will transcribe Mr Bedingfeld's[23] Letter that you
may know it word for word from the first hand, when I have assur'd
you that I always am
                    Dear Sister ever affectionately y[ou]rs M[ary T[asburgh]

Mr Bedingfelds Letter to Mr Tasburgh

you have heard to be sure of poor Hum[phrey] Burgoines misfortune,[24]
an odd accident has occasion'd us several upsets here, the Mahoggany
Slyders on which we set the Bottles were made a present to Mr Tasburgh
by poor Numps, and as he allways testify'd a particular remembrance
for the family when a live, it seems he would leave them a memorandum
of him after his Death, some days before we received the news of it,
one of the said Slyders was stain'd with a parfect Busto of a man, with
Head, neck and Breast, bruis'd, just in the manner one must suppose a
person to be in his Case, and for fear we should not know the meaning
of it, a large B stain'd near the Rim. Bardwell the Painter has drawn an
exact copy of it with China ink upon vellum which we keep in a frame
and Glass, and design by the first opportunity to send the originall to be
ingrav'd on a Copper Plate at London.

26. Delariviere D'Ewes to Sir William Gage, 29 December 1741
[CUL Hengrave MS 88/4/43]

Dear Billy
    I had the pleasure of yours and though not worth a frank think youll
be glad to hear of me[.] I am far from well, and doubt I must take some
Phisick to morrow though the weather is so very cold and I think my
Lodgings are to. I shall be glad to se[e] you and my daughter in town[.]
Mrs Rookwood Gage I hear sets out for Colddem to morrow[.] Mr[s]
Bond has been with me twice she is same[.] I got out yesterday morning
and called upon her. in came old Woods in perfect health, and never
was otherwise[.] I found he was not informed of my being in town, for
he came up to me and ask where I Lodged, and if he might come and
se[e] me[.] Mrs Rookwood Gage and son have had him to diner and
entertained him highly. you and my daughter must se[e] what you can
doe[.] Mrs Dunne and Bond I called upon and intended for Norfolk

---

23 Henry Bedingfield of Coulsey Wood.

24 A Humphrey Burgoyne, Esq. was buried in Bermondsey churchyard in 1735 (see
    D. Lysons, *The Environs of London* (London, 1792), vol. 1, p. 551). He left behind
    a fortune of £12,000 inherited by his daughter Nancy (see *The London Magazine or
    Gentleman's Monthly Intelligencer* (December 1748), p. 571).

Street but was so low spirited I was forced to get home[.] Mrs Boyes
was here on Sunday, and Mrs Townshand[.] indeed I have not had the
heart as yet to send to old acquaintance[.] things are dear this Christmas
time, candle and coal very much so, we all cough still, and I have a
constant head ach. I dont desire tillon should goe free, if you give your
own saddle horses any dry meat once a day, as we ust to doe. I desire
he may share and I will alow for it[.] I have been much alone which
makes me worss[.] I hope your face is well. this weather will try it. my
Blessing atends you and my Daughter

Dear Billy your most afectionate Mother

D[elariviere] Gage

I desire my h[umble] service to Miss Harland
Mr Howard begs his R[everent] service
Dec[ember] the 29 1741

27. Carteret Leathes to Sir William Gage, 13 March 1744 [CUL Hengrave MS 88/4/56]

London 13 March 1743/4

S[i]r
    I did not receive y[ou]r letter of the 9th till last Night, This Morning
I went to the Duke of Grafton's, but unfortunately He was gone to
Croydon to hunt, & will not be at home till late in the Evening, when
I shall not be able to get at him, so that I fear I can have no answer to
what you desire till to Morrow, I will not fail waiting upon him then,
and joyning in what you request; in the mean while you are welcome to
make use of my House, and before my departure, I gave Orders to my
Servants to receive y[ou]r Horses, as Mrs Gerrard will y[ou]r Fowling
Pieces or any other things you think propper to send; and if it should be
necessary you part with them absolutely, If you will present them to me,
I shall alwayes think myself under such obligations for it, as to deserve
a gratefull return whenever opportunitys offer.
    I hear indeed the Justices in most Counties, especially in the North,
are very rigorous and strict in putting the Laws in execution, tho at
the same time it is rumoured here, the Attempt of an Invasion is layd
aside by the bad success of the first Embarkation in which at least 2000
perished, and by the preparations we have made to oppose it. The 6000
Dutch are daily expected. We have rumours from many parts of Admiral
Mathews having gained a complete Victory, but we have yet no letters
or accounts directly from him. I got very safe to town, and have been
in good health ever since; I am obliged to you for y[ou]r kind enquiry.
I hope you have been well, and enjoyed y[ou]r Sports since I left you;

I shall be sorry you should be interrupted in them, and what little I can contribute to prevent it, shall with great readiness & pleasure be done by

S[i]r y[ou]r most obed[ient] & humble servant

Carteret Leathes

APPENDIX 2

HENGRAVE HALL IN THE 1661 INVENTORY

Possible Predecessor in 1603[1]	Name of Room in 1661[2]	Possible Successor in 1775[3]	Value of contents in 1661
The hall	The Hall	Hall (17)	-
The sommer parler	The Summer Parlour	-	£7
The winter parler	The Winter Parlour	Winter parlour (26)	£10
-	The Great Dining Room	-	£50
The cheife or Queen's chamber	The Queenes Chamber	-	£30
The inner chamber to the cheife chamber	The Inward Chamber	-	£4
-	The Gray Bedd Chamber	-	£20
-	The Withdraweing Roome	-	£4
The chappell	The Chappell Chamber	Chapel (6)	£15
The closett to the chapell	The Withdraweing Chamber	-	£4
The chamber over the gate	The Gatehouse Chamber	-	£4
The chamber next to the gate	The Moate Chamber	-	£6
-	The Withdraweing Roome	-	£2
The chamber over the winter parler	The Chamber over the Winter Parlour	-	£15
The inner chamber to the aforesaid chamber	The other Chamber over the Winter Parlour	-	£7
-	The Inward Chamber	-	£4

[1] Taken from the 1603 inventory in Gage, *Hengrave*, pp. 21–22.
[2] CUL Hengrave MS 86.
[3] Taken, with numbers, from the ground plan in Gage, *Hengrave*, facing p. 18.

-	The Chamber over the Pantrie	-	£8
-	The Little Dineing Roome	-	£2
-	The Chamber next the Little Dineing Roome	-	£5
The nurserye	The Great Nourcery	-	£8
-	The Little Nourcery	-	£2
-	The Little Chamber with in the Dineing Roome	-	£2 10s
-	The Closett by the Little Dineing Roome	-	£1
My Ladye Kytson, her chamber	The Ladie Kitson's Chamber	-	£3
-	The Garrett Chamber	-	£2
-	The Chamber in the Upper Matted Gallery	-	£12
-	The Inward Chamber there	-	£3
-	The Brushinge Roome	-	10s
The stewards chamber	The Stewards Chamber	-	£6
The inner chamber to the sayd chamber	The Inward Chamber	-	£4
-	The Stockes Chamber	-	£10
The chapell chamber	The Chamber next the Chappell	-	£2 10s
-	The Inward Chamber	-	£15
-	The Middle Chamber	-	£6
-	The Lower Nurcery	-	£2
-	The Butters Chamber	-	£2
-	The Cookes Chamber	-	£1
-	The Buttery	Buttery (34)	£3
-	The Beere Cellery	-	£8
The kitchen	The Kitchine	Kitchen (33)	£10

The gallery at the tower	At the Tower	Tower (29)	£8
-	The Great Chamber	-	£8
The dyning chamber	The Dineing Roome	Summer dining room (23)	£2
-	The Inward Chamber	-	£2
-	The Chamber over the Dineing Roome	-	£4
-	The Inward Chamber	-	£3
The dayre	The Dayrie	Dairy (40)	£6
The dayrye mayds chamber	The Dayrie Chamber	-	£2
The brewhouse	The Brewhouse	-	£10
The backhouse	The Backehouse	Bakehouse (41)	£1

APPENDIX 3

EXTRACTS FROM RICHARDSON PACK'S
BURY TOASTS, 1725

Miss Molly Spring[1]

In Love's soft Wars She gains a double Prize,
And Triumphs by her Wit, as by her Eyes.

Encore Miss Molly[2]

As that Gay Season of the Youthful Year
That bears her Name, for ever Sweet and Fair.
But She, like Flora, shou'd improve her Charms,
And take an Am'rous Zephyr to her Arms.

Miss Dilly Spring[3]

Her Youthful Charms a Gentle Light convey,
Sweet as the Morning-Star disclosing Day:
Silent She moves, but certain to impart
New Beauties to the Eye, fresh Gladness to the Heart.

Cupid not blind[4]

Not far from the Hide[5] lives a Damsel, so Fair,
I'd Give Her my Heart for one Lock of her Hair.
Her Cheeks are like Roses that Blush in their Prime:
Her Lips sweet as Cherries just Gather'd in Time.
To Gaze on her Eyes might an Hermit inflame;
And Who Looks on her Moles but Thinks o'That same?
Her Bubbies so prettily heave up and down,
The Sight wou'd Please All from a King to a Clown.
Her Waist is as Taper as Mercury's Rod,
And the Treasures below were a Prize for a God.
Those Beauties are Hid – but my Fancy can trace
She's a Venus when Naked, as Dres't She's a Grace.

Now, Cupid, Divine – Who's This Charming Fine Thing?
Well! for once You've Guess'd right: 'tis Dear Molly Spring.

---

[1] Richardson Pack, *Poems on Several Occasions* (1725), p. 29.
[2] Ibid. pp. 29–30.
[3] Ibid. p. 35.
[4] Ibid. pp. 35–36.
[5] Pack's note: 'A Celebrated Wood near Hengrove-Hall [sic] in Suffolk, the Seat of Sir William Gage.'

A Question put upon the Bench in the Hide[6]

Fair, Auspicious, Gentle Maids!
Sweet Oracles of These Blest Shades
Tell Me (for I Know You can)
What will Make a Happy Man?
Is it Wisdom, Wit, or Wealth?
Ancient Blood? Or Youthful Health?
May Conqu'ring Chiefs that title Boast?
Or is the World for Love well Lost?
Fair, auspicious, gentle Maids!
Sweet Oracles of these Blest Shades
Tell Me (for I Know You can)
What will make a Happy Man?

An Answer by ———

I Will Tell You, if I may,
What will make a Happy Day.
Bring back the Rovings of Thy Youth
To bear with the Important Truth:
'Tis None of All That Wanton Train
Summ'd up in Thy Poetick Vain,
Neither is it Venus' Theft,
But it is The World well Left.
I Will Tell You, if I may,
What will make a Happy Day.

Occasioned by the foregoing Verses[7]

A Nightingale That sought This Grove,
The seat of Music & of Love,
Was wont in Artless Strains to Sing
The Bloomy Beauties of the Spring;
When, Lo! She heard a solemn Noise
From the dark Raven's fatal Voice,
That bid the Wanton change her Note,
And Tune to Graver Airs her Throat:
Sighing the Am'rous Bird Reply'd,
Sung This short Dirge, and then she Died.

'Severe are These censorious Days,
When Satire less Offends than Praise.'

Inscribed on a Drinking-Glass[8]

Venus no more shall be Mount Ida's Pride!
The Queen of Beauty now frequents the Hide,

---

6   Ibid. pp. 39–40.
7   Ibid. p. 41.
8   Ibid. p. 43.

Writ on a Seat in the Glade of the Hide[9]

Stay Passenger, Who'er Thou art,
And, if Thou bear'st a Gentle Heart,
Pray for the Soul of One in Love,
That often Haunts this Gloomy Grove.
The Wretch was in a State of Grace,
Whilst He cou'd View Bright Caelia's Charms;
For Paradise is in her Face,
And Heaven, I trust, is in her Arms.
But from That Goddess far Remov'd,
He hovers between Hope and Fear;
And Death-like Absence having Prov'd
Now Mourns in Purgatory Here.

An Extempore Epistle to Mrs. Merelina Spring[10]

The Bards of Old, so Learn'd and Wise,
Nine Female Muses did Devise,
When at the same Time They thought fit
To name but One Male God of Wit;
And still the Charming Six We find
The Noblest Part of Human Kind;
Whilst double Influence They Dispense,
Victorious by their Eyes and Sense:
They Guide our Heads, and Rule our Hearts;
Refine our Manners, and our Parts.
Among the Men the Few who claim
To Wit, or Worth, a lasting Name;
All That, or Give, or Merit Praise,
From Those bright Stars derive their Rays.
'Tis by their Happy Genial Light
The Painters Draw, the Poets write.
Ev'n I, the Meanest of the Tribe,
An Humble Sonneteering Scribe,
Warm'd by your soft Poetick Fire,
To loftier Numbers may Aspire,
Who Now in haste my Thoughts convey
In This Familiar Doggrel Way.
More greedily your Lines I Learn,
Than Graceless Parson stuffs his Barn,
Or Lady's Chaplain crams his Belly
With Whipt cream, Marmalade, or Jelly.
More I would say, but here Comes Dinner,
And I must Eat, as I'm a Sinner.
Commend me then in short to all,
Who Live and Laugh at Hengrave-Hall,

---

9 Ibid.
10 Ibid. pp. 65–67.

From little Dilly sly and sleek,
To Molly with her Dimpled Cheek:
But naming Molly, à propos,
How does the Pretty Cripple do?
I swear That ugly wicked Blow
Just broke my Heart, That bruis'd her Toe.
If Kisses wou'd Allay the Smart,
I wou'd Kiss That, or ——— Any Part.
For 'tis no Wonder I should Love Her,
When Both Coquets and Prudes Approve Her.
Peace, Plenty, Pleasure, from his Soul
He Drinks to All, who Signs This Scroll.

R. P.

APPENDIX 4

THE BENEDICTINE MISSION REGISTER
(*HENGRAVE REGISTER*) 1734–51

Baptisms

Date	Name	Parents	Godparents	Notes
9 December 1734	Richard Gardener	Richard and Rebecca Gardener	John Stockings 'Gardener at Hengrave Hall' and Mary Monker 'housemaid at Hengrave aforesaid'	
19 December 1736	Mary Gardener	Richard and Rebecca Gardener	John Bedingfeld and Jane Crisp 'both of Hengrave'	
31 May 1737	Anne Morley	Thomas Morley	Henry Jermyn Bond and 'Mrs Dowager Gage of Hengrave'	
11 May 1740	Frances Morley	Thomas Morley	William Adams 'Master of the Greyhound Tavern in Bury' and Mary Wilson 'housekeeper to hen: Jermyn Bond Esq.'	
30 May 1740	John Gardener	Richard and Rebecca Gardener	Francis Humbarston 'Steward at Hengave' and Mary Nice 'Housekeeper at Hengrave aforesaid'	
12 October 1742	Laurence Crask	William Crask 'a Shoomaker in Bury'	William Adams and Jane [*illeg.*]	
25 February 1743	Mary Baile	[*illeg.*] Bail 'of Bury'	John Gillett and Mrs Man 'both of Bury'	
3 March 1743	Charles Page	Henry and Sarah Page 'of Bury'	Robert Balls and Charlotte Crisp 'both of Bury'	
22 May 1743	William Morley	Thomas Morley	Sir William Gage and Laelia Huddleston	

13 August 1743	John Horseman	[*illeg.*] Horseman	Thomas Morley and Mary Horseman	
9 August 1744	Edward Sulyard	Francis Sulyard 'of Buxhall'	Edward Sulyard and Mrs Dunne 'both of London'	
24 January 1745	Sarah Hunt	William Hunt	William Adams and Mrs Bambridge, 'Mrs Dillon's Maid'	
20 February 1745	Mary Horseman	[*illeg.*] Horseman	William Adams and Dorothy Wardell	
3 November 1745	Simon Hunt	John and Sarah Hunt	James Hunt and Mary Hunt 'both of Bury'	
20 April 1746	James Hunt	William Hunt	George Simpson and Dorothy Hunt	
19 June 1746	Elizabeth Sulyard	Francis Sulyard 'now living at Haughley Park'	Edward Sulyard and Mrs Sulyard 'both of London'	Child about 6 months old
22 June 1746	Thomas Larret	Thomas and Elizabeth Larret	John Gillett and Mrs Roades 'both of Bury'	
7 August 1746	James Betts	James Betts 'a Prot[estan]t' and Susan Betts 'both of Bury'	Nicholas Brundell and Elizabeth Larret 'both of Bury'	Child 6 or 7 months old
23 September 1746	Susanna Christmas	Emanuel Christmas	James Hunt and Mary Hunt 'both of Bury'	
10 May 1747	Nicholas Horseman	[*illeg.*] Horseman	Thomas Larret and Elizabeth Laudal 'both of Bury'	Child a month old
20 December 1747	Edward Charles Merry	Richard Merry	John Gillett and Elizabeth Laudal 'both of Bury'	
30 December 1747	Edward Cranmer	[*illeg.*] Cranmer	Nicholas Brundell and [*illeg.*] Cranmer 'both of Bury'	
15 January 1748	Thomas Hunt	William Hunt	John Simpson 'of Coldham' and Dorothy Wordell 'of Bury'	

3 April 1748	Mary Larret	Thomas and Elizabeth Larret	Nicolas Brundell and Elizabeth Twite 'both of Bury'	
7 December 1748	Sarah Page	Henry and Sarah Page	Elizabeth Browning	'being then in Danger of Death'; 'the Child died sometime after'
23 April 1749	Joseph Gillet	John Gillet	Richard Merry and Elizabeth Browning 'both of Bury'	
13 June 1749	John Hunt	William Hunt	Thomas Hunt 'of London' and Mary Church 'of Bury'	
21 January 1750	Charles Horseman	[illeg.] Horseman	Joseph Rhodes and Mrs Hunt 'both of Bury'	'These Children died a few days after they were baptiz'd'
11 February 1750	Thomas Larret	Thomas and Elizabeth Larret	Robert Balls and Mrs Crask 'both of Bury'	
25 February 1750	Ann Doleing	Ralph and Margaret Doleing	Robert Balls and Mrs Dobson 'both of Bury'	'the Parents of the Child I think are Irish'
20 June 1750	Charles Page	Henry and Sarah Page	Elizabeth Browning 'of Bury'	
19 August 1750	Henry Hunt	William Hunt	William Davis and Mary Frost	
28 January 1751	Mary Horseman	[illeg.] Horseman	[illeg.] Hunt and [illeg.] Hunt 'both of Bury'	
11 February 1751	Peregrine Cranmer	Peregrine Cranmer	Robert Balls and Elizabeth Rhodes 'both of Bury'	
27 October 1751	Henry Hunt	William Hunt	[illeg.] Adams and Mary Frost	

Confirmations

Date	Name	Location	Bishop
10 June 1720	Thomas Gage	Bury	John Talbot Stonor
10 June 1720	William Gage	Bury	John Talbot Stonor
10 June 1720	Edward Gage	Bury	John Talbot Stonor
27 May 1737	John Stockings	Hengrave Hall	John Talbot Stonor
27 May 1737	Susan Stockings	Hengrave Hall	John Talbot Stonor
27 May 1737	Thomas Stockings	Hengrave Hall	John Talbot Stonor
27 May 1737	John Southgate	Hengrave Hall	John Talbot Stonor
27 May 1737	Jane Crisp	Hengrave Hall	John Talbot Stonor
27 May 1737	Mary King	Hengrave Hall	John Talbot Stonor
27 May 1737	Mary Church	Hengrave Hall	John Talbot Stonor

APPENDIX 5

CATHOLIC NONJURORS IN BURY ST EDMUNDS IN 1745

Alphabetical list of Bury St Edmunds 'papists or reputed papists' listed before the 1745 quarter sessions and in the list of those refusing the Oath of Allegiance to George II[1]

William Adams
Two children of William Adams
Ann Annis, servant to Madam Gage
Henry Baker, glazier
Adam Balls
—— Balls, wife of Adam Balls
Six children of Adam Balls
Robert Balls, victualler
—— Balls, wife of Robert Balls
—— Barker, widow
William Bennet, gardener
Mary Bennet, wife of William Bennet
Grace Bennet, spinster
Ann Beveridge, spinster
George Birch, tailor
Elizabeth Birch, wife of George Birch
Two children of George Birch
Elizabeth Browning, widow
Nicholas Brundle, Butcher
Susan Brundle, wife of Nicholas Brundle
Eight children of Nicholas Brundle
Charles Canion, glover
John Catton, labourer
Emmanuel Christmas, labourer
William Clarke, shoemaker
Elizabeth Clarke, wife of William Clarke
Five children of William Clarke
Thomas Collis, gardener[2]
Charlot Cosin, maidservant

---

[1]   SRO(B) D8/1/3, bundle 2.
[2]   The magistrate adds, 'reputed so'.

Perry Cranmer, shoemaker
Christian Cranmer, wife of Perry Cranmer
Samuel Cranmer snr., taylor
Elizabeth Cranmer, wife of Samuel Cranmer
Samuel Cranmer jnr., gardener
Sarah Cranmer, spinster
William Dobson, joiner
Anne Dobson, wife of William Dobson, joiner
Ann Gage, spinster
Madam Delariviere Gage, widow
Henrietta Gage, spinster
Henry Godfrey, labourer
—— Godfrey, wife of Henry Godfrey
Three children of Henry Godfrey
Richard Harris, labourer[3]
Elizabeth Hawkins, wife of William Hawkins, watchmaker
James Horsman, labourer
Mary Huddlestone, widow
Lelia Huddlestone, spinster
Francis Humberton, farrier
—— Humberton, wife of Francis Humberton
James Hunt, taylor
John Hunt, taylor
Thomas Hunt, taylor
John Kenion, glover
Charlot Lamb, widow
Susanna Larrott, spinster
Thomas Larrott snr., gardener
Agnes Larrott, wife of Thomas Larrott
Thomas Larrott jnr., shoemaker
Elizabeth Larrott, wife of Thomas Larrott
Three children of Thomas Larrott
Sarah Love, widow (lodger)
Elizabeth Lowdall, spinster
Edmund Mann, staymaker
Isabella Mann, widow
Elizabeth Merry, widow (lodger)
Richard Merry, staymaker
Elizabeth Merry, wife of Richard Merry
Five children of Richard Merry
Mary Mount, servant to Madam Gage

---

[3] The magistrate adds, 'reputed so'.

Dr. Nile
——— Nile, wife of Dr. Nile
Dr. Nile's manservant
Henry Page, gardener
Jane Parker, spinster
Joseph Rhodes, butcher
——— Rhodes, wife of Joseph Rhodes
John Salt, woolcomber (lodger)
Charlot Short, spinster
Dr. Henry Short
——— Short, wife of Dr. Henry Short
Peregrina Short, spinster
Thomas Short, gentleman
Sarah Stowe, wife of Robert Stowe
Thomas Tasbrook
Thomas Tasbrook's manservant
Thomas Tasbrook's maidservant
John Tillott, taylor
Mary Tillott, wife of John Tillott
One child of John Tillott
Mary Tinsley, widow
Elizabeth Twite, spinster
Dorothy Wordwell, servant to Madam Gage

Report of arms confiscated from Catholics, 7 October 1745

We the Constables of the Burgh withinmentioned have made Diligent search pursuant to this ward and have taken & seized to his ma[jes]tys use of the persons within named the arms & weapons following that is to say, of Mr Dillon one ffowling piece a Brace of pistols & two swords without Hilts of S[i]r W[illia]m Gage a Brace of pistols & three swords of Mr Bond one sword & no more, But have not taken or seen on such search any Horse of the value of five pounds in our Judgm[e]nt. All which we humbly Codify to the Justices of this Burgh witness our hands the 7th day of October 1745

Tho[ma]s Herring
Jonathan Buller
Lionel Ews
Isaac Bind
John Rose
Martin Webster
Edw[ar]d Elsgood

Jo[h]n Shorter
Rob[er]t Scott
Sam[ue]ll Walker
Sam[ue]l Holt
John Hervey

APPENDIX 6

THE JESUIT MISSION REGISTER
(*BURY REGISTER*), 1756–67

Baptisms (fols 47–52)

Date	Name	Parents	Godparents	Notes
1 January 1756	Elizabeth	'daughter of an Irish traveller'		
18 January 1756	Robert Whitehead	John Mann		
25 January 1756	John Atvers	William Atvers		Foreigner
18 February 1756	Henry Clouting	Mary Clouting		
4 April 1756	Elizabeth Tench	John Tench		
2 May 1756	Charles Beast	John Beast		
20 June 1756	John Beast	William Beast		
8 September 1756	Thomas Perry	Phillip Perry		
5 December 1756	Thomas Ramplin	Mary Ramplin		
2 January 1757	James Cranmer	Perry Cranmer		
18 February 1757	Elizabeth Horseman	James Horseman		
11 February 1758	Mary Goderich	Rupert Goderich	John Beast, Mary Goderich and Susanna Murrel	
12 February 1758	Thomas Hunt	Thomas Hunt	Thomas and Mary Hunt	Died in infancy
26 March 1758	Elizabeth Beast	John Beast	Robert Goderich and Mary Westly	
31 March 1758	Phillip Perry	Phillip and Susanna Perry	James Plummer, Anne Cocksedge and Mary Carr	

31 March 1758	Susanna Betts	Susanna Betts	Charles and Elizabeth Stuart	
9 April 1758	Mary Stuart	Charles and Elizabeth Stuart	Charles and Rachel Kenyon	
27 April 1758	Thomas Ramplin	Mary Ramplin	John Belford and Susan Emmerton	
28 May 1758	Mary Brundle	Mary Brundle	Nicholas Brundle and Agnes Larrett	
25 August 1758	Mary Plummer	James and Mary Plummer		In danger
5 November 1758	Sarah Westly	Mary Westly	John Beast and Elizabeth Merry	
3 December 1758	Mary Beast	William and Alice Beast	Nicholas and Susanna Brundle	
14 December 1758	Susanna Scarf	Clementina Scarf	James Plummer and M. Thorp	
9 May 1759	Mary Magdalene		James and Laelia Farrill	American Negress, 15 years old
21 May 1759	John Horseman	James Horseman	Charles and Charlotte Bond	In Mr. Bond's chapel
13 June 1759	Charlotte Ramplin	Maurice Ramplin	William Olivarez and Charlotte Bond	At home
23 September 1759	Debora Sherwood	Mary Sherwood	John Hunt and Elizabeth Gallant	
5 December 1759	Mary Gardiner	Richard Gardiner	John Jellet and Anne Morley	At Hengrave, at home
16 December 1759	Anne Plummer	James and Mary Plummer	Phillip Perry and Anne Cocksedge	
23 December 1759	Rebecca Beast	John Beast	Charles Stuart and Susanna Murrel	
20 January 1760	Elizabeth Stuart	Charles and Elizabeth Stuart	John Beast and Mary Green	
21 January 1760	Michael Herman	Nicholas Herman	N. Goldsmith and N. Grigg	At Sudbury
10 February 1760	Mary Laelia Scarf	Clementina Scarf	James and Laelia Farrill	
22 February 1760	Robert Goderich	Robert Goderich	John and Anne Hunt	Died in infancy

22 February 1760	Anne Gooderich	Robert Goderich	John and Anne Hunt	In danger
25 February 1760	John Perry	Phillip and Susanna Perry	Charles Kenyon and Anne Morley	
11 April 1760	Thomas Reilly	John and Mary Reilly	William Olivarez and Laelia Farrill	At home
8 February 1761	John Beast	William and Alice Beast	John Beast and Susanna Rutter	
12 April 1761	James Stuart	Charles and Elizabeth Stuart	John Beast and Mary Hunt	
26 April 1761	Susanna Tillson	Elizabeth Tillson	John Hunt and Elizabeth Hounslea	At Fornham All Saints
10 May 1761	Robert Beast	John Beast	Charles Stuart and Rachel Kenyon	
14 June 1761	Sarah Goderich	Robert Goderich	William Hunt and Mary Gardiner	
22 June 1761	John Girt	Elizabeth Girt	Edmund Goderich and Mary Rogers	At Gt. Finborough
21 September 1761	Thomas Melsum	[…] Melsum	Charles and Rachel Kenyon	At home
16 October 1761	Ambrose	Nicholas Herman	Thomas Goldsmith and S. Grigg	At Sudbury
28 December 1761	William Perry	Phillip and Susanna Perry	Joseph Macgowen and Laetitia Waler	
29 December 1761	Mary Plummer	James and Mary Plummer	George Huggens and Mary Sympson	
2 January 1762	William Stuart	William and Elizabeth Stuart (non-Catholic)	Charles and Elizabeth Stuart	
4 March 1762	Elizabeth Reilly	John and Mary Reilly	James and Laelia Farrill	At home
10 May 1762	William Carruthers	William and Elizabeth Carruthers	Joseph Macgowen and Margaret Hatton	At Hargrave
13 June 1762	Elizabeth Westly	Nicholas and Mary Westly	William Beast and Elizabeth Gallant	
26 July 1762	Edmund Hunt	Edmund and Mary Hunt	William and Mary Beast	
9 January 1763	Mary Lott	John and Mary Lott	Daniel Hales and Sarah Norman	At Bulmer Tye

6 March 1763	John Goderich	Robert and Mary Goderich	William Beast and Susanna Rutter	
10 April 1763	Michael Herman	Nicholas Herman	Francis Codlin and N. Grigg	At Sudbury
26 May 1763	James Perry	Phillip and Susanna Perry	John Jellet and Margaret Hatton	
5 June 1763	Ursula Stuart	Charles and Elizabeth Stuart	William Beast and Sarah Cranmer	
29 August 1763	Mary Beast	John Beast	Joan Hunt and Susanna Rutter	
8 September 1763	Mary Vincent	James and Sarah Vincent	James Cooper and Martha Hatton	At Coldham
6 November 1763	James Plummer	James and Mary Plummer	George and Anne Simpson	
21 December 1763	Francis Tillson	Mary Tillson	William Beast and Elizabeth Hounslea	
29 January 1764	Mary Hunt	Edmund and Mary Hunt	William Beast and Elizabeth Gallant	
10 February 1764	Thomas Goldsmith	Thomas Goldsmith	John Gage and Alice Sweetman	At Sudbury
26 February 1764	Elizabeth Sheill	Hugh and Mary Sheill	Thomas Jellet and Elizabeth Gallant	
5 March 1764	Anne Bradshaw	M. Green	John and Mary Jellet	
20 July 1764	Anne Wellum	John and Susanna Wellum	Francis and Mary Codlin	At Melford
28 July 1764	John Lott	John and Mary Lott	Francis Codlin and Mary Hales	At Bulmer Tye
30 September 1764	Elizabeth Merry	Richard and Susanna Merry	Thomas Jellet and Elizabeth Merry	
21 October 1764	Thomas Spark	Thomas and Sarah Spark	Charles Stuart and Elizabeth Cranmer	
28 October 1764	Elizabeth Stuart	Charles and Elizabeth Stuart	William and Alice Beast	
3 July 1765	Mary Rebecca Reilly	John and Mary Reilly	John Reilly and Anne Fergus	
7 July 1765	William Goderich	Robert Gooderich	William Beast and Mary Gooderich	

28 July 1765	Robert […]	Felicity […]	William Beast and Elizabeth Merry
21 September 1765	Sarah Plummer	James and Mary Plummer	William Morley and Susanna Huggens
10 November 1765	Susanna Perry	Phillip and Susanna Perry	Thomas Melsum and Agatha Annis
10 August 1766	Mary Jellet	John and Elizabeth Jellet	William Morley and Helen Whitlock
28 September 1766	Susanna Merry	Richard and Mary Merry	Charles Kenyon and Elizabeth Gallant
29 December 1766	Elizabeth Hunt	Edmund and Mary Hunt	John Beast and Mary Westly
11 January 1767	William Beast	William and Alice Beast	Thomas Jellet and Mary Green
19 April 1767	William Goderich	Robert and Mary Goderich	William Morley and Joan Larritt
22 April 1767	John Plummer	James and Mary Plummer	Edward and Mary Simpson
5 July 1767	Thomas Beast	John Beast	Charles Kenyon and Elizabeth Gallant
21 November 1767	Sarah Perry	Phillip and Susanna Perry	In danger

Deaths (fols 63–65)

Date	Name	Age	Notes
3 January 1756	Mary Hunt	19	Confirmed, virgin
9 March 1756	Henry Clouting	Infant	
31 October 1756	Margaret Honslea	59	Confirmed, married
17 November 1756	Frances Honslea	14	Confirmed, virgin
9 January 1757	Christina Cranmer		
25 January 1757	Francis Honslea	26	
30 January 1757	Margaret Plummer		
1 March 1757	Mary Larrett	9	

4 March 1757	Mary Clowting	36	Confirmed
18 March 1757	Elizabeth Emmerton	22	Confirmed
21 March 1757	James Westly	2	
1 April 1757	Thomas Ramplin	Infant	
23 April 1757	Henry Page		
27 April 1757	James Stuart	2	
8 June 1757	Mary Bloss	60	
25 June 1757	Henrietta Gage		Confirmed
31 July 1757	Mary Bennet		
24 September 1757	Alice Beast	4	
4 October 1757	John Beast	Infant	
26 August 1758	Mary Plummer	Infant	
30 January 1759	Elizabeth Gage	76	Confirmed
5 April 1759	Teresa Hunt		Confirmed
1 July 1759	Elizabeth Moore	66	Confirmed
14 April 1759	Mary Ramplin	30	Confirmed
22 November 1759	Isabella Mann		Suddenly
27 January 1760	Elizabeth Stuart	Infant	
15 February 1760	Charlotte Crisp	70	
22 February 1760	Robert Goderich	Infant	
29 March 1760	Ann Gage		Confirmed
13 April 1760	Elizabeth Browning	80	Confirmed
22 October 1760	Mary Rhodes		Confirmed
22 October 1760	Catharine Brundle		Confirmed
27 April 1761	Robert Balls	72	Suddenly
19 July 1761	John Cocksedge	69	Convert
13 October 1761	Elizabeth Lowdell		Confirmed
Day uncertain	John Horseman	Infant	
29 December 1761	William Hunt		Confirmed

14 February 1762	William Stuart	Infant	
17 April 1762	John Rhodes	68	Confirmed
24 May 1762	Mary Jones	79	Confirmed
21 July 1762	William Stuart		Confirmed
30 September 1762	Barbara Thomson	80	
20 October 1762	Elizabeth Merry		Suddenly
Day uncertain (1762)	William Caruthers	Infant	
Day uncertain (1763)	Sarah Norman		At Cornard, accident
29 June 1763	William Macgowen		Confirmed
20 July 1763	Frances Gage	58	Confirmed
12 August 1763	Dorothy Wordwell		Confirmed
9 January 1764	Margaret Brundle	10	
17 January 1764	Thomas Bedingfield	69	Confirmed
21 April 1764	Elizabeth Bedingfield		Confirmed
7 October 1764	Robert Oxer	70	In the hospital
31 October 1764	Joan Parfery	100	'In the hospital; whose noise was so great that she was deprived of the Sacrament out of the envy of non-Catholics and especially of the minister Crask'
30 November 1764	Rebecca Gardiner		Confirmed, at Hengrave
16 February 1765	Sarah Sullyard	84	At Woolpit
19 April 1765	Robert Gurney	72	Confirmed
27 August 1765	Mary Rebecca Reilly	Infant	
4 September 1765	Mary Simpson		Suddenly
13 September 1765	Phillip Perry	7	
27 September 1765	Thomas Perry	9	

2 November 1765	Susanna Rutter		Confirmed
5 November 1765	Elizabeth Reily	5	At Tours in France
29 November 1765	Anne Bradshaw	Infant	
27 March 1766	William Goderich	Infant	
31 March 1766	James Birtch	80	Confirmed
14 October 1766	Joan Tindesley	77	Confirmed
18 December 1766	Elizabeth Beast	7	
17 May 1767	Sir William Gage	55	Confirmed, at London
18 June 1767	Martha Brockfield	38	At Bradfield
19 October 1767	James Farrill	75	
8 December 1767	Sarah Casey	84	Confirmed
28 December 1767	Sarah Perry	Infant	

Marriages (fols 81–82)

Date	Names	Witnesses	Notes
27 January 1757	Robert Goderich and Mary Frost (non-Catholic)		
13 November 1757	James Plummer and Mary Cocksedge		
8 October 1759	Mary Coppin and William Brook (non-Catholic)	Anne Cocksedge and Susanna Murrell	At Westley
19 January 1760	John Jellet and Mary Herman	Thomas Miller	
27 April 1760	Luke Moore and Bridget Clark (non-Catholic)	Thomas and Mary Miller	
7 July 1760	Robert Tillson (non-Catholic) and Elizabeth Birtch		'That it might be done prudently, no witnesses here'

17 August 1760	William Caruthers (non-Catholic) and Elizabeth Cross	John and Rebecca Macgowen	
2 December 1760	Elizabeth Goderich and John Girt (non-Catholic)	Anne Cocksedge	
3 May 1761	François Le Comte and Anne Morley	Philippe Lemazurier, John Jellet and Anne Annis	Died at London in 1764
24 April 1762	John King and Elizabeth Needle (non-Catholic)	John Hunt and Rachel Kenyon	
23 October 1763	William Best (non-Catholic) and Elizabeth Brunning	Mrs Tindesley and Thomas Hunt	
10 June 1764	Thomas Jellet and Elizabeth Gibben	Charles Kenyon and Mary Jellet	
12 July 1764	Richard Merry and Susanna Molton (non-Catholic)	John Jellet and Elizabeth Merry	
27 April 1767	John Thwaite and Mary Holland	John and Thomas Jellet	
5 November 1767	Anne Cocksedge and John Clark (non-Catholic)	John Larrett	
4 December 1767	William Last and Mary Gibben	John Martellet	By dispensation of the Reverend Vicar Apostolic, private

Easter Communions (?) 1766

Communicant	Number of times communion received or age at first communion (unclear)
George Beast	
William Beast junior	
Joan Beast	
Charlotte Beast	10
Elizabeth Beast	8
Joanna Beast	
Susanna Beast	

Mary Beast	8
Catherine Gage	
Mary Goderich	8
Mary Gallant	
Sarah Gallant	
Anne Goderich	7
Mary Horseman	
Charlotte Horseman	
Ann Horseman	
Elizabeth Horseman	9
Nicholas Hunt	
Charlotte Macgowen	
Elizabeth Plummer	
Anne Plummer	5
Joanna Perry	7
Susanna Rutter	
Anne Scarf	
Clementina Scarf	
Charlotte Stuart	
Mary Stuart	9
Susanna Scarf	8
Mary Westly	
Ann Westly	
Sarah Westly	8
Francisca Ramplin	
Thomas Ramplin	8
Charlotte Ramplin	7
Alice Frost	
Henrietta Farrill	
Susanna Betts	10
Rebecca Beast	6
Robert Beast	5
James Betts	5
William Betts	
John Betts	
Ann Wilkinson	
Mary Brundle	8

Christmas and Easter Communicants (fols 101–3)

Date	Number of Communicants	Notes
Christmas 1755–Epiphany 1756	73	
Easter 1756	103	
Christmas 1756–Epiphany 1757	74	
Easter 1757	87	2 converts
Christmas 1757–Epiphany 1758	67	
Easter 1758	100	3 converts
Christmas 1758–Epiphany 1759	90	
Easter 1759	107	
Christmas 1759–Epiphany 1760	83	
Easter 1760	103	
Christmas 1760–Epiphany 1761	85	
Easter 1761	101	2 deathbed converts
Christmas 1761–Epiphany 1762	78	
Easter 1762	113	1 convert
Christmas 1762–Epiphany 1763	74	
Easter 1763	106	1 convert
Christmas 1763–Epiphany 1764	80	
Easter 1764	100	
Christmas 1764–Epiphany 1765	80	
Easter 1765	93	
Christmas 1765–Epiphany 1766	82	
Easter 1766	89	4 converts
Christmas 1766–Epiphany 1767	63	
Easter 1767	91	1 convert

APPENDIX 7

CATHOLIC FAMILIES IN BURY ST EDMUNDS AND DISTRICT, 1715–67[1]

No.	Surname	1715	1734–51	1745	1756–67	1767	Notes
1	*Adams*	-	Adams	Adams	-	Adams	Innkeeper
2	*Allen*	-	-	-	-	Allen	Glover
3	*Annis*	-	-	Annis	Annis	Annis	Shoemaker
4	Atvers	-	Atvers	-	-	-	'Foreigner'
5	Baile	-	Baile	-	-	-	
6	Baker	-	-	Baker	-	-	
7	*Balls*	-	Balls	Balls	Balls	-	Victualler
8	Bambridge	-	Bambridge	-	-	-	Servant
9	*Barker*	-	-	Barker	-	Barker	Mantua maker
10	Beast	-	-	-	Beast	Beast	Woolcomber, tailor
11	Bedingfield	-	Bedingfeld	-	Bedingfield	-	
12	Belford	-	-	-	Belford	-	
13	*Bennet*	-	-	Bennet	Bennet	Bennett	Gardener
14	*Betts*	-	Betts	-	Betts	Betts	Smith

[1] This list includes Catholics in neighbouring villages such as Hengrave, the Fornhams and Stanningfield; it does not include Catholics from further afield who appear in the mission registers. Non-Catholics and visiting Catholics who appear in the registers are also excluded. Surnames that feature in the 1695 tax assessment of the Parish of St James (SRO(B) 508/1) are given in italics.

No.							Occupation
15	Beveridge	-	-	Beveridge	-	Beveridge	Servant
16	Birch	Birch	-	Birch	Birtch	Birch	Tailor
17	Bloss	-	-	-	Bloss	-	-
18	*Bond*	-	Bond	Bond	Bond	-	Gentry
19	Bradshaw	-	-	-	Bradshaw	-	-
20	Brockfield	-	-	-	Brockfield	-	-
21	Browning	-	Browning	Browning	Browning	-	-
22	Brundle	-	Brundell	Brundle	Brundle	Brundell	Butcher
23	*Burton*	Burton	-	-	-	-	Gentry
24	Carruthers	-	-	-	Carruthers	-	-
25	Casey	-	-	Casey	Casey	Casey	Labourer
26	Catton	-	-	Catton	-	-	-
27	Charles	-	-	-	-	Charles	Labourer
28	*Christmas*	-	Christmas	Christmas	-	-	-
29	Church	-	Church	-	-	-	-
30	*Clarke*	-	-	Clarke	-	-	Shoemaker
31	Clouting	-	-	-	Clouting	-	-
32	*Cocksedge*	-	-	-	Cocksedge	Cocksedge	Servant
33	Collis	-	Collis	Collis	-	-	-
34	*Cooper*	-	-	-	Cooper	Cooper	Labourer
35	Coppin	-	-	-	Coppin	Copping	-
36	Cosin	-	-	Cosin	-	-	-
37	Cranmer	-	Cranmer	Cranmer	Cranmer	Cranmer	Shoemaker, tailor
38	*Craske*	-	Craske	-	-	-	-

No.	Name						Occupation
39	*Crisp*	–	Crisp	–	Crisp	–	–
40	Cross	–	–	–	–	Cross	–
41	*Curtis*	–	–	–	–	Curtis	Servant
42	Davis	–	Davis	–	–	–	–
43	Dillon	–	Dillon	Dillon	–	–	Gentry
44	Dobson	–	Dobson	Dobson	–	–	Joiner
45	Ely	–	–	–	–	Ely	Servant
46	Emmerton	–	–	–	Emmerton	–	–
47	Farrill	–	–	–	Farrill	Farrell	Gentry
48	Fergus	–	–	–	Fergus	Fergus	Gentry (?)
49	Fox	–	–	–	–	Fox	–
50	*Frost*	–	Frost	–	Frost	Frost	Servant
51	Gage	Gage	Gage	Gage	Gage	Gage	Gentry
52	*Gallant*	–	–	–	Gallant	Gallant	Servant
53	Gardener	–	Gardener	–	Gardiner	Gardener	Labourer
54	*Gibben*	–	–	–	Gibben	–	–
55	Gillett	–	Gillett	–	Jellet	Jellet	Tailor
56	*Goderich*	–	–	–	Goderich	Goodrich	Servant
57	*Godfrey*	–	–	Godfrey	–	–	Labourer
58	*Green*	–	–	–	Green	Green	–
59	Gurney	–	–	–	Gurney	–	–
60	Hann	–	–	–	Hann	Hann	–
61	Harris	–	–	Harris	–	–	–
62	Hatton	–	–	–	Hatton	–	Labourer

63	Hawkins	-	-	Hawkins	-	-	Watchmaker
64	Holland	-	-	-	Holland	-	-
65	Horseman	-	Horseman	Horsman	Horseman	Horseman	Labourer, shoemaker
66	Hounslea	-	-	-	Honslea	Hownsley	-
67	Huddleston	-	Huddleston	Huddlestone	Huddlestone	Huddlestone	Gentry
68	Huggens	-	-	-	-	Huggins	Innkeeper
69	Humbarston	-	Humbarston	Humberton	Humberton	-	Steward, farrier
70	*Hunt*	-	Hunt	Hunt	Hunt	Hunt	Tailor, staymaker, glover, breeches maker
71	Jones	-	-	-	Jones	-	-
72	*Kenyon*	-	-	Canion, Kenyon	Kenyon	Kenyon	Glover
73	*King*	-	King	-	-	King	Servant, tailor
74	*Lamb*	-	-	Lamb	-	-	Gentry
75	Larret	-	Larret	Larrott	Larrett	Larratt	Gardener, shoemaker, schoolmistress
76	Last	-	-	-	Last	-	-
77	Laudal	-	Laudal	Lowdall	Lowdell	Lawdall	Tailor
78	Le Comte	-	Le Comte	-	-	-	-
79	Lemazurier	-	Lemazurier	-	-	Masurier	Barber
80	Love	-	-	Love	-	-	Widow
81	MacGowen	-	-	-	Macgowan	McGovan	Draper
82	*Mann*	-	-	Mann	Mann	Mann	Staymaker, shoemaker
83	Martellet	-	-	-	Martellet	-	-
84	Melsum	-	-	-	Melsum	-	-

85	Merry	-	Merry	Merry	Merry	Merry	Staymaker, shoemaker
86	Miller	-	-	-	Miller	-	
87	Monker	-	Monker	-	-	-	
88	*Moore*	-	-	-	Moore	-	
89	Morley	-	Morley	-	Morley	Morley	Woolcomber
90	*Mount*	-	-	Mount	-	-	Servant
91	*Murrell*	-	-	-	Murrel	Murrells	Servant
92	Nice	-	Nice	-	-	-	
93	Nile	-	-	Nile	-	-	Gentry, physician
94	Norman	-	-	-	Norman	-	
95	Olivarez	-	-	-	Olivarez	-	Gentry (?)
96	*Oxer*	-	-	-	Oxer	Oxer	Woolcomber
97	*Page*	-	Page	Page	-	-	Gardener
98	Parfery	-	-	-	Parfery	-	
99	*Parker*	-	-	Parker	-	-	
100	*Perry*	-	-	-	Perry	Perry	Gardener
101	Plummer	-	-	-	Plummer	Plummer	Barber
102	*Prettiman*	Prettiman	-	-	-	-	
103	Ramplin	-	-	-	Ramplin	Ramplee	Innkeeper
104	Reilly	-	-	-	Reilly	-	Gentry
105	Rhodes	-	Rhodes	Rhodes	Rhodes	-	Butcher
106	Rookwood	-	-	-	Rookwood	-	
107	*Rutter*	-	-	-	Rutter	Rutter	
108	Salt	-	-	Salt	-	-	Woolcomber

#	Name						Occupation
109	Scarf	-	-	-	Scarf	-	Carpenter
110	Seales	-	-	-	-	Seales	
111	Sheill	-	-	-	Sheill	-	
112	Sherwood	-	-	-	Sherwood	-	Physician, gentry
113	*Short*	Short	-	Short	-	-	
114	*Simpson*	-	Simpson	-	Simpson	-	
115	Southgate	-	Southgate	-	-	-	
116	*Spark*	-	-	-	Spark	-	
117	*Steward*	-	-	-	-	Steward	Breeches maker
118	Stockings	-	Stockings	-	-	-	Gardener
119	Stowe	-	-	Stowe	-	-	
120	Stuart	-	-	-	Stuart	-	
121	Sulyard	Sulyard	Sulyard	-	Sullyard	-	Gentry
122	Tasbrook	-	-	Tasbrook	-	-	Servant
123	Tench	-	-	-	Tench	-	
124	Thomson	-	-	-	Thomson	-	
125	*Thorp*	-	-	-	Thorp	-	
126	Thwaite	-	-	-	Thwaite	-	
127	*Tillott*	-	-	Tillott	-	-	Tailor
128	Tillson	-	-	-	Tillson	Tilson	
129	Tyldesley	Tyldesley	-	Tinsley	Tindesley	-	Gentry
130	Toop	-	-	-	-	Toop	
131	Twite	-	Twite	Twite	Twite	Twights	Woolcomber
132	*Vincent*	-	-	-	Vincent	-	

133	Wordwell	-	Wordell	Wordwell	-	Servant
134	Westly	-	-	Westly	-	
135	Whitehead	-	-	Whitehead	-	
136	Whitlock	-	-	-	Whitlock	Operator for the teeth
137	Wilkinson	-	-	Wilkinson	Wilkinson	Servant
138	Wilson	-	-	-	Wilson	

BIBLIOGRAPHY

Manuscript collections

Birmingham Archdiocesan Archives
A14
A38
C935f

British Library, London
Add. MS 30267
Add. MS 61457

Cambridge University Library, Cambridge
Add. MS 4403
Hengrave MSS

Downside Abbey, Stratton-on-the-Fosse
Benedictine mission register for Hengrave and Bury St Edmunds, 1734–51 with the North Province Cash Book, 1806–9
South Province Book R, 1717–1826

The National Archives, Kew
PROB 11/375
PROB 11/615
PROB 11/715

Private Collection, Bury St Edmunds
Jesuit mission register for Bury St Edmunds, 1756–89

Suffolk Records Office, Bury St Edmunds Branch
326
449
508
558
712
744
806
942.64 BUR
D8
E2

FL550
FL571
HA 507
HA 528

Archives of the Archbishop of Westminster
A 40
N 125

Printed primary sources

Allanson, A. (ed. A. Cranmer and S. Goodwill), *Biography of the English Benedictines* (Ampleforth: Ampleforth Abbey, 1999)

Anstruther, G., *The Secular Priests* (Ware: St Edmund's College, 1969–77), 3 vols

Bellenger, D. A. (ed.), *English and Welsh Priests 1558–1800* (Bath: Downside Abbey, 1984)

Bernardi, J., *A Short History of the Life of Major John Bernardi* (London, 1729)

Berry, W., *County Genealogies: Pedigrees of the Families in the County of Sussex* (London, 1830)

Bevan, A. B., *Brief Records of St. James' Church* (Bury St Edmunds, 1878)

Birt, H. N., *Obit Book of the English Benedictines, 1600–1912* (Edinburgh: Mercat Press, 1913)

Boutauld, M., *Les Conseils de la Sagesse, ou le Recueil des Maximes de Salomon les plus necessaires à l'homme pour se conduire sagement* (Paris, 1677)

Boutauld, M. (trans. 'E. S.'), *The Counsels of Wisdom or, A Collection of the Maxims of Solomon; Most Necessary for a Man towards the Gaining of Wisdom: With Reflexions upon the Maxims* (London, 1680)

Burke, J., *A Genealogical and Heraldic History of the Commoners of Great Britain and Ireland* (London, 1836), 4 vols

Castle, E. (ed.), *The Jerningham Letters* (London: Richard Bentley and Son, 1896), 2 vols

Catalogue of the Whole of the Very Interesting and Historical Contents of Hengrave Hall, Bury St Edmunds (London: Hampton and Sons, 1897)

Clarke, J. S., *The Life of James the Second King of England* (London, 1816), 2 vols

De Rochefoucauld, F. (trans. and ed. N. Scarfe), *A Frenchman's Year in Suffolk* (Woodbridge: SRS, 1988)

Dodd, C. [Hugh Tootell], *The Secret Policy of the English Society of Jesus* (London, 1715)

Dodd, C. [Hugh Tootell], *The Church History of England* (Brussels, 1737–42), 3 vols

Dominicana (London: CRS, 1925)

Estcourt, E. E. and J. O. Payne (eds), *The English Catholic Non-Jurors of 1715* (London: Burns and Oates, 1885)

Foley, H. (ed.), *Records of the English Province of the Society of Jesus* (London Burns and Oates, 1877–83), 8 vols

Fouquet, N. (attrib., trans. E. Gage), *Essays suppos'd to be written by Monsieur Fouquet: being reflections upon such maxims of Solmon as are most proper to guide us to the felicity of both the present and the future life* (London, 1694)

Gage, H. (ed.), 'Pedigree and Charters of the Family of Rookwood' in *Collectanea Topographica et Genealogica* (London, 1835), 2 vols

Gerard, J., *The Autobiography of an Elizabethan* (London: Longmans, Green and Co., 1951)

Gillow, J., *A Biographical Dictionary of the English Catholics* (London: Burns and Oates, 1885–1902), 5 vols

Gillow, J. and R. Trappes-Lomax (eds), *The Diary of the 'Blue Nuns'* (London: CRS, 1910)

Green, M. A. (ed.), *Calendar of Proceedings of the Committee of Compounding, 1643–1660* (London: HMSO, 1889–92), 5 vols

Gumbley, W., *Obituary Notices of the English Dominicans from 1555 to 1952* (London: Blackfriars Publications, 1955)

Hallett, N., *Lives of Spirit: English Carmelite Self-Writing of the Early Modern Period* (Aldershot: Ashgate, 2007)

Hermans, T., *The Franciscans in England 1600–1850* (London: Art and Book Co., 1898)

Hervey, S. H. A. (ed.), *Letter-Books of John Hervey, First Earl of Bristol* (Wells: E. Jackson, 1894), 3 vols

Hervey, S. H. A. (ed.), *Rushbrook Parish Registers with Jermyn and Davers Annals*, (Woodbridge: G. Booth, 1903)

Hervey, S. H. A. (ed.), *Suffolk in 1674, being the Hearth Tax Returns* (Woodbridge: G. Booth, 1905)

Hervey, S. H. A. (ed.), *Biographical List of Boys educated at King Edward VI Free Grammar School, Bury St Edmunds from 1550 to 1900* (Bury St Edmunds: Paul and Mathew, 1908)

Hervey, S. H. A. (ed.), *Bury St. Edmunds, St. James Parish Registers, Baptisms 1558–1800* (Bury St Edmunds: Paul and Mathew, 1915)

Hervey, S. H. A. (ed.), *Bury St. Edmunds St. James Parish Registers: Burials 1562–1800* (Bury St Edmunds: Paul and Mathew, 1916)

Hervey, S. H. A. (ed.), *Bury St. Edmunds St. James Parish Registers, Marriages 1562–1800* (Woodbridge: G. Booth, 1916)

Hervey, W. (ed. J. Jackson Howard), *The Visitation of Suffolk* (Lowestoft: Whittaker and Co., 1866–71), 2 vols

Holt, G., *St. Omers and Bruges Colleges, 1593–1773: A Biographical Dictionary* (London: CRS, 1979)

Holt, G., 'Some Letters from Suffolk, 1763–80: Selection and Commentary', *Recusant History* 16 (1983), pp. 304–15

Holt, G., (ed.), *The English Jesuits 1650–1829: A Biographical Dictionary* (London: CRS, 1984)

Hovenden, R., *A True Register of all the Christenings, Marriages and Burials in the Parishe of St. James, Clarkenwell* (London: Mitchell and Hughes, 1884–93), 6 vols

Hunter, T., *An English Carmelite: The Life of Catharine Burton, Mary Xaveria of the Angels, of the English Teresian Convent at Antwerp* (London, 1876)

Kendall, J., *A View of the South Front of Hengrave Hall, the Seat of Sir Thomas Gage Bart* (Bury St. Edmunds, 1775), engraving

Luttrell, N., *A Brief Historical Relation of State Affairs from September 1678 to April 1714* (Oxford: Oxford University Press, 1857), 6 vols

Marchant, J., *A History of the Present Rebellion* (London, 1746)

Miscellanea VII (London: CRS, 1911)

Miscellanea VIII (London: CRS, 1913)

Moorman, J., *The Franciscans in England* (London: Mowbray, 1974)

The Names of the Roman Catholics, Nonjurors, and others, who refus'd to take the Oath of Allegiance to his late Majesty King George (London, 1745)

Pack, R., *Poems on Several Occasions* (London, 1725)

Palmer, C. F. R., *Obituary Notices of the Friar-preachers, or Dominicans, of the English Province* (London: Burns and Oates, 1884)

Palmer, C. F. R., *Acta Capitulorum Provincialium Provinciae Angliae Ord. Praed. 1730–1916* (London: Westminster Press, 1918)

Payne, J. O. (ed.), *Records of the English Catholics of 1715: compiled wholly from original documents* (Burns and Oates: London, 1889)

'Popish Recusants in Suffolk', *EANQ* 1 (1885–86), pp. 345–6

The Report to the Honourable the House of Commons ... of the Commissioners ... Appointed to Execute the several Trusts and Powers ... contained in Two several Acts of Parliament (London, 1719)

Reynolds, E. E. (ed.), *The Mawhood Diary* (London: CRS, 1956)

Rowe, J. (ed.), 'Norwich Diocesan Return of Papists 11 November 1767 (NRO: DN/DIS 9/16)', in D. Chadd (ed.), *Religious Dissent in East Anglia III* (Norwich: University of East Anglia, 1996), pp. 202–34

Rylands, W. H. (ed.), *A Visitation of the county of Suffolk, begun Anno Dni 1664 & finished Anno Dni 1668* (London: Mitchell, Hughes and Clarke, 1910)

Ryves, B., *Mercurius Rusticus: Or, The Countries Complaint of the barbarous Out-rages Committed by the Sectaries of this late flour-ishing Kingdome* (London, 1646)

Scarisbrick, E., *The Holy Life of Lady Warner* (London, 1691)

Trappes Lomax, R. (ed.), *Franciscana* (London: CRS, 1922)

Ware, J. (ed. W. Harris), *The whole works of Sir James Ware concerning Ireland* (Dublin, 1739–45), 2 vols

Whiteman, A. and M. Clapinson (eds), *The Compton Census of 1676: A Critical Edition* (London: British Academy, 1986)

Worrall, E. S. (ed.), *Returns of Papists Volume 2: Dioceses of England and Wales, except Chester* (London: CRS, 1989)

Newspapers and magazines

'Hengrave Hall manuscripts saved', *Cambridge University Library Readers' Newsletter* 34 (October 2006)

The London Courant, 18 December 1688

The London Evening Post 2121 (13–16 June 1741)

The London Magazine or Gentleman's Monthly Intelligencer, December 1748

The London Mercury or Orange Intelligence, 31 December 1688–3 January 1689

The Universal Intelligence, 15 December 1688

Secondary works

Airs, M., 'The Designing of Five East Anglian Country Houses, 1505–1637', *Architectural History* 21 (1978), pp. 58–107

Anderson, J. H., 'More, Cressacre' in *ODNB*, vol. 39, p. 36

Ashton, R., *Counter-Revolution: The Second Civil War and its Origins, 1646–8* (New Haven, CT: Yale University Press, 1994)

Aveling, J. C. H., *Northern Catholics: The Catholic Recusants of the North Riding of Yorkshire 1558–1790* (London: Chapman, 1966)

Aveling, J. C. H., *The Handle and the Axe* (London: Blond and Briggs, 1976)

Bastow, S., 'The Catholic Gentry and the Catholic Community in the City of York, 1536–1642: The Focus of a Catholic Country?', *York Historian* 18 (2001), pp. 12–22

Bastow, S., *The Catholic Gentry of Yorkshire, 1536–1642: Resistance and Accommodation* (Lampeter: Edwin Mellen Press, 2007)

Battely, J., *Antiquitates S. Eadmundi Burgi ad Annum 1272 Perductae* (Oxford, 1745)

Bishop, P., *The Sacred and Profane History of Bury St. Edmunds* (London: Unicorn, 1998)

Blackwood, B. G., 'Lancashire Catholics, Protestants and Jacobites in the 1715 Rebellion', *Recusant History* 22 (1994), pp. 41–59

Blackwood, G., *Tudor and Stuart Suffolk* (Lancaster: Carnegie, 2001)

Blatchly, J. M., 'D'Ewes, Sir Simonds' in *ODNB*, vol. 16, pp. 1–4

Blatchly, J. M., 'Pack, Richardson' in *ODNB*, vol. 42, pp. 305–6

Blomefield, F., *An Essay towards a Topographical History of the County of Norfolk* (London, 1805–10), 11 vols

Boothman, L. and R. Hyde Parker (eds), *Savage Fortune: An Aristocratic Family in the Early Seventeenth Century* (Woodbridge: SRS, 2006)

Bossy, J., *The English Catholic Community 1570–1850* (London: Darton, Longman and Todd, 1975)

Brown, D., 'John Wilbye, 1574–1638', *The Musical Times* 115 (1974), pp. 214–16

Brückmann, P., 'Virgins Visited by Angel Powers: *The Rape of the Lock*, Platonick Love, Sylphs, and some Mysticks' in G. S. Rousseau and P. Rogers (eds), *The Enduring Legacy: Alexander Pope Tercentenary Essays* (Cambridge: Cambridge University Press, 1988), pp. 3–20

Callow, J., 'The Last of the Shireburnes: The Art of Life and Death in Recusant Lancashire 1690–1754' *Recusant History* 26 (2002–3), pp. 589–615

Callow, J., *King in Exile* (Stroud: Sutton, 2004)

Callow, J., *James II: The Triumph and the Tragedy* (London: Sutton, 2005)

Carter, C., 'Hervey, John, first earl of Bristol', *ODNB*, vol. 26, pp. 861–62

Chambers, L., *Michael Moore c.1639–1726: Provost of Trinity, Rector of Paris* (Dublin: Four Courts, 2005)

Clark, R., *Strangers and Sojourners at Port Royal* (Cambridge: Cambridge University Press, 1932)

Cockayne, G. E., *Complete Baronetage* (Exeter: Pollard, 1900–9), 6 vols

Collinson, P., 'Godly Preachers and Zealous Magistrates in Elizabethan East Anglia: The Roots of Dissent' in idem (ed.), *From Cranmer to Sancroft* (London: Continuum, 2006), pp. 25–44

Cooper, T., (rev. D. Milburn), 'Gage, Francis' in *ODNB*, vol. 21, p. 249

Cooper, T., (rev. J. M. Blatchly), 'Rokewode, John Gage' in *ODNB*, vol. 47, pp. 605–6

Coppinger, W. A., *The Manors of Suffolk* (Manchester: Fisher Unwin, 1905–11), 9 vols

Cowell, F., *Richard Woods (1715–1793): Master of the Pleasure Garden* (Woodbridge: Boydell Press, 2009)

Croft, P., 'The Catholic Gentry, the Earl of Salisbury and the Baronets of 1611' in P. Lake and M. Questier (eds), *Conformity and Orthodoxy in the English Church, c. 1560–1660* (Woodbridge: Boydell Press, 2000), pp. 262–81

Davies, O., *The Haunted: A Social History of Ghosts* (Basingstoke: Palgrave MacMillan, 2007)

Dovey, Z., *An Elizabethan Progress: The Queen's Journey into East Anglia, 1578* (Stroud: Sutton, 1996)

Duffy, E., 'A Rub-up for Old Soares; Jesuits, Jansenists, and the English Secular Clergy, 1705–1715', *Journal of Ecclesiastical History* 28 (1977), pp. 291–317

Durrant, C. S., *A Link Between Flemish Mystics and English Martyrs* (London: Burns and Oates, 1925)

Dymond, D., 'Suffolk and the Compton Census of 1676', *Suffolk Review* 3 (1966), pp. 103–18

Elliot, R. W., *The Story of King Edward the Sixth School Bury St. Edmunds* (Bury St Edmunds, 1963)

Evans, N., 'The Tasburghs of South Elmham: The Rise and Fall of a Suffolk Gentry Family', *PSIAH* 34 (1980), pp. 269–80

Everitt, A., *Suffolk and the Great Rebellion 1640–1660* (Ipswich: SRS, 1960)

Farrer, E., *Portraits in Suffolk Houses (West)* (London: B. Quaritch, 1908)

Fellowes, E. H., 'John Wilbye', *Proceedings of the Musical Association* 41 (1915), pp. 55–86

Gage, J., *The History and Antiquities of Hengrave in Suffolk* (Bury St Edmunds, 1822)

Gage, J., *The History and Antiquities of Suffolk: Thingoe Hundred* (London, 1838)

Gardiner, A. B., 'Defenders of the Mystery', *Recusant History* 30 (2010), pp. 241–60

Gillingwater, E., *An Historical and Descriptive Account of St. Edmund's Bury, in the County of Suffolk* (Bury St Edmunds, 1804)

Glickman, G., *The English Catholic Community 1688–1745: Politics, Culture and Ideology* (Woodbridge: Boydell Press, 2009)

Glover, S., *The History of the County of Derby* (Derby, 1829), 2 vols

Gooch, L., '"The Religion for a Gentleman": The Northern Catholic Gentry in the Eighteenth Century', *Recusant History* 23 (1997), pp. 543–68

Haggar, A. L. and L. F. Miller, *Suffolk Clocks and Clockmakers* (Ramsgate: Antiquarian Horological Society, 1974)

Hallett, N., '"As if nothing had belonged to her": the Lives of Catherine Burton (1668–1714) as a Discourse on Method in Early Modern Life-writing', *Early Modern Literary Studies* 7 (2002), pp. 1–30

Handley, S., 'Petre, Sir Edward', *ODNB*, vol. 43, pp. 706–7

Haswell, J., *James II: Soldier and Sailor* (Hamilton: London, 1972)

Henning, B. D., *The History of Parliament: The House of Commons 1660–1690* (London: HMSO, 1983)

Hickes, G., *Devotions in the Ancient Way of Offices* (London, 1701)

Higham, T., *Excursions in the County of Suffolk* (London, 1818–19)

Hodgetts, M., *Secret Hiding Places* (Dublin: Veritas, 1989)

Hodgetts, M., 'The Yates of Harvington, 1631–1696', *Recusant History* 22 (1994), pp. 152–81

Holmes, C., *The Eastern Association in the English Civil War* (Cambridge: Cambridge University Press, 1974)

Holt, G., *The English Jesuits in the Age of Reason* (Tunbridge Wells: Burns and Oates, 1993)

Holt, G., 'Edward Scarisbrick (1639–1709): A Royal Preacher', *Recusant History* 23 (1996–97), pp. 159–65

Hopkins, P., 'Rookwood, Ambrose' in *ODNB*, vol. 47, pp. 700–1

Hughes, A., 'Feilding, Basil' in *ODNB*, vol. 19, pp. 238–41

'Illustrative Memoir of the Right Honourable Lady Emily Feilding', *La Belle Assemblée* 2:11 (1825), pp. 185–88

Joyce, M. B., 'The Haggerstons: The Education of a Northumberland Family', *Recusant History* 19 (1978), pp. 175–92

'The Junior Branches of the Howards', *The Gentleman's Magazine* 103 (1833), pp. 404–406

Kenyon, J. P., *The Popish Plot* (London: Penguin, 1974)

Kimber, E. and R. Nicholson, *The Baronetage of England* (London, 1771), 2 vols

Kingston, A., *East Anglia and the Great Civil War* (London: E. Stock, 1897)

Krook, D., *John Sergeant and his Circle: A Study of Three Seventeenth-Century Aristotelians* (Leiden: Brill, 1993)

Langhans, E. A., 'The Theatre' in D. P. Fiske (ed.), *The Cambridge Companion to English Restoration Theatre* (Cambridge: Cambridge University Press, 2000), pp. 1–18

Loomie, A. J., 'Aston, Walter, Baron Aston of Forfar' in *ODNB*, vol. 2, pp. 793–94

Loomie, A. J., 'Gage, Sir Henry' in *ODNB*, vol. 21, pp. 250–51

Lunn, D., *The English Benedictines 1540–1688* (London: Burns and Oates, 1980)

Lunn, J., *The Tyldesleys of Lancashire: The Rise and Fall of a Great Patrican Family* (Astley, 1966)

Lysons, D., *The Environs of London* (London, 1792)

MacCulloch, D., *Suffolk and the Tudors: Politics and Religion in an English County 1500–1600* (Oxford: Clarendon Press, 1986)

Mackinlay, J. B., *Saint Edmund, King and Martyr* (London: Art and Book Co., 1893)

Macaulay, T. B., *The History of England* (London: Penguin, 1968)

McCoog, T., 'Wright, William' in *ODNB*, vol. 60, p. 503

Marshall, P., *Beliefs and the Dead in Early Modern England* (Oxford: Oxford University Press, 2002)

Marshall, P. and G. Scott, 'Introduction: The Catholic Gentry in English Society' in idem (eds), *Catholic Gentry in English Society: The Throckmortons of Coughton from Reformation to Emancipation* (Farnham: Ashgate, 2009), pp. 1–30

Martin, E., 'Hundreds and Liberties' in D. Dymond and E. Martin (eds), *An Historical Atlas of Suffolk* (Ipswich: Suffolk County Council, 1988), pp. 18–19

Martin, J., 'Hanmer, Sir Thomas' in *ODNB*, vol. 25, pp. 64–65

Meeres, F., *A History of Bury St. Edmunds* (Chichester: Phillimore, 2002)

Miller, J., *James II*, 3rd edn (New Haven, CT : Yale University Press, 2000)

Murphy, M., 'A House Divided: The Fall of the Herberts of Powys 1688–1715', *Recusant History* 26 (2002–3), pp. 88–101

Murrell, P. E., 'Bury St. Edmunds and the Campaign to Pack Parliament, 1687–8', *Bulletin of the Institute of Historical Research* 54 (1981), pp. 188–206

Nixon, G., *Old Inns and Beerhouses of Bury St. Edmunds* (Brandon, 1996)

'Obituary: John Gage Rokewode, Esq.', *The Gentleman's Magazine* (December 1842), pp. 660–61

The Old Brotherhood of the English Secular Clergy: Catalogue of Part of the Archives (London: CRS, 1968)

Paine, C., (ed.), *The Culford Estate 1780–1935* (Ingham: Ingham Local History Group, 1993)

Questier, M., 'Conformity, Catholicism and the Law' in P. Lake and M. Questier (eds), *Conformity and Orthodoxy in the English Church, c.1560–1660* (Woodbridge: Boydell Press, 2000), pp. 237–61

Questier, M., *Catholicism and Community in Early Modern England: Politics, Aristocratic Patronage and Religion, c.1550–1640* (Cambridge: Cambridge University Press, 2006)

Quintrell, B., 'The Practice and Problems of Recusant Disarming', *Recusant History* 17 (1983), pp. 208–22

Rogers, N., 'Popular Jacobitism in a Provincial Context: 18th Century Bristol and Norwich' in E. Cruickshanks and J. Black (eds), *The Jacobite Challenge* (Edinburgh: J. Donald, 1988), pp. 123–41

Rowe, J., *The Story of Catholic Bury St. Edmunds, Coldham and Surrounding District* (Bury St Edmunds, 1981)

Rowe, J., 'Roman Catholic Recusancy' in D. Dymond and E. Martin (eds), *An Historical Atlas of Suffolk* (Ipswich: Suffolk County Council, 1988), pp. 88–89

Rowe, J., 'The 1767 Census of Papists in the Diocese of Norwich: The Social Composition of the Roman Catholic Community' in D. Chadd (ed.), *Religious Dissent in East Anglia III* (Norwich: University of East Anglia, 1996), pp. 187–234

Rowe, J., '"The Lopped Tree": The Re-formation of the Suffolk Catholic Community' in N. Tyacke (ed.), *England's Long Reformation 1500–1800* (Abingdon: UCL Press, 1998), pp. 167–94

Rowe, J., 'Drury Family' in *ODNB*, vol. 16, pp. 997–1000

Rowe, J., 'Everard, Thomas' in *ODNB*, vol. 18, p. 788

Rowe, J., 'Kitson family' in *ODNB*, vol. 31, pp. 843–46

Rowlands, M. B., (ed.), *English Catholics of Parish and Town 1558–1778* (London: CRS, 1999)

Ryan, G. H. and L. J. Redstone, *Timperley of Hintlesham: A Study of a Suffolk Family* (London: Methuen, 1931)

Scarisbrick, J. J., *The Reformation and the English People* (Oxford: Blackwell, 1984)

Scott, G., *Gothic Rage Undone: English Monks in the Age of Enlightenment* (Bath: Downside Abbey, 1992)

Scott, G., 'The Throckmortons at Home and Abroad, 1680–1800' in P. Marshall and G. Scott (eds), *Catholic Gentry in English Society: The Throckmortons of Coughton from Reformation to Emancipation* (Farnham: Ashgate, 2009), pp. 171–211

Sheridan, R. B., *Sugar and Slavery: An Economic History of the British West Indies, 1623–1775* (Baltimore, MD: Johns Hopkins University Press, 1974)

Shield, A. and A. Lang, *The King over the Water* (London: Longmans, Green and Co., 1907)

Smith, G., *Royalist Agents, Conspirators and Spies: Their Role in the British Civil Wars, 1640–1660* (Farnham: Ashgate, 2011)

Spurr, J., *The Restoration Church of England 1646–1689* (New Haven, CT: Yale University Press, 1991)

Statham, M., *The Book of Bury St. Edmunds* (Whittlebury: Baron Birch, 1996)

Storey, G., 'Culford Hall, Near Bury St. Edmunds' in *People and Places: An East Anglian Miscellany* (Lavenham: Dalton, 1973), pp. 93–198

Suckling, A., *The History and Antiquities of the County of Suffolk* (London: John Weale, 1846), 2 vols

Tymms, S., *An Architectural and Historical Account of the Church of St. Mary, Bury St. Edmunds* (Bury St Edmunds: Jackson and Frost, 1854)

Walter, J., 'Anti-Popery and the Stour Valley Riots of 1642' in D. Chadd (ed.), *Religious Dissent in East Anglia III* (Norwich: University of East Anglia, 1996), pp. 121–40

Walter, J., *Understanding Popular Violence in the English Revolu-*

tion: The Colchester Plunderers (Cambridge: Cambridge University Press, 1999)

Walter, J., 'Savage [née Darcy], Elizabeth, suo jure Countess Rivers' in *ODNB*, vol. 49, pp. 67–68

Whitelock, A. and D. MacCulloch, 'Princess Mary's Household and the Succession Crisis, July 1553', *Historical Journal* 50 (2007), pp. 265–87

Wiseman, S., *Drama and Politics in the English Civil War* (Cambridge: Cambridge University Press, 1998)

Wotton, H., *The English Baronetage* (London, 1727), 4 vols

Yates, R., *An Illustration of the Monastic Antiquities of the Town and Abbey of St Edmund's Bury*, 2nd edn (London: J. B. Nichols and Son, 1843)

Young, A. R., *The English Emblem Tradition: Emblematic Flag Devices of the English Civil Wars 1642–1660* (Toronto: University of Toronto Press, 1995)

Young, F., 'Mother Mary More and the Exile of the Augustinian Canonesses of Bruges in England: 1794–1802', *Recusant History* 27 (2004), pp. 86–102

Young, F., '"An Horrid Popish Plot": The Failure of Catholic Aspirations in Bury St. Edmunds, 1685–88', *PSIAH* 41 (2006), pp. 209–55

Young, F., 'The Shorts of Bury St. Edmunds: Medicine, Catholicism and Politics in the Seventeenth Century', *Journal of Medical Biography* 16 (2008), pp. 188–94

Young, F., 'Catholic Exorcism in Early Modern England: Polemic, Propaganda and Folklore', *Recusant History* 29 (2009), pp. 497–498

Young, F., 'The Tasburghs of Bodney: Catholicism and Politics in South Norfolk', *Norfolk Archaeology* 46 (2011), pp. 190–98

Young, F., 'The Tasburghs of Flixton and Catholicism in North-east Suffolk, 1642–1767', *PSIAH* 42 (2012), pp. 455–70

Young, F., *English Catholics and the Supernatural, 1553–1829* (Farnham: Ashgate, 2013)

Young, F., 'Elizabeth Inchbald's "Catholic Novel" and its Local Background', *Recusant History* 31 (2013), pp. 573–92

Index of People and Places

Index of Subjects